Marco Mazzone

Cognitive Pragmatics

Mouton Series in Pragmatics

Volume 20

Marco Mazzone

Cognitive Pragmatics

Mindreading, Inferences, Consciousness

DE GRUYTER
MOUTON

ISBN 978-1-5015-1612-2
e-ISBN (PDF) 978-1-5015-0773-1
e-ISBN (EPUB) 978-1-5015-0767-0
ISSN 1864-6409

Library of Congress Cataloging-in-Publication Data
A CIP catalog record for this book has been applied for at the Library of Congress.

Bibliographic information published by the Deutsche Nationalbibliothek
The Deutsche Nationalbibliothek lists this publication in the Deutsche Nationalbibliografie; detailed bibliographic data are available in the Internet at http://dnb.dnb.de.

Typesetting: Compuscript Ltd., Shannon, Ireland
Printing and binding: CPI books GmbH, Leck
♾ Printed on acid-free paper Printed in Germany

MIX
Papier aus verantwortungsvollen Quellen
FSC www.fsc.org
FSC® C083411

www.degruyter.com

Table of contents

Introduction

Paul Grice (1989) has famously described human communication as a case of expression and recognition of intentions, thus laying "the foundations for an inferential model of communication, an alternative to the classical code model" (Wilson and Sperber 2002: 249). According to the inferential model, speakers have communicative intentions that normally exceed the meanings conventionally conveyed by utterances; as a consequence, comprehension requires the addressees to inferentially reconstruct those intentions from those meanings. Thanks to this model, Grice is among the founders of the discipline that is called "pragmatics", and whose primary subject matter is in fact the understanding of the implicit meanings that we express through language on specific occasions of use.

Grice and his model have importantly inspired cognitive pragmatics, a recent discipline whose aim is to identify the actual psychological mechanisms underlying the phenomena that he had recognized at a purely conceptual level of analysis. Given this aim, cognitive pragmatics may be naturally expected to interact with a subject of psychological research which is now forty years old and has prompted a huge amount of experimental studies on children and adults, but also on other species – especially, other primates. This subject is mindreading, also called "(folk) theory of mind", that is, the ability – which is characteristic for humans but possibly present to some degree in other primates – to understand observed behaviours as driven by intentions and other mental states. The debate on the implied mechanisms is still open, but some aspects have been widely analysed and some experimental results appear robust. If Grice was right in conceiving of language understanding in context as a case of (communicative) intentions' recognition, this line of research could not leave cognitive pragmaticists cold.

As a matter of fact, the relationship between pragmatics and mindreading has been explicitly acknowledged by Dan Sperber and Deirdre Wilson, among the most influential scholars within the field of cognitive pragmatics. To this field, they have contributed a rich theoretical model under the name of "Relevance Theory" (from now on RT). *Relevance* is actually the name of the book in which, in 1986, Sperber and Wilson gave a first systematic account of their approach. More than fifteen years later, in Sperber and Wilson (2002), they discuss the relationship between that approach and the research on mindreading.

The present book aims to provide a focussed discussion of the relationship between cognitive pragmatics and mindreading, through a systematic analysis of, and comparison with, the model proposed by relevance theorists. Besides Sperber and Wilson, I will also take into consideration works of Robyn Carston, Paula Rubio-Fernández and Diana Mazzarella, who to various degrees are related

https://doi.org/10.1515/9781501507731-001

to that theoretical tradition. The discussion will be mainly focussed on some basic issues to which I have devoted my theoretical efforts in the last ten years and that led me to outline a general approach to cognitive pragmatics that is potentially divergent from the one defended by RT.

When I say that my approach is *potentially divergent* from RT, my caution is justified. RT is a very rich theory developed over three decades with the contribution of many scholars, among whom, besides Sperber and Wilson, a crucial role has been played by Robyn Carston. By now, the theory has become an indispensable reference point for the debate on linguistic comprehension, raising objections as well as theoretical contributions and attempts at experimental verification. When one is confronted with such a rich and complex theoretical framework, it is hard to say which aspects constitute its central and indispensable core and which instead could be revised without serious consequences. Nevertheless, by using the phrase "potentially divergent" I put the emphasis more on the intention to revise the theory than to contribute to it. The reason is that, while I accept some ideas of RT entirely and attempt to clarify and refine others, I put nonetheless into question some basic assumptions that the theory receives from classical cognitive science: most of all, a commitment to modularity, and the assumption that rule-based processing cannot be accounted for by simple associations. Such background assumptions, I submit, make it difficult to provide a satisfying account of the relation between pragmatic comprehension and mindreading.

This is especially evident when one considers the very notion of relevance adopted by Sperber and Wilson, an aspect that can hardly be considered marginal: this notion, I will argue, can hardly be reconciled with the claim that comprehension is after all "an exercise in mind-reading" (Sperber and Wilson 2002: 3), and therefore a special case of intentions' understanding. The crucial issue is that RT defines relevance in terms of how widely information enables us to modify our world knowledge. We might call this a quantitative-informational view of relevance. Thus, to say that comprehension is driven by the search for relevance equates to saying that the process has a sort of intrinsic purpose of its own: the maximisation of cognitive effects. This implies in turn thinking of communication as an activity essentially aimed at knowledge transmission, in contrast with the intuition of Grice (and the other founders of philosophical pragmatics: the late Wittgenstein, Austin) according to which communication may pursue an indefinite plurality of purposes, and comprehension is recognition of the current purposes of the speaker in the first place. Within this traditional framework, communication is a special case of action – and therefore, of practical reasoning – while knowledge transmission is just one of its very many possible purposes.

However, in accordance with our previous considerations about the richness and complexity of RT, it must be said that the theory has provided clues to a different notion of relevance than the quantitative-informational one. Moreover, some of the cognitive mechanisms proposed are entirely compatible with the view that relevance is a function of the plurality of speakers' purposes. But to the extent that one takes the quantitative-informational notion of relevance at its face value, RT has to face serious problems. These problems will be addressed in chapter 1.

Chapters 2 and 3 will be devoted instead to some basic features of the cognitive mechanisms underlying comprehension. In chapters 2, specifically, I will analyse RT's proposal according to which the cognitive processes responsible for comprehension are inferential. Not only does RT accept the Gricean idea that communication can *be described* in terms of an inference from conventional meanings to communicative intentions, but it is also committed to the claim that the psychological processes involved imply the actual construction of non-demonstrative inferences, constituted by a certain number of premises and some conclusions. However, this inference-based interpretation process is conceived as automatic, instead of conscious and controlled, and therefore it is not considered a form of explicit reasoning. I will claim that such an inferential process can be accounted for in terms of simple associative mechanisms, which are not specialized for pragmatic comprehension. This amounts to assigning a crucial role to the organization of memory: associative recovery is not erratic; on the contrary it is driven and motivated by the structure of encoded information. In chapter 2 I will especially focus on the hierarchical organization of memory in schemata that lie at different levels of abstraction, and on how this organization enables a bottom-up/top-down dynamic which is capable of guiding and constraining the basic mechanism of associative activation. As I will show, there are reasons to think that this dynamic is apt to provide explanations of different domains of cognition, including pragmatic comprehension, language processing, action control and action understanding (i.e., mindreading). Action goals might indeed be represented by high-level schemata, apt to coordinate complex perceptual and motor configurations.

On the one hand, the hypothesis that an associative mechanism is responsible for the inferential process described by RT can be seen as entirely compatible with that theory. To this effect, we have to assume that by speaking of inferences between propositions RT intends to provide a functional, high-level description, while the associative hypothesis would describe how those inferences are actually implemented in our memory networks. There are reasons to believe that this is the case, in other words, that there is compatibility between RT's inferential account and its associative implementation. I will mainly consider two such reasons. First, on occasion relevance theorists explicitly embrace the idea that the organization of memory is crucial for comprehension processes. Second, in recent years relevance theorists have regularly characterized the pragmatic inferential process as a case of bidirectional and parallel (instead of sequential) processing, these features being typical of associative models of explanation.

But, on the other hand, there are also reasons to believe that RT would not subscribe to the view that inferential and associative accounts of pragmatics are compatible. First of all, RT explicitly assigns a role to associative processes, but clearly differentiates them from the properly pragmatic, inferential process and provides an argument against the view that the latter is reducible to the former. Another important issue is RT's commitment towards the modularity thesis, that is, with a rough simplification, the thesis that cognitive processes are largely specialized, specific for domains and autonomous. The modularity thesis is essentially trivialized if one thinks of it in terms of a single associative mechanism ensuring, at a functional level, a plurality of processes that are (relatively) autonomous due to mere organization of memory in bodies of knowledge – that is, portions of the associative network characterized by strong internal connections. It can be doubted that RT would be happy to concede, in particular, that this is the case for pragmatics. In other words, if pragmatic inferential processes are implemented by basically associative mechanisms then pragmatics can be modular only in a very weak sense, which implies the organization of memory in different bodies of knowledge, but not the existence of specific processes for this domain. And it is not clear that RT would welcome that weak notion of modularity. However, the modularity thesis is at times presented in such loose terms (see Sperber 2005) that one cannot rule out this possibility altogether.

Even the other objection, that is, RT's explicit argument against associative accounts, can possibly be overcome thanks to a distinction between two senses of "associative". The idea is that the sense of "associative" which is involved when we consider inferential and associative processes as mutually exclusive is different from the one at issue in my proposal that inferential processes are implemented by associative mechanisms. This distinction has important consequences for cognitive science in general, also with regard to the issue of consciousness – as we will see in a moment. However, the question whether RT is compatible with an associative account has to remain open, since the theory does not provide unambiguous answers to it.

In chapter 3 I will discuss the nature of automatic and controlled processing and their relationship, in general and with respect to pragmatic comprehension. The topic is closely related with that of the two senses of "associative", one at the level of functional descriptions, the other at the level of the underlying implementation mechanisms. At the former level, associative processes are conceptually opposed to those involving conscious control: for the sake of clarity, it is therefore convenient to call them, respectively, "automatic" and "controlled" processes.

At the implementation level, the point is that both automatic and controlled processes are presumably implemented by (different) dynamics of activation of the same network of nodes and links that constitutes the associative memory of the organism. What distinguishes the two dynamics of activation is in essence their temporal course: automatic processes are characterized by rapidly decaying activations, while activation in controlled processes is sustained through time. But what is activated in the two conditions is the same network of associative representations, which contains the information required to properly connect perception and action. To put it differently, one can embrace an associative explanation of pragmatics and mindreading, in the sense of an explanation essentially based on the structure of associative memory, without being forced to deny that pragmatic comprehension and mindreading involve controlled processes, not just automatic ones.

In more general terms, I will attempt to provide a unified picture of the relationship between automatic and controlled processes, based on the idea that there is a constant interaction between them, to the point that it is hard to find purely automatic processes displaying no interactions with episodes of conscious control, and it is even harder to find controlled processes not involving a number of automatisms.

These considerations must be applied back to the previous discussion regarding pragmatic comprehension. My claim that inferential pragmatic processes can be explained in associative terms has to be understood in the sense that they are based on the organization of associative memory, which is normally activated by a mixture of automatic and controlled components. This means that in linguistic comprehension a non-marginal role is probably played by conscious attention and working memory – an aspect that RT tends to overlook, and that might help instead to explain some debated pragmatic phenomena. By way of example, I will analyse two such phenomena: the role played by conscious attention, respectively, in making speaker-related information especially prominent, and in the construction of emergent properties.

Chapter 4 directly addresses the issue of mindreading and its connection to pragmatic comprehension. The framework outlined in chapters 2 and 3 is strongly unitary: according to it, comprehension of action and comprehension of utterances rest on the same mechanism, that is, the integration of automatic and controlled activation within associative networks of memory. In chapter 4, the processes subserving action are indeed argued to display a feature that, according to RT, characterizes utterance understanding as well: the mutual adjustment between forward and backward inferences, a feature that is hardly surprising to the extent that we conceive the mechanisms at play as activations through an associative network. But they are not only, presumably, processes of the same kind, they also appear to require reciprocal integration, if it is true that communicative intentions can be sub-goals of larger plans of action. In this sense, I will analyse the ability to construct chains of means and ends that cross the boundary between language and action. At the same time, I will propose that such chains are built out of both perceptual and motor information and, finally, that they can integrate our own and others' goals into shared intentional contexts.

In such a unitary approach, goals and intentions can be thought of as special cases of the representational schemata that impose a motivated structure on associative memory. Is this view compatible with the state of research on mindreading? In particular, in chapter 4 I summarize the debate between empiricist and nativist approaches to mental concepts (intentions and the like), with the aim to show that they share a notion of mental state that is in essence compatible with the one defended here. Mental states are in fact conceived as "intermediate variables", that is, unobservables entities mediating between – and generalizing over – classes of environmental stimuli and behavioural responses. Even accepting this notion, however, one might argue that a purely associative view of mental concepts is nonetheless insufficient. I will examine two arguments to this effect. The first comes from nativist theories of mental concepts, which are sceptical towards the possibility that these are formed thanks to generalization from experience. Against this argument I will contend that nativists cannot have it both ways: on the one hand, they want mental concepts – that is, generalizations over classes of stimuli and responses – to be innate; on the other hand, they do not seem ready to accept that, if this is the case, it is the entire pattern of correlations between stimuli and responses that has to be innate. The second argument is based on the consideration that typical mindreading tasks appear to involve abilities, such as the ability to construct and manipulate mental models of situations, which exceed the mere formation and activation of schemata abstracted from regularities. This argument is correct, I think, but it does not speak against the claim that mental concepts are schemata in associative memory. It calls our attention instead to the other sense of "associative" we considered above. In other words, the point is that the tasks cannot be passed unless subjects not only activate the appropriate mental schemata, but also do this by way of a controlled dynamic of activation, so that situation models can be formed and then maintained for all the time required.

I will also analyse the consequences of the above framework with regard to the modularity issue. As already noted, to say that pragmatic processes are essentially of the same type as mindreading processes, since both are implemented by associative mechanisms, allows only for a trivial and uncontroversial notion of modularity. I will argue that this is in fact the case and that the alternative option is hardly viable: an interesting notion of modularity would require a plurality of processes that differ in themselves rather than as a function of the bodies of knowledge they apply to. If, on the contrary, the very same associative dynamic operates differently, and on different domains of inputs, just because of the organization of memory, then there is no plurality of modular processes in any interesting sense.

Finally, in chapter 5, I will analyse in more detail the issue of how rational is spontaneous pragmatic comprehension. My general claim is that pragmatic processing is not only inferential, but it is also a special case of practical rationality. I will defend this view against the objection that communication is rational at a completely different (normative) level than that of cognitive explanations. On the contrary, I will argue, spontaneous comprehension shares important features with the sort of rational reconstructions provided in pragmatics: in practice, the latter make use of the same schemata that have presumably played a key role in ensuring the former. On the other hand, I will analyse a couple of aspects for which rational reconstructions are not entirely reliable indicators of what happens in spontaneous comprehension.

To sum up, what I am going to propose is a cognitive approach to pragmatics according to which spontaneous comprehension is a case of practical rationality, operating in strict continuity with action understanding, and implemented by a non-modular associative mechanism based on the schematic organization of memory. As it should be clear, by discussing the special case of pragmatic comprehension I aim, in fact, to sketch the general lines of a unitary, non-modular account of cognition, in which not only pragmatics and mindreading, but also linguistic and non-linguistic processing on the one hand, spontaneous and controlled ("rational") processes on the other, are seen under the perspectives of their underlying common mechanisms and their strict integration. Since the associative organization of memory is key to this account, the analysis also aims to shed light on the crucial issue of what concepts are, on the related notion of schema, and on how schematic associations in memory allow for both spontaneous and controlled inferencing.

This book is the result of almost ten years of work in cognitive pragmatics, in the course of which I had fruitful discussions with many people. Among those to whom I am deeply indebted, I want to mention at least: Robyn Carston and Deirdre Wilson who hosted me at the University College London for one week (May 2013) during which I gave an informal talk and took part in a seminar on one of my papers; Agustin Vicente who invited me to a workshop at the University of the Basque Country (September 2013); Mark Jary who invited me to a workshop at the Roehampton University (London, July 2014). A special thanks goes to Diana Mazzarella who, in the course of her PhD, raised a number of issues that made me change my mind on a couple of topics. Also, I have to thank Francesca Ervas: her invitation to give a talk on the notion of relevance at the seminar series she organized for the University of Cagliari (May 2015) was not only a great opportunity to discuss my ideas, but also contributed to give its present form to the first chapter of this book.

I have published a somewhat different and incomplete version of these ideas in a book in Italian, “Pragmatica cognitiva e mindreading” (edited by Bonanno, Acireale-Roma, 2016). And I have re-used materials from a number of papers, namely: “Pragmatics and Cognition: Intentions and Pattern Recognition in Context” (2009); “Intentions as Complex Entities” (2011a); “Schemata and associative processes in pragmatics” (2011b); “Attention to the speaker. The conscious assessment of utterance interpretations in working memory” (2013a); “Crossing the associative/inferential divide: ad hoc concepts and the inferential power of schemata” (2014c); “Being nativist about mindreading: More demanding than you might think” (2015a); “Trivializing modularity. An associative-representational account of cognition” (2015b); “Constructing the context through goals and schemata: Top-down processes in comprehension and beyond” (2015c); “What kind of associative and inferential processes? A response to Rubio-Fernández (2016)”; “Why don’t you tell it explicitly? Personal/subpersonal accounts of implicitness” (2017); “Distributed intentionality: A model of intentional behaviour in humans” (Mazzone and Campisi 2013). I thank the editors and publishers of the relevant journal and volumes for their permission to re-use those materials.

1 Relevance

1.1 Introduction

Central to the theoretical framework proposed by Sperber and Wilson (1986/1995) is a specific notion of relevance, which the scholars define explicitly and carefully distinguish from the ordinary meaning of the term. The basic idea is that the relevance of a stimulus is its capacity to modify the information represented within a cognitive system, and a relevant interpretation is one that processes the stimulus so as to maximise its cognitive effects. The process of utterance understanding is said to be just a special case of the general tendency of cognitive systems to interpret stimuli so as to maximise their impact. Comprehension would thus be driven by search for relevance.

The main thesis I am going to defend is that, to the precise extent that it departs from the ordinary meaning of the term, the notion of relevance put forth by Sperber and Wilson is not able to accomplish the theoretical function assigned to it, that is, the function to guide the comprehension process. I will argue in fact that the mechanisms described by RT for the construction and evaluation of relevant – i.e., maximally informative – interpretations are unsatisfactory. According to RT, utterances cause expectations of relevance in addressees, and interpretations that have enough cognitive effects to meet those expectations are accepted.[1] One would then need an explanation both of how the cognitive system forms specific quantitative expectations of relevance, whose satisfaction by a sufficient amount of cognitive effects is needed to accept a given interpretation, and of how the cognitive effects would be measured and compared with those expectations. However, in order to answer the second question – how cognitive effects are measured? – relevance theorists provide a speculation with no independent theoretical or empirical support, while no explanation at all is provided regarding how addressees form quantitative expectations of relevance, to which the amount of actual cognitive effects should be compared.

Interestingly, however, RT explores a quite different strategy that is not based on the notion of relevance as maximisation of cognitive effects, thus making it possible to avoid both the above difficulties. On the one hand, RT suggests that a mechanism for measuring cognitive effects might not be needed, since the construction of relevant interpretations is already guaranteed by a mechanism

1 I will clarify below the reasons of my emphasis on cognitive effects in contrast to cognitive costs.

https://doi.org/10.1515/9781501507731-002

that is far more established in cognitive science, that is, competitive access based on the organization of memory. On the other hand, with an even more radical theoretical turn, RT has recently proposed that expectations of relevance are not related to the *amount* of cognitive effects but to their *type* instead. As I will show, these suggestions pave the way for a more traditional view, according to which relevance is not defined with regard to informational states, but rather to the plurality of the speakers' goals. This in turn will have important consequences for the issue of the relationship between cognitive pragmatics and mindreading.

1.2 Some assumptions

It is important to make explicit from the beginning some basic assumptions that will guide my analysis of the notion of relevance in RT.

In the first place, I do not subscribe to some radical form of epistemological holism, that is, to the idea that theories face the tribunal of experience as inseparable wholes. On the contrary, I assume that theories may have more or less cohesive and logically consistent parts, and that as a general rule those parts can be assessed separately. Specifically, with regard to RT, there are a number of claims that I find entirely convincing, but I assume that these claims can be separated from the explicit definition of relevance provided by Sperber and Wilson, which in my opinion raises instead serious theoretical problems. At the same time, I will show that in the writings of relevance theorists there are clues to a different notion of relevance, which is closer to the ordinary meaning and free from the above problems.

To put it a bit differently, what I aim to do is – so to speak – the pruning of a luxuriant theory. Even as far as the notion of relevance is concerned, we can find formulations (or at least suggestions) that are immune to my criticisms; and this also occurs with respect to other issues I will discuss. As a consequence, my criticisms may occasionally seem ungenerous and not entirely justified. I am well aware of this, and I know that RT can be held to support (also) different views than the ones I criticize. However, there are important pieces of their theory that are repeated on many occasions and that I find problematic, both in themselves and with respect to other formulations and parts of the theory. The explicit definition of relevance and the comprehension procedure described in this chapter are one example; their criticism to the idea of associative processing is another (see chapter 2); the little attention given to the role of consciousness is still another (chapter 3); and finally, I do not think their commitment to modularity is fruitful (chapter 4).

In the second place, I subscribe to RT's thesis that the notion of relevance has an important role to play not only in a theory of communication but also in a theory of cognition – as a matter of fact, the complete title of Sperber and Wilson (1986/1995) is *Relevance. Communication and Cognition.* To be sure, we may presume that different notions of relevance lead to different views of communicative and cognitive processes. More specifically, in accordance with an assumption that is traditional in pragmatics, I propose that we should look to human (and especially, to verbal) communication as a special case of action, and therefore that the notion of relevance should be thought as related to the practical means-ends reasoning ability that is characteristic of humans. The main thesis I will be defending is that, in this perspective, the required notion of relevance is not the quantitative-informational one that we must attribute to RT if we take seriously both their definition of relevance and the heuristic they propose for its detection, but instead a qualitative one with regard to which, however, relevance theorists provide some clues, too.

1.3 The Gricean background

To fully understand RT and, more generally, what is at stake in current cognitive pragmatics it is necessary to start from the analyses of Paul Grice. He proposes an inferential model of communication, and specifically of comprehension, as opposed to a model based on mere coding and decoding. The idea is that what a speaker means with an utterance (Grice refers to this meaning with the phrase "what is meant") normally exceeds what the utterance says on the basis of its conventional meaning ("what is said"). In practice, the speaker selects an utterance insofar as she assumes that the addressee, given a context, is able to draw an inference from what the utterance says to what the speaker means with it in that context. Coding and decoding are thus merely components of a larger process, which also depends on information provided by the context and background knowledge that the speaker expects the addressee to exploit when interpreting an utterance.

For one simple example, if a telephone rings and someone shouts "I'm having a shower", she plausibly intends to communicate something more than what the utterance says literally, for instance that she is not able to answer the phone and asks for someone else to do it. The context (the telephone ringing) and the knowledge we have of this kind of situations (a person who is having a shower is not in the best position to answer the phone; people living in the same flat expects a certain degree of cooperation from each other, etc.) allow the addressee to infer what is meant by the speaker in that circumstance from what is actually said.

On the whole, linguistic communication is conceived as a special case of intentional action, embedded within the larger framework of non-communicative intentional actions. In other words, the speaker is thought to be driven by a communicative intention that usually acquires its entire meaning as part of the specific activity it is embedded in. Participants to communicative interactions are thus seen as rational agents that pursue a variety of goals, both communicative and non-communicative, and adopt the contextually appropriate means – including linguistic ones – to pursue those goals. On the other hand, linguistic comprehension is conceived as a special case of the understanding of purposive action.

This is the background against which key Gricean notions such as the cooperative principle and conversational maxims have to be framed. In current pragmatics these notions are sometimes presented as if they were conventions that speakers have to conform to, while their crucial connection with rational action is somewhat neglected. In particular, more to our point, relevance theorists criticize the cooperative principle under the assumption that it is a normative convention prescribing the adoption of cooperative goals in communication. If this were the case, they would be right to object that speakers are sometimes guided by selfish, not cooperative, goals. But if we take a look at the way in which Grice (1975: 45) expresses it, it is rather apparent that the principle can be intended differently: "Make your conversational contribution such as is required, at the stage at which it occurs, by the accepted purpose or direction of the talk exchange in which you are engaged". Speaker and hearer have to share a common goal relative to the direction of the verbal exchange they are engaged in; they do not need to be cooperative relative to their behaviour as a whole. In other words, the speaker has to be cooperative in the limited sense of producing an utterance that, given the context and the shared knowledge, is rationally appropriate for the addressee to infer her communicative intention, and the addressee has to assume that the speaker will be rational in this precise sense.

In a sense, relevance theorists accept this minimal notion of cooperation, too (see also Reboul 2017 for a related distinction between altruistic and mutualistic – i.e., minimal – cooperation). As Sperber and Wilson (1986/1995: 268) put it, "we ourselves have stressed that interlocutors always share at least one common goal, that of understanding and being understood." According to them, Grice is wrong insofar as he presumes instead that the participants to verbal exchanges need to be cooperative *beyond* what is required by merely understanding one another. Is this correct? On the one hand, Grice may in fact be suggesting that altruistic cooperation has a more fundamental relation to human communication than deceptive behaviour: which is not exactly the same as claiming that communication must always be cooperative in the strong sense – a few lines below, I mention a similar argument proposed by Tomasello. But I think that the main disagreement lies elsewhere: Grice's approach is "normative" in the sense of assuming that human communication (be it truthful or deceptive) is a special case of means-ends reasoning, while according to RT this is not the case. In other words, what I think is really required by Grice is not that participants to verbal exchanges are not deceptive; it is rather that verbal exchanges – even when deceptive – are understood on the background of human activities and systems of goals.

Similar considerations apply to conversational maxims. By these Grice does not intend to provide a list of moral norms of communication. They are instead thought as key components (and there might be others) of the cooperative principle, accounting for how it actually ensures rationality. In other words, the maxims specify dimensions of rationality of the speaker's communicative behaviour, and the related rational expectations on the part of the addressee. The maxims proposed by Grice (1975: 45–6) are four, and can be summarized as follows: try to make your contribution one that is true (quality); be informative (quantity); be relevant (relation); be perspicuous (manner). Of these, only the first may actually seem a sort of moral norm, although it should be noted that, since maxims are intended to describe general expectations, it has a clear rational ground, too: presumably, there would not be communication at all if speakers were not truthful as a normal case. Lies and deceptive communicative behaviour can only emerge on a background of cooperative expectations (on this, see Tomasello 2008: 190). The connection with practical reasoning is even more evident for the other maxims. Let us consider, for instance, how Grice (1975: 45) formulates the maxim of quantity (more precisely, its first half): "Make your contribution as informative as is required (for the current *purposes* of the exchange)" (my emphasis: notably, the word "purposes" appears in the cooperative principle as well). As it can be seen, the amount of information is requested to be appropriate *relative to the purposes of the exchange*. In sum, the maxims aim to capture different respects in which an utterance can be rational as a means of accomplishing the communicative goals of the speaker.

The theoretical move made by RT with regard to the principle and the maxims is twofold. On the one hand, relevance theorists point out that their intent is to lay the foundations of *cognitive* pragmatics. Grice was aware that he was providing post hoc, rational reconstructions of comprehension processes, and that those reconstructions might not be implemented by actual reasoning-based psychological processes.[2] RT, on the contrary, aims to provide an analysis of the actual cognitive processes, and coherently it proposes to replace the notions (the cooperative principle and the maxims) on which Grice

2 But on this, see chapter 5 below.

based his rational reconstructions with specific cognitive mechanisms, that are maintained to be automatic and then quite different from explicit reasoning. On the other hand, the idea is that these mechanisms are essentially based on the search for relevance. The notion of relevance was explicitly mentioned by Grice in the maxim of relation (expressible as "be relevant"). In this respect, then, RT's theoretical move amounts to assigning to this notion a more central, not to say exclusive, role.

Before I describe RT's view in more detail, let me make two further comments on these theoretical moves. First, RT does not completely abandon the Gricean idea that utterance comprehension is a rational process, despite its being automatic. The idea is preserved in the assumption that the addressee builds up an inferential structure, formed by premises and conclusions, and that this non-demonstrative inference is in fact the core of the comprehension process. In Grice, however, as we noted, side-by-side with this propositional sense of rationality (the construction of inferences from premises to conclusions) a different sense of the word was at play: the one related to practical means-ends reasoning. This latter sense of rationality is indeed put in the background in RT's theoretical framework. Second, as we will see, the notion of relevance adopted by RT has a quantitative character, being based on the idea of a cognitive tendency to maximise information. If we compare this idea with Grice's maxim of quantity, the theoretical shift is evident: Grice speaks of the appropriateness of the amount of information with respect to the purposes of the communicators, while RT proposes an automatic mechanism aimed at maximising information without regard to the goals and the forms of rational action in which participants are involved.

1.4 Relevance theory: a prologue

I have just claimed that RT gives up the Gricean intuition of comprehension as a form of practical reasoning *based on goal recognition* (cfr. Mazzone 2009), and replaces it with a mechanism based on the maximisation of information. Does any textual evidence support this view? This is actually the case. One year after *Relevance*, Sperber and Wilson published a synopsis of their book as a target article for the journal *Behavioral and Brain Sciences*, and in answer to objections raised by commentators they wrote the following:

> Some commentators [...] think our definition of relevance fails to do justice to pretheoretical intuitions. Utterances are relevant, they feel, to *purposes*, *goals*, topics, questions, interests, or matters in hand. We define relevance in a context and to an individual. [...] One reason *we*

> *did not set out to define relevance to purpose, goal, and so on*, is that we had no idea how to answer the analogous questions for any of these terms [...] Given a definition of relevance in a context, and a method of context construction, however, there is no reason that assumptions about the goals and purposes of the individual, or of the participants in a conversation, should not form part of the context and give rise to contextual effects in the usual way. (Sperber and Wilson 1987: 742; my emphases)

Sperber and Wilson acknowledge that their notion of relevance, contrary to pretheoretical intuitions, is not defined relative to the goals of communicators. Nevertheless, they suggest that in their perspective goals can still play a role indirectly, to the extent that they are part of the context and apt to produce contextual effects. In practice, neither their definition of relevance grants a positive theoretical role to goals, nor are the cognitive mechanisms they have in mind based on the recognition and manipulation of goals. Goals are only indirectly involved as a side effect of a mechanism that recovers contextual assumptions in view of the derivation of sufficient cognitive effects, to the extent that those assumptions may concern goals.

1.5 Cognition and communication

A key thesis of RT is that both cognition and communication are guided by expectations of relevance. "According to relevance theory, utterances raise expectations of relevance not because speakers are expected to obey a Co-operative Principle and maxims or some other specifically communicative convention, but because the search for relevance is a basic feature of human cognition, which communicators may exploit" (Wilson and Sperber 2002: 251).[3] In practice, since our cognitive system receives a large number of perceptual inputs on a continuous basis, their processing cannot but be selective. RT expresses this point in terms of a "Cognitive Principle of Relevance", according to which cognition has a tendency to maximise relevance. Leaving aside for a moment the issue of precisely how relevance is to be defined, the hypothesis is that the cognitive system tends to process the most relevant stimuli, searching their most relevant interpretations. The case of communication is partially different, since here the cognitive system is not faced with a haphazard presentation of

3 In this introductory part I will repeatedly refer to Wilson and Sperber (2002), that is a useful synopsis of Relevance Theory written about fifteen years after *Relevance*, and therefore takes into account the main recent innovations in the theory.

stimuli, it is instead in presence of a message that has been deliberately produced by a speaker for an addressee. In this case, the "Communicative Principle of Relevance" applies, according to which every ostensive stimulus – that is, every communicative act manifestly addressed to an interlocutor – conveys a presumption of its own optimal relevance (Wilson and Sperber 2002: 256–7). This means that it produces the expectation to be relevant enough to be worth the audience's processing effort – otherwise, why should the speaker bother to address it to the addressee? – and the most relevant one compatible with the communicator's abilities and preferences.

1.6 The definition of relevance

What is then relevance for RT? Let us start from an informal and intuitive description.

> When is an input relevant? Intuitively, an input (a sight, a sound, an utterance, a memory) is relevant to an individual when it connects with background information he has available to yield conclusions that matter to him: say, by answering a question he had in mind, improving his knowledge on a certain topic, settling a doubt, confirming a suspicion, or correcting a mistaken impression. (Wilson and Sperber 2002: 251)

First of all, this quotation introduces the idea of an inferential mechanism that, starting from some elements (an input and background information), draws some conclusions. But most of all, relevance to an individual is intuitively understood by conceiving individuals in terms of informational systems – or, if you prefer, in terms of pure subjects of knowledge. Input processing is relevant to the extent that it produces cognitive effects into those systems, by modifying their informational status. In particular, there is no mention of goals of the subject apart from that of acquiring knowledge. The key notion here is that of "cognitive effects", described by exemplification in the following way:

> The most important type of cognitive effect achieved by processing an input in a context is a contextual implication, a conclusion deducible from the input and the context together, but from neither input nor context alone. For example, on seeing my train arriving, I might look at my watch, access my knowledge of the train timetable, and derive the contextual implication that my train is late (which may itself achieve relevance by combining with further contextual assumptions to yield further implications). Other types of cognitive effect include the strengthening, revision or abandonment of available assumptions. (Wilson and Sperber 2002: 251)

The picture is thus as follows. The relevance of cognitive inputs depends on the cognitive effects obtained by their processing; specifically, an input is relevant to the extent that, by combining with assumptions suggested by the context, it allows reaching contextual conclusions. To gain new knowledge is the most important type of cognitive effect; others include the strengthening of already possessed knowledge and its revision or abandonment. Let me also observe in passing that these intuitive descriptions make no mention of cognitive *efforts*: the emphasis is entirely on cognitive *effects*. I will turn to this in a moment.

The example of the train might suggest that the individual's goals have a role to play here; specifically, it suggests a situation in which a subject intends to take a train with the purpose of getting somewhere. It is important, then, to be clear about it. The theoretical point is not that RT's notion of cognitive effect is incompatible with assigning a role to goals. On the contrary, it is fair to assume that there is a sort of logico-conceptual connection between goals and cognitive effects, and some considerations of relevance theorists encourage such an assumption. For instance, in the context of the same example Wilson and Sperber (2002) claim that a delay of the train of only one minute would have few cognitive effects since it would not imply a reorganization of the agent's plans; that is, the delay would not have important consequences on the informational status of the agent *in that* it would not modify her system of goals. However, as relevance theorists have recognized (see above), the definitions and the mechanisms they propose do not assign any explicit role to goal recognition. In other words, RT explains the role played by goals only indirectly, as a side effect of mechanisms based on the amount of cognitive effects – instead of explaining cognitive effects only indirectly, as a side effect of goal recognition. As we will see below, this raises the question – which is, I will argue, unanswered – of explaining how the amount of cognitive effects can be measured and play the theoretical role assigned to it.

We can now introduce the formal definition of relevance for an input and an individual. Relevance is defined as directly proportional to the amount of cognitive effects obtained, and inversely proportional to the effort expended in obtaining them:

a. Other things being equal, the greater the positive cognitive effects achieved by processing an input, the greater the relevance of the input to the individual at that time.
b. Other things being equal, the greater the processing effort expended, the lower the relevance of the input to the individual at that time. (Wilson and Sperber 2002: 252)

To be sure, these two parts of the definition are of unequal importance. The second one, related to effort, is introduced in order to put a realistic constraint on the first. It would be, in fact, of little use to define maximisation of cognitive effects without considering to what extent it can actually be pursued by a cognitive system. What if the process by which one obtains the greatest amount of cognitive effects requires an entire life, or a devastating effort? It is apparent that the processing of inputs, and the interpretation of utterances, that we daily perform are not compatible with such a scenario. As a consequence, maximisation of effects must be balanced against minimisation of effort.

Thus, we can say that the key point of input processing and utterance interpretation is the maximisation of effects, and often relevance theorists encourage this view – they speak of expectations of relevance in terms of expectations about the amount of cognitive effects. Minimisation of effort is not what cognitive processing aims to; it is rather a realistic constraint on its actual functioning.

1.7 Implicit and explicit meaning, construction of context

The fundamental thesis of RT is that utterance understanding is driven by the search for relevance, defined as we just saw. We have to look now at the specific mechanism through which this is accomplished. We already know that this mechanism involves the production of a non-demonstrative inference. Now we are going to analyse in more detail the structure of this inference, in the next section we will see how it is constructed.

In the picture outlined by Grice, "what is said" is a proposition endowed with a truth-value, that is, a unitary and completely specified thought that can be judged either true or false. This requires that the addressee goes beyond simple decoding of the words contained in utterances, and therefore beyond their conventional linguistic meaning, to the extent that this meaning does not usually provide unambiguous and completely specified thoughts. For instance, if I say "this dog is little" one cannot decide whether the utterance is true or false unless something that is not part of the conventional meaning – that is, which individual in the world I refer to with the phrase "this dog" – is grasped. This requirement is often expressed by saying that certain linguistic forms need "reference assignment". Similarly, the utterance "I put my money in the bank" has quite different truth-conditions depending on whether "bank" is intended as FINANCIAL INSTITUTION or RIVERSIDE. In such cases, it is said that "disambiguation" of ambiguous words is needed.

According to Grice, as soon as lexical decoding is accomplished, reference assignment and disambiguation are the only pragmatic processes required in order to get "what is said" – recently, it has become customary to call it also the "explicit" meaning of utterances. However, reference assignment and disambiguation are generally considered pragmatic processes in a quite peripheral and little interesting sense. Although they require the addressee to go beyond conventional meaning and make an appeal to context, as is characteristic of pragmatic processes, the common belief is that this occurs quite trivially and under strict control of conventional meaning. An ambiguous word suggests by itself the need for disambiguation; a generic expression as the definite description "this dog" automatically guides the addressee towards the search for a referent in the context. The pragmatic phenomena that Grice considered interesting were the ones requiring a far less predictable inferential derivation, which could be reconstructed in terms of a practical argument containing premises and conclusions, and only the transition from what is said to what is meant (also called the "implicit" meaning) was thought to match that description.

In the last decades, it has become common to think that Grice was wrong with regard to the construction of explicit meaning: nowadays, this is generally thought to require other pragmatic processes beyond disambiguation and reference assignment. Specifically, according to the so-called contextualists, conventional meaning largely underdetermines explicit meaning and only the context (together with background knowledge and possibly even consideration of the speaker's intentions) allows obtaining a proposition that can be judged either true or false. To continue the previous example, in order to determine whether the utterance "this dog is little" is true, more is needed than identifying the entity that is referred to by the expression "this dog": we need to determine, too, the comparison class against which the dimensions of the animal have to be evaluated ("little with respect to what?").

However, in line with Grice's view, utterance understanding is still thought to require the construction of an inference taking the explicit meaning as one of its premises and the implicit meaning as a conclusion. What else do these inferences contain? A certain number of contextually suggested assumptions that, together with the explicit meaning, feature as premises from which a certain number of conclusions – including the implicit meaning – can be drawn. Precisely because assumptions and conclusions are suggested by the context, RT speaks of the interpretation process as a process of context construction. More precisely, RT reserves the term "context" not for the entirety of the circumstance in which the conversation takes place and that we might call the "physical context", but instead for the entirety of the cognitive entities that must be activated with the help of the physical context in order to provide the pragmatic interpretation. In sum, RT conceives comprehension as the construction of the relevant cognitive context, and a key aspect of this is the construction of an inference involving a certain number of contextual assumptions and conclusions.

These claims are easily agreed on. As we will see in the next section, problems arise when RT attempts to specify a mechanism, based on the notion of relevance, for the construction of cognitive context.

1.8 The comprehension procedure and its problems

In the end, how is the context – and, more specifically, the inference in which the interpretation consists – constructed? Sperber and Wilson's answer is that this occurs by means of a heuristic that they call "relevance-based comprehension procedure". By the term "heuristic", it is intended a process or procedure that accomplish a certain task in an approximate manner; that is, the process is not perfectly satisfactory but on the other hand it ensures economy of effort.[4] The heuristic proposed by RT is constituted by two steps:

a. Follow a path of least effort in computing cognitive effects: Test interpretive hypotheses (disambiguations, reference resolutions, implicatures, etc.) in order of accessibility.
b. Stop when your expectations of relevance are satisfied. (Wilson and Sperber 2002: 260)

This heuristic should account for the fact that the search for relevant interpretations is satisfied in an approximate but realistically feasible manner. One might imagine a different, more systematic method consisting in producing all the possible interpretations, assessing the amount of cognitive effects against the related effort for each of them, and then comparing the results in order to establish which interpretation is the most relevant. But this method would be extremely expensive from a computational point of view. On the other hand, the above heuristic does not grant that the most relevant interpretation in an absolute sense will be selected, but allows individuating an interpretation that is apt by definition to satisfy the addressee's expectations of relevance at a quite reasonable cost.

First of all, let us consider how the procedure achieves these goals, that is, maximisation of cognitive effects and minimisation of cognitive efforts. The effort is reduced by the simple fact that the system constructs only one interpretation at a time and, what is more, the most accessible one, which also means the least expensive. The construction process needs to be repeated only in case, at the second step, the accessed interpretation turns out not to satisfy expectations of relevance. Thus, the procedure as a whole ensures economy of effort, without any explicit computation of the costs. As to cognitive effects, at the first step of the procedure these are computed for one single interpretation at a time, and then, in the second step, they are assessed against expectations of relevance. There is a key point here, to which we must draw attention. If we take seriously the analysis of relevance provided by RT, we have to leave aside our intuitions about the notion and apply instead the formal definition we are provided with, according

4 On this issue, see Kahneman et al. (1982), Gigerenzer et al. (1999).

to which relevance is a direct function of the amount of cognitive effects and an inverse function of the effort required for their processing. More precisely, RT holds that the essential component of relevance is the one related to cognitive effects – while reference to effort essentially acts as a constraint. In any case, as we saw, economy of effort is granted by the overall structure of the procedure. Thus, the assessment described at the second step of the procedure – as to the satisfaction of expectations of relevance – can be presumed to concern whether the cognitive effects are quantitatively sufficient with respect to expectations.[5]

Why is this important? Because, I claim, there is here a specific problem for the relevance-based approach. We already saw that the notion of relevance proposed by RT suggests a different view than the Gricean one, insofar as comprehension is conceived as aiming at the maximisation of information instead of at goal recognition. This may appear disputable, in the first place, and possibly incoherent with relevance theorists' claim that comprehension is a form of mindreading. In addition, we are now going to see that the actual mechanisms proposed to ensure maximisation of information have a theoretical blind spot. Specifically, it is far from clear how the second step of the procedure – related to the satisfaction of expectations about the amount of cognitive effects – may be accomplished.

There is here a sharp difference between the two steps of the procedure. The first step can most naturally be understood in terms of associative processes, that is, in terms of processes whose existence and functioning are not actually controversial in cognitive science. On the contrary, how the second step is to be performed is far from clear, and as a matter of fact RT seems to explore different hypotheses, apparently incompatible with each other and partly resting on very weak empirical grounds.

One possibility that is repeatedly mentioned is that the assessment of relevance is not quantitative and absolute but instead comparative:

> While quantitative notions of relevance might be worth exploring from a formal point of view, it is the comparative rather than the quantitative notion that is likely to provide the best starting point for constructing a psychologically plausible theory. (Wilson and Sperber 2002: 253)

5 The emphasis on the quantitative dimension of the relevance-based mechanism is well attested in relevance theorists' writings. For one example, see the following quotation: "when similar *amounts* of effort are required, the effect factor is decisive in determining degrees of relevance, and when similar *amounts* of effect are achievable, the effort factor is decisive" (Wilson and Sperber 2002: 251; my emphases). For another example: "On this approach, any utterance addressed to someone automatically raises an expectation of relevance, which will be satisfied by deriving *enough* true contextual implications (or other positive cognitive effects), at a low enough processing cost, to make it relevant in the expected way" (Wilson and Carston 2006: 408; my emphasis).

In other words, what would be needed is not a mechanism for assessing the absolute amount of cognitive effects derived by a single interpretation; rather, there might be an intuitive comparison between different interpretations with regard to the respective amount of cognitive effects.

It should be noted, however, that the comprehension procedure and, specifically, its second step, seems committed to a different idea. Interpretations would be constructed one at a time, and the procedure would stop as soon as one of them succeeds in providing a sufficient amount of cognitive effects. In sum, the procedure does not predict the construction of a plurality of interpretations in competition with one another. It predicts instead that the amount of cognitive effects produced by a single interpretation is measured and then compared with expectations of relevance. Coherently with this quantitative – versus comparative – view, in more than one occasion relevance theorists have outlined what Sperber and Wilson (1986/1995: 130) explicitly called "a speculation": the hypothesis according to which cognitive effects and mental efforts might be perceived, by analogy with bodily movements and the related efforts, through certain "symptomatic physico-chemical changes" (ibidem). This would allow gross evaluations, not mediated by a precise numerical measurement, of the effects and efforts related to single interpretations, and occasionally even finer comparative judgments between interpretations:

> Relevance, as it affects cognition, is not computed or numerically measured but monitored or assessed, yielding only gross absolute judgments and, in certain types of cases only, finer relative judgments. Suppose that the brain is sensitive to the amount of reorganization brought about by the processing of some information and to the expenditure of energy thus incurred, just as it is sensitive to changes of posture and expenditure of energy in the case of bodily movement. This is very vague – hopelessly so, some AI people may think – but it is not so vague that it could not be false, and it is what we are claiming anyhow. (Sperber and Wilson 1987: 742)

In sum, it seems that RT is exploring two different hypotheses, one involving comparison between interpretations and the other based on absolute measurement of the cognitive effects of single interpretations. Only the latter seems coherent with the comprehension procedure, but unfortunately it has a serious flaw: it depends on a speculation – by analogy with the capacity to perceive bodily movements and the related effort – that is not further investigated, and for which there are, to my knowledge, neither empirical evidence nor independent theoretical grounds. To make matters worse, even if that speculation turned out to be correct there is another problem to be solved. In order to establish whether cognitive effects are sufficient to stop the comprehension procedure, it is not enough to have a non-numerical perception of their amount. This assessment also requires quantitative expectations against which the system may assess whether the amount of cognitive effects is sufficient. Without such *quantitative* expectations, there is nothing with respect to which the perceived amount of cognitive effects can be said either to be *sufficient* or not. But in RT there is no explanation of how such quantitative expectations would be formed. For all these reasons, it is not clear how the second step of the comprehension procedure is to be ensured.

What if we choose the other option, that is, the hypothesis of a comparison between possible interpretations? With regard to this hypothesis, too, RT is not very explicit about the mechanisms involved. A rather natural view, however, is that such a competition may be performed by the same dynamic of accessibility described as the first step of the procedure. In other words, the degree of accessibility of different interpretations would by itself provide a comparative evaluation of their respective relevance. It should not go unnoticed, however, that if we equate comparison/competition between interpretations to simple accessibility, then the second step of the procedure becomes superfluous: interpretations would be recognized as relevant – in an absolute sense, that is, with regard to both cognitive effort and cognitive effects – by the simple fact that they are less expensive (i.e., more accessible) than the alternatives. As we are going to see in a moment, there is at least one occasion in which relevance theorists suggest exactly this: that minimisation of cognitive effort is sufficient by itself to guide the cognitive system towards maximisation of effects.

1.9 Is it possible that cognitive effort does the whole job?

In Sperber and Wilson (1996) there is a passage in which cognitive effort is considered at first, as one would expect, as the other side of cognitive effects with regard to relevance, but then an unexpected question is raised (below in italics):

> when expectations of effect are wholly indeterminate, the mind should base itself on considerations of effort: pick up from the environment the most easily attended stimulus, and process it in the context of what comes most readily to mind. *Ceteris paribus*, what is easier is more relevant, if it is relevant at all. *But what are the chances that what comes more easily to mind is, in fact, relevant?* [my emphasis] They would be close to nil, if saliency in the environment and accessibility in memory were both random, and moreover uncorrelated. (Sperber and Wilson 1996: 531)

The question is unexpected because there seems to be no reason why "what comes more easily to mind" should be relevant except for the fact that, *ceteris paribus*, it is relevant by definition simply because it requires minimum effort. Stimuli and interpretations that we process easily might result not relevant at all on the side of cognitive effects, that is, they might have little or no cognitive effect. Precisely in order to avoid this, the second step of the procedure appears to be required: an easily accessible interpretation might not be relevant enough to stop the search for interpretations. Nevertheless, Sperber and Wilson seem to ask here whether easy accessibility ensures *by itself* a sufficient degree of relevance.

And in fact, the previous quotation is followed by an evolutionary argument aimed at showing that what requires little processing effort is automatically "the right kind of information" (so to speak), with no need of further mechanisms to assess whether a sufficient amount of cognitive effects is achieved:

> But humans are evolved organisms with learning capacities of sorts, so it is not too surprising to find that they spontaneously pay more attention [...] to objects and events that, on average, are more likely to be relevant to them.
>
> For the same reason, it is not surprising that the perceptual categorization of a distal stimulus should tend to activate related information in memory. [...] Nor is it surprising that memory is so organized that pieces of information that are likely to be simultaneously relevant tend to be co-accessed or co-activated in chunks variously described in the literature as "concepts", "schemas", "scripts", "dossiers", etc. (Sperber and Wilson 1996: 531)

In practice, the suggestion is that accessibility of information depends on a mechanism selected by evolution to single out what is more important for the agent. More specifically, it is suggested that – thanks to the organization of information in memory via schemata, concepts etc. – accessibility of contents is a reliable sign of the fact that they are "simultaneously relevant".

This proposal is quite different from the view that the notion of effort is mainly a constraint – due to considerations of economy – on the search for cognitive effects. Here the effort is presumed to function instead as a self-sufficient sign of relevance. This suggestion goes in the same direction as the thesis that we will explore in chapter 2, according to which, thanks to the organization of memory, simple associative mechanisms are sufficient to ensure motivated cognitive processes such as pragmatic inferencing. Nevertheless, on many occasions relevance theorists maintain on the contrary that simple accessibility is not sufficient to constrain interpretations, and further constraints are therefore required. This is precisely the function performed by the second step of the procedure: the most easily accessed interpretations are then evaluated with regard to their capacity to satisfy quantitative expectations of relevance.

To sum up, one has to choose between two distinct hypotheses. The one prevailing in RT predicts that there are quantitative expectations of relevance against which interpretations selected by simple accessibility have to be further assessed. The other proposes instead that accessibility alone does the whole job. The former hypothesis raises the problem that we lack satisfactory answers to how cognitive effects are measured, how quantitative expectations of relevance are determined, and how the amount of effects is assessed against expectations.

As we will see in a moment, however, relevance theorists have also explored a different approach according to which expectations of relevance would not concern the quantity but the type of cognitive effects.

1.10 Expectations about the type of cognitive effects and mutual adjustment process

Relevance theorists have explicitly spoken of expectations about the *type* of cognitive effects, occasionally side by side with the more standard reference to their *quantity*. For one example in which type and quantity are mentioned together, consider the following passage of Carston (2007: 20; my emphasis): "an utterance automatically triggers quite specific expectations of relevance in its addressee, that is, expectations concerning *both the quantity and the kind* of cognitive effects (implications) it will yield if optimally processed".[6]

Mention of the type has become especially frequent in more recent writings of RT, characterized by the introduction of the mutual adjustment process (for instance, Sperber and Wilson 1998; Wilson and Sperber 2004; Wilson 2004; Carston 2002). The idea is that pragmatic comprehension processes do not operate sequentially, that is, exclusively by means of forward inferences from explicit meaning to contextual conclusions – passing through the production of appropriate contextual assumptions. On the contrary, there would be a combination of forward and backward inferences operating in parallel, yielding reciprocal adjustment between explicit meaning, contextual assumptions and contextual conclusions.

> Mutual adjustment is seen as taking place in parallel rather than in sequence. The hearer does not first identify the proposition expressed, then access an appropriate set of contextual assumptions and then derive a set of cognitive effects. In many cases [...] he is just as likely to reason backwards *from an expected cognitive* effect to the context and content that would warrant it. (Wilson 2004: 353; my emphasis)

As the last sentence suggests, the backward inferences involved in the mutual adjustment process depend on expectations about specific cognitive effects.

---

6 More extensively, consider the following quotation: "According to relevance theory, utterance interpretation in general is goal directed. Every utterance addressed to someone creates a presumption of relevance, *together with more specific expectations* about how relevance is to be achieved (and in particular, *about the type* of contextual implications to be derived)" (Wilson and Carston 2006: 421; emphases mine).

For one example (from Wilson and Carston 2007), let us consider the following exchange:

(1) Peter: Will Sally look after the children if we get ill?
Mary: Sally is an angel.

Clearly, the implicit meaning conveyed by Mary's utterance is an affirmative answer to Peter's question, something like SALLY WILL LOOK AFTER THE CHILDREN IF WE GET ILL. This meaning can be seen as the conclusion of an inference having as premises the explicit meaning of Mary's utterance and some contextual assumptions. As to the explicit meaning, however, the concept that the word "angel" hands over to it is not, of course, the encoded concept ANGEL having among its features SUPERNATURAL BEING. It has to be instead a different concept obtained by adapting the encoded concept to the context. A natural way to explain this adjustment is precisely in terms of a backward inference triggered by an expected conclusion. Peter's question, insofar as it requires a yes/no answer, raises in fact the expectation that Mary intends to claim either SALLY WILL LOOK AFTER THE CHILDREN IF WE GET ILL or its negation, and this expectation can cause in turn a backward inference toward the explicit meaning, which has to be coherent either with that claim or with its negation. Thus, the concept ANGEL must be adjusted until the explicit content is apt to provide a premise (for instance, SALLY IS KIND AND CARING) that licences the claim or its negation as a conclusion.

The example clearly shows how backward inferences involve expectations about specific cognitive effects. This makes the notion of *type* of cognitive effects importantly different from that of their expected *amount* or *quantity*: while the former involves specific contents that in turn impose constraints on the content of the premises, the latter does not involve any specific content and only allows for a quantitative comparison with the actual cognitive effects. Moreover, the notion of type of cognitive effects admits of a natural explanation in terms of accessibility. In the previous example, the expected cognitive effect that Mary intends to give a yes/no answer to Peter depends on a conventional schema connecting yes/no questions and yes/no answers. It is reasonable to assume that Peter's question associatively activates such a schema, which in turn activates an expectation about the implicit meaning intended by Mary.

This last point is important in that it allows giving a unitary explanation of the comprehension process. We considered above the hypothesis that, thanks to the organization of memory, associative accessibility alone is sufficient to ensure the relevance of interpretations. Now we see that, according to RT, the physical context may trigger backward inferences towards specific cognitive effects and this seems to admit of a simple associative explanation. Thus, the entire process must not be thought of as the combination of two mechanisms: an associative one based on accessibility of interpretations and a non-associative one assessing those interpretations against expectations of relevance. On the contrary, one can think of it as a unitary mechanism based on associative access of contextual assumptions and conclusions: these can be accessed both via forward inferences prompted by the linguistic meaning and via backward inferences prompted by the context. In this case, expectations of relevance are expectations about types of cognitive effects prompted by the context.

As we are going to see, this is compatible with the traditional view of comprehension as goal recognition.

1.11 Recognition of goals is back again

In the overall, the situation we have outlined so far is the following. On the one hand, RT's standard view conceives relevance as maximisation of cognitive effects (constrained by minimisation of efforts); in practice, comprehension would be explained by a procedure – based on the quantitative notion of relevance – that accepts the most accessible interpretation provided that it ensures a sufficient amount of cognitive effects. On the other hand, RT seems to consider an alternative hypothesis according to which accessibility is by itself sufficient to grant relevance, and expectations of relevance are described in qualitative terms, involving specific contextual conclusions. I intend to show now that, when conceived in accordance with this alternative hypothesis, expectations of relevance are coherent with the kind of goal recognition that Grice had in mind.

As already noted, Grice (1989) has described comprehension as a rational enterprise in the following sense: the addressee sees the speaker as a rational agent pursuing communicative goals and producing utterances that can be interpreted as means for the expression of those goals. In sum, utterance comprehension is taken to consist in the contextually appropriate reconstruction of coherent means-ends structures. In this perspective, Grice makes an appeal to the physical context as a source of information about the non-communicative goals of the speaker, and these goals can yield backward inferences toward what is nowadays called the explicit meaning of the utterance. Let us consider the following quotation:

> in cases where there is doubt, say, about which of two or more things an utterer intends to convey, we tend to refer to the context (linguistic or otherwise) of the utterance and ask which of the alternatives would be *relevant to other things he is saying or doing*, or which intention in a particular situation would fit in with *some purpose he obviously has* (e.g., a man who calls for a "pump" at a fire would not want a bicycle pump). (Grice 1957: 387; emphases mine)

In this example, to the extent that the context suggests the non-communicative goal of extinguishing a fire, the interpretation of "pump" must be adjusted accordingly. There is a noteworthy structural similarity with the example (1) above, in which Peter's question plays the same role that is played here by the extra-linguistic context: it sets the goal to which, through a backward inference, the addressee must adjust the explicit meaning of Mary's answer. In other words, thanks to contextual information, goals are recognized and then employed to trace back the communicative means apt to pursue them.

Thus, RT's recent proposal of a mutual adjustment process – based on forward and backward inferences and on specific expectations about the cognitive effects intended by the speaker – appears coherent with the Gricean picture based on goal recognition: both involve the construction of chains of means and goals that may cross the boundaries between communication and action. While in the example (1) Mary's goal is to answer Peter's yes/no question (a communicative goal, which in turn sets the goal of giving a yes/no answer as a means to pursue it), in Grice's example the ultimate goal is extinguishing a fire, that is, a non-communicative one. It seems, then, that backward inferences can be drawn from both communicative and non-communicative goals recognized by the context. If this picture is correct, pragmatic comprehension must be incorporated into a more general mindreading ability. This is explicitly acknowledged by Sperber and Wilson (2002), who cite approvingly Grice for having described human communication as a case of expression and recognition of intentions, define pragmatic understanding as "an exercise in mind-reading" (Sperber and Wilson 2002: 3), and propose that the relevance-based comprehension procedure is a "sub-module of the human mind-reading ability" (idem: 21). Although Sperber and Wilson do not draw this conclusion, it seems reasonable to conclude that communicative intentions are embedded within wider goal structures and that this plays some role in linguistic production and comprehension.[7]

An interesting contribution to this idea is offered by Levinson (1992) with his notion of "activity types". These are defined as social patterns of goal-directed behaviours in specific scenarios. As such, activity types produce specific expectations about the goals – including communicative ones – at play in social actions. In practice, communicative actions are thought of as moves embedded

7 However, as I am going to say in a moment (see the Conclusions), this is controversial. The idea of means-ends chains is coherent with the mutual adjustment process, but probably not with the standard RT's view based on the notion of relevance and the comprehension procedure. On the construction of chains of goals crossing the boundary between pragmatics and mindreading, see below §§ 4.2 and 4.3.

within the currently performed activity types and apt to pursue sub-goals of their overall goals. Levinson gives the following example: the sentence "C'mon Peter" may have a variety of meanings, but if one hears it during a basketball game it acquires a very clear sense, based on the kind of goal the speaker may have in that context. Trials and lessons are other examples of activity types provided by Levinson, in order to show how questions in English may have very specific uses (i.e., goals), which "are closely tied – indeed, derived from – the overall goals of the activities in which they occur" (Levinson 1992: 82).

1.12 Conclusions

In this chapter we have analysed the notion of relevance proposed by RT and contrasted it with pretheoretical intuitions according to which the notion is relative to goals and interests of the subject. Sperber and Wilson conceive instead of relevance mainly as maximisation of cognitive effects. Under the assumption that utterance comprehension is guided by the search for relevance, this means that the amount of information gained by the addressee is seen as a goal in itself, independently from the activities in which she is involved. From this perspective, RT takes a step away from the traditional Gricean view, according to which communication and comprehension are thought of as forms of practical rationality in the context of human action and, as such, they require the representation of goal structures. In other words, while for Grice relevance is essentially adequacy to (and coherence with) action goals,[8] for RT it is essentially informativity.

More specifically, RT describes a relevance-based mechanism for comprehension in two steps: a first one in which interpretations are constructed in order of accessibility, and a second one in which those interpretations are assessed for their capacity to satisfy expectations about the amount of cognitive effects. This proposal faces at least two problems, both affecting the second step: a speculation devoid of empirical or theoretical support is offered for how cognitive effects are measured, and no explanation at all is offered for how quantitative expectations of cognitive effects are determined.

On the other hand, the writings of relevance theorists contain suggestions going in a different direction. To start with, the idea is explored that the assessment of cognitive effects is not absolute but comparative. It is not easy to understand how this is compatible with the *two-steps* comprehension procedure.

8 Recall Grice's quotation in § 1.11: the communicative intention we attribute to a speaker has to be "relevant to other things he is saying or doing".

The comparison between interpretations is rather to be identified with the first step alone: the construction of the most accessible interpretation equates to a competition that selects the least expensive interpretation. This is compatible with the further suggestion according to which minimisation of effort is sufficient to single out the (relatively) most relevant interpretations, thanks to the organization of memory. In the same direction as these two suggestions, RT explores the hypothesis that expectations of relevance concern the type, not the amount, of cognitive effects. If this is the case, cognitive effects can be activated not only by forward inferences from explicit meaning, but also by backward inferences from contexts. These backward inferences can therefore substitute for the second step of the comprehension procedure, in the sense that they allow assessing the relevance of the interpretations that are constructed through forward inferences from conventional meaning: an interpretation would be sufficiently relevant to the extent that it is coherent with contextual expectations about the type of cognitive effects intended by the speaker. In sum, each of these suggestions contributes to outline an alternative picture to the standard RT's view based on the satisfaction of quantitative expectations of relevance. In this way, one might avoid precisely the component of the comprehension procedure that we argued to be problematic.

One might find disputable that what I call "the standard RT's view" is actually their standard view: I then need to be clear on this point. There are a couple of specific issues to be mentioned.[9] First, one might feel that my insistence on a quantitative-informational view is incompatible with relevance theorists' emphasis on a comparative-rather-than-quantitative account. Second, and relatedly, I insist on cognitive effects, thus downplaying the role that RT assigns to effort in a way that may seem unjustified. Third, I contrast expectations about the type and the amount of cognitive effects, while these two aspects might both be present and cooperate with each other. One important answer is: I am well aware of these issues, and of their importance whenever relevance theorists get to the heart of their analyses of actual episodes of communication; but my point is, first of all, that when they summarize their theory, they give the place of honour to such things as the relevance-based comprehension procedure. And according to this procedure, the process is *not* comparative (the hearer constructs and assesses one interpretation at a time), and the expectations of relevance primarily concern cognitive effects (since the effort is already ensured by the first step). Moreover, this is coherent with a number of explicit formulations – I mentioned a couple of them – concerning expectations *about the amount of cognitive effects*. But what

9 I have to thank two anonymous reviewers for their help in detecting these issues.

about the possibility that both expectations about the amount and the type of effects have a role to play? For instance, is it possible[10] that expectations about type drive the recovery of strongly communicated implicatures, while expectations about quantity are responsible for the recovery of weak implicatures? Here my key point is twofold: we lack any clear proposal about the mechanism that might provide expectations about quantity, and then assess cognitive effects against them; we may count instead on a well-established mechanism for expectations about type (based on organization of memory and associative activation), and there are reasons – as Sperber and Wilson (1996) recognize – for thinking that this mechanism does the whole job (with no reason to distinguish here between strong and weak implicatures).

Most of all, it is important to recall my metaphor of a luxuriant theory that requires pruning. I do not think that my criticisms can be appropriately rejected by pointing to parts of RT that are immune to them. If I am right that RT has explored different theoretical options, then the problem is which ones are compatible with each other, and which should be probably dismissed altogether. Even if one disputes that what I criticise is the *standard* view of RT, the point still stays: relevance theorists repeatedly suggest that there are quantitative expectations of relevance, and in any summary of the theory they propose that, in the second step of the relevance-based comprehension procedure, the amount of cognitive effects is assessed against those expectations – a claim that I argue is quite problematic. On the other hand, they explore an alternative picture that is comparative rather than quantitative, is entirely framed in terms of effort (and associative activation), and is based on expectations about type.

Moreover, this alternative picture is more coherent with the spirit of the Gricean view, since backward inferences can easily be thought of as inferences from goals made manifest by the context to communicative intentions that provide the means for those goals. Nevertheless, it is not clear whether this hypothesis of continuity between pragmatics and mindreading is coherent with the general RT's approach: if, on the one hand, this theory conceives of utterance comprehension as a special case of mindreading, on the other hand it does not assign any explicit role to the connection between communicative intentions and non-communicative goals. This is not surprising, given the above analysis of the notion of relevance and the comprehension procedure: the standard RT's view describes comprehension essentially as a self-sufficient mechanism – specifically, as a mechanism that does not depend on goal recognition. As we saw, Sperber and Wilson (1987) makes it explicit that RT describes relevance (and the processes involved in utterance

10 One anonymous reviewer has actually raised this issue.

understanding) with regard to a context and an individual, since they have no idea of how this could be done with regard to goals.

In sum, relevance theorists occasionally explore hypotheses compatible with the Gricean idea of pragmatic comprehension as a form of practical reasoning based on goal recognition. In their standard view, however, comprehension is a form of mindreading in the limited sense of a procedure for the attribution of communicative intentions to speakers, independently from the attribution of any other goal.

A related question is that of modularity: RT describes pragmatic comprehension as a modular process, operating with mechanisms that are different from those involved in mindreading. In chapter 2 I will develop instead the proposal that pragmatics and action understanding are implemented by the same kind of process, that is, an associative process driven by schemata. A key purpose of that chapter is to argue that two different notions of "associative" might be involved, respectively, in my claim that utterance understanding is essentially associative and in RT's argument against associative approaches in pragmatics. At the same time, I will claim (in chapter 3) that this distinction between two notions of associative implies a role for controlled and conscious processes that RT tends to neglect. Later, I will analyse (chapter 4) the consequences of that distinction for the issue of modularity.

2 Associative and inferential processes

2.1 Introduction

The topic of this chapter is the distinction between associative and inferential processes and the role that they play in utterance understanding.

The issue has gained attention in recent pragmatics thanks to a debate between François Recanati (2004; 2007) and relevance theorists (Carston 2007; Wilson and Carston 2006, 2007; Sperber and Wilson 2008; Rubio-Fernández 2013).[11] The former has claimed that some pragmatic phenomena require conscious inferential processes, while others are explained by simple associative processes, which are neither conscious nor inferential in a proper sense. In contrast, RT has insisted on its view based on a unique mechanism, an automatic process that does not assign any special role to consciousness and yet is genuinely inferential – instead of associative.

The picture is made more complex if we consider the existence of some non-standard hypotheses in RT (see chapter 1): markedly, the hypothesis that simple accessibility is sufficient to single out relevant interpretations thanks to the organization of memory; and the hypothesis that the context determines expectations about the type of cognitive effects. These hypotheses, I will argue, are compatible with an associative account that can be developed by generalization of the associative view proposed by Recanati.[12] In this picture, a crucial theoretical role is played by the organization of memory, and specifically by the idea that memory is organized in hierarchies of associative schemata, each of which prescribes how the entities represented at lower levels of the hierarchy can be combined with each other. This hierarchical organization based on schemata can explain how simple associative access is able to constrain and guide cognitive processing in a non-accidental way.

Would such an associative explanation amount to a radically non-inferential account of pragmatic processes? It would rather provide a mechanism for the implementation of inferences in general, and of those invoked in pragmatic explanations in particular. However, we must be very careful about the terminology, here. In some research areas in psychology, the two terms "associative" and "inferential" are used as equivalent to, respectively, "automatic" and "controlled".

11 On this issue, see also Mazzarella (2011, 2013a), Mazzone (2011b, 2013a, 2016a), Kehler and Cohen (2016); Cohen and Kehler (submitted).
12 But, as we will see, the view that I defend has also important differences from Recanati's one.

https://doi.org/10.1515/9781501507731-003

This latter distinction is essentially based on a different temporal course of activation: automatic processes are characterized by rapidly decaying activations, while controlled ones have activations that are sustained through time. In practice, except when required by the discussion – and in this case I will mostly use graphic conventions to disambiguate the intended senses – I prefer not to use "associative" and "inferential" in the sense of "automatic" and "controlled". I will mostly reserve the notions of associative and inferential to the use that is largely dominant in pragmatics: that is, I will speak of associative processes to refer to any dynamic of activation through associative networks, whereas I will speak of inferences with regard to processes that can be described in terms of rational derivations (be they demonstrative or not). It should be noted that, if we take the latter description at its face value, a process might be considered as inferential (in case it can be *described* in terms of derivations) even if implemented by activations through associative networks. As a consequence, "inferential" and "associative" are not necessarily incompatible. There is, however, a further complication. Some think that it is in principle impossible to implement inferential processes by way of associative mechanisms, and assume that *genuinely inferential* processes are inferential at the implementation level, too – in other words, the underlying mechanisms would be based on symbols and symbolic rules for their manipulation. In this view, processes are conceived as inferential not only with regard to the phenomena to be explained – transitions between mental contents that can be described in terms of inferences – nor in the specific sense of controlled processes with sustained activation, but in yet another sense: with regard to a model of explanation (based on symbols and symbolic rules), which is alternative to the one based on activations in associative networks.

Given the previous definitions, I will claim in the first place that associative mechanisms actually implement the processes that can be described as inferential. In favour of this view, there is the fact that our brain is nothing but an associative network in which activation spreads, and therefore any cognitive process must in the end be explained in those terms. In the second place, one can claim without contradiction both that pragmatic inferential processes *are associative*, in the sense that they are implemented by activations in associative networks, and that they are *inferential instead of (merely) associative*, in the sense of the distinction between controlled and automatic processes. This is because activation through associative networks can occur with each of the two temporal courses described above, the rapidly decaying one and the one sustained across time. In sum, associative implementation is compatible with both automatic and controlled processes. In practice, in this chapter I will defend the thesis that pragmatic inferences (mental transitions that can be described inferentially) are implemented by associative processes (against the view that they are inferential in the sense of "implemented by a symbolic mechanism"); in the next one I will defend the thesis that pragmatic processes are at least partly controlled processes (i.e., inferential in this special sense). Is it possible to understand in this perspective RT's claim that inferential processes are not reducible to associative processes? There are two reasons to question this.

First of all, in more than one occasion relevance theorists have denied that activation through associative networks can account for inferential processes – in my opinion, essentially due to confusion between the two notions of association. Second, if RT were contrasting pragmatic inferential processes with merely associative ones on the basis of the distinction between automatic and controlled, then the theory should acknowledge a role to sustained activation and conscious attention. But this is not the case (see chapter 3).

To sum up, in this chapter I will argue that pragmatic inferential processes are implemented by associative mechanisms, and that this view does not equate to RT's thesis of automatic inferential processes for two reasons: my view predicts that (pragmatic) inferences are implemented in terms of activations through associative networks, and that these activations can be sustained through time and cause conscious attention; on the contrary, RT seems to exclude a role for conscious attention, and deny that inferences can be implemented by activations in associative networks (alone).

As I said, a crucial role in my argument will be played by the notion of schema. It allows capturing the motivated and hierarchical organization of memory thanks to which associative processes are able to produce non-accidental outcomes. A schema prescribes, in fact, the possible combinations between elements lying at lower levels of the representation hierarchy. Thanks to that notion, in particular, we can provide a comprehensive model of how not only pragmatic inferences, but also inferential processes of sort can be performed, through a double bottom-up/top-down dynamic. At the same time, the notion of schema is general enough to capture mental notions such as goal or intention, which can be characterized as high-level schemata in action representation. By this account, goals can guide the whole dynamic of top-down activations through associative networks of memory.

This proposal that mental notions are to be conceived as representational schemata must be defended with respect to the recent debate on mindreading: I will do this in chapter 4.

2.2 Associative and inferential processes in Recanati

As we saw, Grice has conceived the transition from explicit to implicit meaning as a rational inference requiring consideration of the speaker's goals. Despite his insistence that this description ought to be considered an idealized reconstruction rather than a genuine psychological thesis about the processes underlying comprehension, in a form or another his appeal to inferential processes performed by rational agents has shaped recent cognitive accounts.[13] The most straightforward manifestation of this influence is Recanati's (2004) view of what he calls secondary pragmatic processes.

Recanati is among those who think that Grice has underestimated the role played by context in the determination of explicit meaning: in Recanati's opinion, explicit meaning is the result of pragmatic processes just as implicit meaning is. As we saw above, according to Grice the transition from the conventional meaning of linguistic forms to the explicit meaning of utterances requires, so to speak, only "minor" pragmatic processes (disambiguation and reference resolution), in which the role of the context is strictly constrained by conventional meanings. Among others, Recanati thinks instead that the construction of explicit meaning also requires pragmatic processes depending on the context in more free and unpredictable ways, due to the fact that conventional meanings importantly underdetermine what is said by the speaker – a view also known as "contextualism".

This notwithstanding, according to Recanati Grice was right in suggesting that a fundamental difference exists between the two levels of meaning, the explicit and the implicit, or to say better, between the processes delivering them. While the processes responsible for explicit meaning, which are called by Recanati "primary pragmatic processes", are described as sub-personal and associative, implicit meaning would be instead the outcome of genuinely inferential processes involving personal awareness, which he calls "secondary pragmatic processes". Let us analyse this proposal in more detail.

In Recanati's (2004) account, primary pragmatic processes are conceived of as local and associative. By "local", it is intended that these processes concern transitions between concepts, not complete thoughts. By "associative", it is intended that the transitions at issue are based on the propagation of activation through conceptual networks and the resulting degree of activation of concepts in memory networks. In other words, a concept would be contributed to the explicit content of the utterance insofar as that concept is the most accessible (i.e. the most activated) for the system given the situation. In practice, the literal meaning of an expression

13 Two instructive discussions of this issue are in Allott (2005) and Geurts and Rubio-Fernández (2015). See below, chapter 5.

> is accessed first and triggers the activation of associatively related representations. That literal meaning is a natural candidate for the status of semantic value, but there are others: some of the representations activated by association contribute further candidates for the status of semantic value. All candidates, whether literal or derived, are processed in parallel and compete. (Recanati 2004: 28)

The literal meaning would then have an initial advantage over other possible candidates, that is, over concepts less directly associated to the word. But this cannot imply, of course, that literal meanings – or, more generally, concepts endowed with an initial advantage – always win the competition. Recanati (2004) emphasizes the importance of what he calls "accessibility shifts": in the course of processing, contextual information may change the accessibility of any concept activated previously, by adding a new train of activation to the process. According to Recanati, a key role in accessibility shift is played by abstract schemata coded in our long-term memory. Consider the following example:

(2) John was arrested by a policeman yesterday; he had just stolen a wallet.

Here the focus is on how to assign a reference to the pronoun "he" in the second sentence. At the moment when the pronoun is uttered we may assume to have two candidates, John and the policeman, and even supposing that, for any reason, the policeman is initially a more accessible candidate than John, the situation can be expected to change when the whole sentence is processed. The reason is that the predicate "had stolen" can be thought to recall a frame or schema such as the following

STEAL (x) → IS ARRESTED (x)

where stealing and being arrested are connected in such a way that one and the same person is the subject of both.

> This schema is jointly activated by the predicates "was arrested" and "had stolen". An interpretation in which the same person steals and is arrested (and in which he is arrested because he has stolen [...]) satisfies the schema, and is more likely to be selected than one which violates it. (Recanati 2004: 36).

In this way, schemata promote the search for coherence in utterance interpretation: "Coherent, schema-instantiating interpretations [...] tend to be selected and preferred over non-integrated or 'loose' interpretations" (Recanati 2004: 37). It must be emphasized that this coherence-producing role of schemata is assumed to depend on a simple associative mechanism operating in a double direction: on the one hand, from the word to the concept and then to the schema of which that concept is a component; on the other hand, as soon as the schema has been activated, from it to the other concepts by which it is composed.[14] Schemata thus play the role of constraints on interpretations: for any given schema, the greater the number of its components activated by items in the context, the more the schema itself is activated, and the more it enhances the activation of its components in turn. Consider how similar this is to what Sperber and Wilson (1996) have claimed (see the above quotation in § 1.9), when they propose that schemas, concepts, scripts etc. can co-activate "pieces of information that are likely to be simultaneously relevant". In other words, schemata allow predictions from items in the context to other items that can be simultaneously relevant, and when a prediction (a schema) is confirmed by subsequent items, it is reinforced and becomes part of our understanding of the situation. We will see below how this applies to other cases than the example (2).

Once explicit content has been recovered by means of associative processes as the ones just described, Recanati proposes that a quite different process leads to the determination of implicit content. In Carston's (2007: 19) words, "secondary pragmatic processes are to be understood as part of a more general theory of human action and interpretation and so having the philosophically central property of being rational, personal-level (as opposed to subpersonal) processes". In practice, secondary pragmatic processes are said to be "transparently or consciously inferential" in that they satisfy the "availability condition" (Recanati 2004: 44): they are accessible to consciousness, that is, the subject is aware of what is said, of the implicature, and of the inferential process leading from the former to the latter.

A thorough assessment of this proposal would require us to consider the issue of conscious access, and therefore it must be postponed to chapter 3. Let us now focus instead on the distinction between associative and inferential in itself, and specifically on how it is drawn in RT.

2.3 Associative and inferential in RT

In cognitive science, associative mechanisms are the standard explanation for storage of information in memory and its subsequent recall.[15] These mechanisms

---

14 In Recanati's (2004: 37) words, on the one hand "a schema is activated by, or accessed through, an expression whose semantic value corresponds to an aspect of the schema"; on the other hand, the "schema thus activated in turn raises the accessibility of whatever possible semantic values for other constituents of the sentence happen to fit the schema".

15 In order to make this claim reasonably uncontroversial, I should rather say "for *automatic* storage of information in memory". The reason why I do not restrict my claim to automatic processes alone will be clarified below, when I will analyse the ambiguity of the term "associative".

have a solid reputation at various levels of description, including neuroscientific descriptions of the brain. In particular, there is the largest possible evidence that we collect information from the environment by coding regularities thanks to the strengthening of synaptic connections between neurons and between neuron assemblies, and that we can subsequently exploit that information thanks to a simple dynamic of accessibility: the more two pieces of information are regularly connected in our experience, the more the connections between them (between their representations) are strong, and the more accessible they are to each other. Since this is basically the way in which we detect and store information, it can be expected that associative access forms the basis of the brain's activity every time we have to resort to our stored knowledge. I see no reason why pragmatic processes should be an exception to this generalization: to the extent that they need to resort to information of sorts – whether lexical information linked to words, or more general world knowledge – it is reasonable to expect that associative processes of the kind described above are at play.[16]

As a matter of fact RT assigns some role to associative processes: the point is whether they are considered sufficient to explain utterance understanding. RT defends a negative answer to this question. Specifically, its standard view is that comprehension additionally requires automatic processes that are inferential, not associative. Let us address in more detail this view, and in particular the limited role that RT assigns to associative processes.

For instance, let us consider Wilson and Carston's (2007) explanation of how, in accordance with RT, the word "angel" could be interpreted metaphorically in the following question-answer pair (this is the example (1), that we repeat for convenience):

(1) Peter: Will Sally look after the children if we get ill?
Mary: Sally is an angel.

Wilson and Carston (2007: 247) make an appeal to the fact that "the stereotypical angel is a good angel, and the encyclopaedic properties of stereotypical category members are likely to be highly accessible as a result of frequent use". This would cause that certain properties – such as EXCEPTIONALLY GOOD AND KIND, WATCHES OVER HUMANS AND HELPS THEM WHEN NEEDED, etc. – "are likely to be strongly activated" (ibidem). These properties could then "receive additional activation from other items in the context" (ibidem): for instance, Peter's

16 These claims may appear in contrast with the modularity hypothesis, and especially with the notion of domain-specific processes. I will turn to this issue in chapter 4. More detailed accounts of my view on modularity and the brain are in Mazzone (2015b) and Plebe and Mazzone (2016).

question may arguably reinforce the features of goodness and helpfulness. Although this account is presumed to be embedded in a relevance-theoretic framework, a key role is clearly assigned here to the dynamics of accessibility: stereotypicality and frequency of use are said to account for the accessibility of concepts and properties, and hence for their degree of activation; moreover, activation may change as an effect of new contextual inputs – an accessibility shift, in Recanati's terms. Up to this point, the picture is not sensibly different from that outlined by Recanati with regard to primary pragmatic processes.

Apart from specific examples, a vast number of explanations in RT's writings are framed in terms of accessibility and activation of representations. Such a propensity has also been explicitly theorized on occasion. For instance, Wilson and Carston (2006) ask themselves how much their explanation of metaphors should

> mesh with psycholinguistic investigations of the online comprehension process designed to show, for instance, [...] at what stage a particular feature *associated* with the encoded concept may *be activated or suppressed*. Let's suppose that the feature FEMALE ROYAL *is closely associated with, hence activated by*, the encoded concept PRINCESS [...]. (Wilson and Carston 2006: 405; emphases mine).

Wilson and Carston's answer is that RT, along with other cognitively oriented approaches, ought to be coherent with the kind of explanations invoked here. But there is a point at which, they claim, such considerations must give way to RT's specific model of explanation. There is here an important difference with the account of metaphor provided by cognitive linguistics, which makes an appeal to

> (non-inferential) associative mechanisms based on domain mappings of one sort or another [...] on our inferential account, such associative links may affect the outcome of the mutual adjustment process by altering the accessibility of contextual assumptions and implications, but the resulting overall interpretation *will only be accepted as the speaker's intended meaning if it satisfies the hearer's expectations of relevance and is properly warranted by the inferential comprehension heuristic* discussed [above in that paper]. (Wilson and Carston 2006: 429; emphasis mine)

What this quotation suggests is that associative mechanisms may play a role in the stages that precede pragmatic processing proper,[17] by causing the activation of the premises and conclusions that have to be handed over to the inferential component of the process. As we saw, according to RT utterance comprehension requires the construction of non-demonstrative inferences involving contextual assumptions and implications. Such interpretations must then be assessed

17 "Precede" from a logical, rather than temporal, point of view. We will turn to this in a moment.

against expectations of relevance, an assessment that is described as the second step of the relevance-based comprehension procedure. If the process were sequential, the associative mechanisms accounting for the generation of premises and conclusions should be followed by a further stage, in which the resulting interpretation is either accepted or not, based on a comparison with expectations of relevance. If this were the case, the initial associative stage would hardly be distinguishable from primary pragmatic processes as described by Recanati.

But, as we said, RT proposes instead a non-sequential process of mutual adjustment, in which forward and backward inferences can occur in parallel, without a rigid sequential order. This has a crucial consequence: the explicit meaning (just as the other contextual premises) is not determined once and for all by the associative component of the process. On the contrary, the final assessment based on expectations of relevance can retroact on the premises and modify them through backward inferences. Consequently, the distinction proposed by Recanati between primary pragmatic processes, responsible for the explicit meaning, and secondary ones that derive from it the implicit meaning, cannot be drawn anymore. Rather, according to RT, we would have associative processes affecting from the outside the interpretation process through mechanisms of accessibility, and a unique, pragmatic process that determines both the implicit *and the explicit* meaning: a process in which the non-demonstrative inference constituting the interpretation is evaluated and, if necessary, changed backwards, based on expectations of relevance.

To sum up, both Recanati and RT distinguish sharply between the associative and the inferential component. But while for Recanati the associative component alone is sufficient to ensure a certain class of pragmatic processes – the primary ones responsible for the explicit meaning – according to RT the associative component is extra-pragmatic. The only pragmatic process is *non-associative*: it is inferential, in that it involves the construction of an inference, and automatic, that is, non-conscious.

Let us now analyse in more detail this alleged distinction between associative processes and the automatic inferential process involved in comprehension. Since according to RT the pragmatic inferential process is automatic, the distinction cannot depend on the fact that the latter is conceived as reflective and conscious, a possibility that we will consider in chapter 3. We need to understand, then, on which grounds the distinction is drawn. I will claim that the arguments provided by RT to this effect are disputable; in particular, they seem to depend on a confusion between different levels of explanation and underestimate the importance of the schematic organization of memory. In fact, I will argue that the pragmatic inferential process is implemented by associative processes, and I will show that in RT there are suggestions entirely compatible with this view – provided that one redefines the notion of relevance in the direction suggested above, and gives up the argument against associative accounts that we are going to analyse.

2.4 The argument against associative accounts

Relevance theorists have explicitly contrasted associative explanations with their own approach in a number of papers (Carston 2007; Wilson and Carston 2006, 2007; Sperber and Wilson 2008). The most extensive argument against the associative account is provided by Wilson and Carston (2007), and it deserves to be analysed, as it is indicative of a more general attitude towards this issue. Wilson and Carston (2007: 243) claim that statistical associations "provide no basis for drawing warranted conclusions". The argument is based on considerations of statistical associations among lexical items in a corpus, as they are represented in the connectionist model discussed by Kintsch (2000, 2001). Wilson and Carston presume that there is a general cognitive lesson to be learned from the discussion of this model, and it is that although all inferential relationships are also associations, not all associations are inferential:

> In the minds of many speakers of English, for instance, "shark" is non-inferentially associated with "diver", "salt" with "pepper", "love" with "hate", and so on. (Wilson and Carston 2007: 244)

As a consequence, we are told that associative processes "will vastly overgenerate, and some method of filtering out unwanted associations will be required" (Wilson and Carston 2007: 252). In this sense, associative processes are unconstrained with respect to drawing warranted conclusions. I can see two related problems in this argument.

In the first place, by saying that "shark" is non-inferentially associated with "diver", the authors apparently mean that only a specific class of associative relationships can properly be considered inferential. For instance, they observe that, based on co-occurrences in the corpus, the word "shark" can be expected to have the words "fins", "dolphin", "diver" and "fish" as its close associates, but while "x is a shark" entails "x is a fish" it is not the case that it also entails "x is a diver" or "x is a dolphin". Thus, the claim that *not all associations are inferential* seems to be intended in the sense that, while the transition from "x is a shark" to "x is a fish" is inferential, the one from "x is a shark" to "x is a diver" or "x is a dolphin" is not. However, it is disputable that the domain of inferences should be delimited in such a way. Specifically, it can be doubted that inferences have to be equated to logical entailments based on category inclusion ("shark" implies "fish").

In pragmatics as well as in other cognitive domains a variety of probabilistic inferences can be drawn on the basis of regularities of different sorts. For one example, on the basis of regularities concerning sharks, from "x is a shark" we can infer "x has fins".

Here is where the second problem comes in. Let us suppose to adopt, as I will propose, a liberal notion of inference and admit that any associative relation can be considered inferential in some sense. At this point, a large number of conclusions may be reached associatively and therefore a way to select the contextually appropriate associations/inferences is needed. In other words, since activation spreads to all the associated elements, one needs a mechanism to select the relevant activations. Is this something exceeding the explanatory power of associative accounts? Let us note that Wilson and Carston only consider the initial accessibility of the nodes in a network as a result of activation spreading *from one single node*: for instance, their concern is about which nodes are accessible starting from the node "shark". They do not take into account the possibility that the nodes surrounding "shark" receive further activation from the context, so as to cause what Recanati calls "accessibility shift". To be sure, without such contextual adjustments activation can only spread unconstrained from a node to all its associates, with no sensitivity to what is contextually relevant. But this limitation is contingent on the specific model discussed by Wilson and Carston; it does not depend on intrinsic limitations of associative mechanisms as such.

Both these points deserve to be further analysed, since as I said Wilson and Carston's argument is but an example of a general attitude towards associations. The general idea is that associations are low-level mechanisms that can at most encode and recover very simple correlations from experience but cannot account for more sophisticated cognitive performances. This idea, I will claim, does not stand up to scrutiny.

2.5 Two kinds of associative accounts

Let us start from a specific example. Wood et al. (2007) have conducted a study on nonhuman primates' ability to perceive actions as goal-directed. Specifically, they have shown that different kinds of nonhuman primates understand a pointing gesture produced with the elbow as directed towards a goal (pointing to the location of food) only in case the experimenter's hands are not free to move. If, on the contrary, the hands are free, the animals seem uncertain about how to interpret the gesture. The authors' conclusion is that the ability of those animals to understand goal-directed actions "extends beyond [...] *associative mechanisms*, drawing upon *inferences about an agent's goals* in the context of particular environmental constraints" (Wood et al. 2007: 1405; my emphases).

Here, associative mechanisms are contrasted with a more sophisticated understanding, based on inferences about the agents' goals. In practice, the idea is that the tested animals go beyond the simple association between a gesture and the location of food: they are engaged in an episode of practical reasoning, in the course of which the elbow is taken as an appropriate means to signal the food only in case a more standard or convenient one (i.e., the index finger) is not available.

This distinction is largely common in psychology, where the term "associative" is standardly used to refer to a specific low-level mechanism for learning, and its counterpart for the recovery of information. In this sense, the term is contrasted with "cognitive" or "inferential" as used to designate a different mechanism of knowledge acquisition and exploitation involving conscious attention (see Shanks 2010 for a review).[18] This is a first point to be kept in mind. The criterion of the presence of conscious attention with the related manifestations – information maintained active in working memory, different courses of activation, etc. – gives precise content to this notion of inferential (versus associative) processing.[19]

On the other hand, there is another use of the terms "associative" and "cognitive" (or "inferential") that is probably no less common. As pointed out by Buckner (2011), the terms can also be used to refer not to psychological processes but instead to models by which psychological processes are explained. In this sense, "cognitive" applies to models constructed from things like symbols and propositional rules, while "associative" applies to models built from nodes that represent stimuli and links that represent associations between them. Since these

18 One may doubt that mention of controlled (instead of automatic) processes is in itself sufficient to account for an episode of practical reasoning as the one described by Wood et al. (2007). Intuitively, episodes of practical reasoning dealing with the pursuit of goals, and with the appropriate means for their accomplishment, appeal to information that differs from simple associative relations. It is exactly this kind of intuitions that I will call into question in the next sections. The core idea is that associative relations have a schematic structure, based on various types of schemata situated at different hierarchical levels, and that goals are nothing but schemata at the highest level of the hierarchy. In chapter 4 I will turn back to the understanding of goal-directed behaviour, and to the reason why this presumably requires controlled processes. In short, controlled processes guarantee that bits of information either separated by temporal intervals, or not directly associated, are sustained until they can interact as required.

19 In what follows, I will mainly adopt the terms "controlled" and "automatic" for these two notions. But in this section the more ambiguous terms "inferential" and "associative" need to be used, precisely because I intend to analyse their ambiguity.

models are essentially thought of as possible *implementations* of psychological processes, when necessary I will use the labels "associative-I" and "inferential-I" to refer to these latter senses, while I will use "associative-B" and "inferential-B" to refer to the former ones, which concern instead psychological processes characterized in terms of their *behavioural* manifestations. A key point for my argument is that associative-I mechanisms can implement both associative-B and inferential-B processes. In other words, from a neurocomputational point of view, given a network constituted by links connecting nodes, it is possible to have both local activation with rapid decay – and therefore low-level processes without conscious attention (associative-B processes), and sustained activation through circuits that are widely distributed in the cortex – and therefore high-level processes characterized by conscious attention (inferential-B processes).

These terminological clarifications issue a warning against a possible equivocation. From the fact that an increasing number of inferential processes seem to admit of associative explanations (see Shanks 2010), one might be tempted to conclude that inferential processes will finally turn out to be nothing but associative processes. As Buckner observes, in the light of the previous clarifications, we risk here a form of misguided deflationism: it is one thing to say that inferential-B processes can be implemented by associative-I mechanisms; it is quite another to presume that inferential-B processes can eventually be reduced to associative-B ones. In other words, conscious processes with activation sustained through time and unconscious processes with rapidly decaying activation remain different even if both are increasingly explained in terms of associative-I mechanisms.[20]

On the other hand, we must also be careful to avoid a complementary fallacy: from the existence of clear differences between associative-B and inferential-B processes at the cognitive behavioural level, we should not conclude that the latter cannot be reduced to associative-I mechanisms. Indeed there is a sense in which, at the implementation level, inferential-B processes must necessarily admit of an explanation in associative-I terms: since our brain can be described as a network of nodes and connections between them supporting representations, both associative-B and inferential-B processes must in the end be implemented by processes involving the associative activation of those nodes. From this point of view, it can be doubted that the notions of associative-I and inferential-I actually lie at the same explanatory level. While in fact the notions of nodes and connections between them are compatible with the basic elements of the neurocomputational dynamic of the brain, the notions of symbol and

20 For more details on these explanations, see § 2.11 below.

symbolic rule seem to be lying at a definitely more abstract explanatory level: they presumably result from complex combinations of operations at the level of associative-I mechanisms.

In sum, my view is as follows: processes supporting clearly distinct cognitive behaviours, respectively characterized as inferential-B and associative-B, must be implemented by associative-I mechanisms; it is misleading both to presume that the cognitive behavioural distinction between inferential-B and associative-B can be cancelled, and to deny that inferential-B processes can be implemented by associative-I mechanisms.

Turning back to our initial example, the above considerations are wholly compatible with the conclusions of Wood et al. (2007): on the basis of the reported experiments, nonhuman primates seem to show abilities that are better described as inferential than as associative (at the level of cognitive behaviours). It must be clear, though, that this does not allow one to conclude that those abilities cannot be implemented by associative-I mechanisms.

With a further step back, what do these considerations suggest with regard to RT's view and, specifically, to Wilson and Carston's (2007) argument? There are two distinct issues.

The first concerns the criteria for drawing the boundary between inferential and associative, at the level of cognitive behaviours. As we saw, in psychology the distinction is essentially based on the presence (or absence) of conscious attention, on the fact that information is maintained active for the time required by current cognitive tasks, and on the kind of complex manipulations that this makes possible. However, while Recanati actually characterizes inferential pragmatic processes as conscious, RT conceives of them as automatic and does not assign to consciousness any interesting role. In this sense, we are left without clear criteria for the distinction between associative and inferential processes.

In sum, I claim in the first place that RT's distinction between associative and inferential is scarcely compatible with the use of these notions in current psychology. Moreover, our previous considerations about the two notions of association suggest the existence of a further problem in Wilson and Carston's (2007) argument. They deny that inferential pragmatic processes can be accounted for in terms of activations in associative networks. But this is exactly one of the equivocation fallacies we warned about. It is one thing to insist on the existence of inferential (versus associative) processes at the level of the behaviourally manifest cognitive processes (leaving aside the fact that RT lacks of clear criteria for that distinction); it is quite another to maintain that inferential processes cannot be explained in terms of associative-I mechanisms. In other words, the intuition that the processes are different at the cognitive behavioural level must not be used to draw conclusions regarding the implementation.

The key theoretical point, on which we are now going to focus our attention, is that the limitations of associative-B processes (and the related representations) must not be taken as limitations of associative-I mechanisms. Associative networks constituted by nodes and connections between them are the mechanism by which information is encoded in every part of our brain – and especially, for what concerns us here, of our cortex. Consequently, the question is not *whether* these networks are able to implement inferential pragmatic processes. The only sensible question is *how* this may occur. The answer I propose assigns a crucial role to the notion of schema already introduced by Recanati, provided that it is defined in a sufficiently general way. In the light of this generalized notion of schema, inferences can be described as cases of pattern completion, as we are going to see in a moment.

2.6 Inferences as pattern completions

As we observed above, in pragmatics as well as in other cognitive domains a variety of probabilistic inferences can be drawn on the basis of regularities of different sorts – well beyond the case of logical entailment based on category inclusion. Inferences in this wide sense, I maintain, can be performed by associative processing, provided that sufficient information about the nature of associative relations is encoded. In practice, any such association licences inferences of some kind, and precisely of the kind that the nature of its represented relation allows it to licence. For instance, spatial relationships allow spatial inferences, and so on and so forth.

That information-rich associative relations allow inferences has been claimed by otherwise very different psychological theories of concepts such as semantic network models and Barsalou's theory.

To start with, one of the key intuitions underlying the development of semantic network models in the 70's was precisely that concepts may be connected by different classes of relations licensing different types of inferences. For instance, to the extent that the node SHARK is connected to the node FISH by means of a ISA (a category inclusion) link, the semantic network licenses the inference from SHARK to (ISA) FISH. But with equal right, provided that the node SHARK is connected to the node FINS by means of a HAS link, the semantic network licenses the inference from SHARK to (HAS) FINS and so on and so forth.

The connection between associative relations and inferences is also recognised by Barsalou, in a paper where semantic network models are nevertheless criticised for conceiving concepts as amodal and decontextualized symbols (Barsalou 2005: 621–622). Specifically, the inferences enabled by the conceptual system are described by Barsalou (2005) in terms of statistical pattern completions. In his view, concepts are not isolated and context-independent entities, detached from information on settings in which objects appear. Against this view he proposes the notion of "situated conceptualization", according to which concepts are encoded as components of specific settings to which they are specifically tuned. Situated conceptualizations are maintained to play a key role in drawing inferences:

> The situated conceptualization that becomes active constitutes a rich source of inference. The conceptualization is essentially a pattern, namely, a complex configuration of multimodal components that represent the situation. When a component of this pattern matched the situation, the larger pattern became active in memory. The remaining pattern components-not yet observed-constitute inferences, that is, educated guesses about what might occur next. Because the remaining components co-occurred frequently with the perceived components in previous situations, inferring the remaining components is justified. (Barsalou 2005: 628)

Let me focus on a couple of points touched in this quotation. First, patterns are suggested here to play the same role that Recanati (2004) assigns to schemata. According to Recanati, a schema receives activation from any of its components and, once activated, it enhances in turn the accessibility of its other components. In short, a schema enables inferences – that is, schematically motivated transitions – from any of its components to the other components. This is also the kind of mechanism described in semantic network models. For instance, thanks to the labelled link HAS the nodes SHARK and FINS enter into a pattern (a schema) such that whenever SHARK is activated FINS can be inferred via that pattern. I find it important to note that this mechanism has the structure of what in logic is called "modus ponens": given the pattern IF A THEN B, and given A, we are justified in concluding B. In practice, the mechanism we are describing is a generalised form of modus ponens, in various senses: because inferences are probabilistic, because As and Bs can be connected via a number of different patterns besides material implication (IF-THEN), and because more than two entities can be connected within a given pattern.

Second, the above quotation not only establishes a direct link between inferences and frequency of co-occurrence in experience, thus emphasizing the statistical character of inferences, but it even suggests that frequency of co-occurrence is the reason why one is justified to infer the remaining components of patterns. In a sense, this is an appeal to induction as a form of justification. For instance, it is the frequency with which sharks and having fins co-occur in our experience that justifies the inference form SHARK to (HAS) FINS. It should be kept in mind, however, that in another sense once a schema is encoded in our conceptual system, it is this schema that justifies the transition from one to another of its components. In this sense, what properly justifies the inference from SHARK to FINS is the pattern SHARK HAS FINS. An interesting application – which I will address below – of this distinction between inductive and schematic justification is that the transition from one mental content to another can be justified even in the absence of direct inductive evidence of the correlation, provided that there are schemata indirectly justifying that transition.

Based on a distinction that is common in philosophy, one could object that given the *descriptive* purposes of this book, *normative* issues of justification had better be left aside. Specifically, my use of the term "justifies" in the previous context might ultimately be just a misleading way to describe the fact that a schema *causes* the activation of a concept. There is, however, a cognitive reason for speaking of justification and not of cause: while associations in a restrictive sense can only be causes of concept activation, schematic associations in my sense can be thought to justify concept activation, to the extent that they can act as premises in rules of inference having certain concepts as their conclusions. In practice, the presence of a schema connecting two concepts not only allows one of them to automatically activate the other, but also permits the subject to actively recall (in a controlled way) the schema and employ it as a criterion for the validity of that transition. In this sense I find it legitimate to speak of a generalized modus ponens.[21]

To sum up, cognitive inferences can be conceived of as probabilistic completions of patterns (schemata), based on a generalized form of modus ponens.

2.7 Structure of schemata and sensorimotor representations

Another point raised by Barsalou is that concepts are neither amodal symbols nor decontextualized entities. This view implies that concepts are even richer in information than they are presumed to be by semantic network models. Let me focus on the first point, the criticism of concepts as amodal symbols.

Barsalou has famously insisted on the thesis that concepts are based on sensorimotor representations. This is not intended to mean that our conceptual system is "a collection of holistic images like those in a camera, video recorder, or audio recorder" (Barsalou 2005: 621). On the contrary, in Barsalou's view situations and objects are analysed in components and features

---

21 On consciousness as a mechanism for the evaluation of transitions between mental content, I will say something below, in chapter 4. For a wider discussion, see Mazzone (2016b). See also below, § 5.3, for a recapitulation of how the present considerations on schematic associations and the considerations on consciousness may account together for the problem of predication: in short, the problem of how concepts can be composed into complex thoughts.

whose sensorimotor representations are organised hierarchically in the brain, so that those components "can be combined productively to produce infinite conceptual combinations" (Barsalou 2005: 625). In other words, the idea is that structural (or schematic) organization and sensorimotor format of representations can coexist. I now propose to analyse further this idea by connecting it to the notion of schema.

Schemata or patterns, as I have described them above, are structures of representation constituted by a certain number of components and their relations. Recanati (2004) has adopted a notation for schemata an example of which is

STEAL (x) → IS ARRESTED (x).

This notation, although very abstract and simplistic from a cognitive point of view, can be a useful approximation for certain purposes. One of its merits is that a schema is represented as a relation between concepts, and concepts are represented in turn as predicates with slots for variables. This notation is reminiscent of Frege's (1952a, 1952b) theory according to which concepts are functions that take individuals as arguments and return truth values. For instance, the concept DOG (x) is a function that gives the truth value TRUE by substituting for "x" the name of any individual which is an actual dog.

My suggestion is that schemata have this general structure, that is, they are constituted by relations between nodes with slots that must be filled by selecting a single item from a range of possible arguments. However, I also propose that a cognitively plausible notion of schema has to be richer than the above notation suggests, in two senses.

In the first place, schemata must specify the nature of the relations between their components. As we saw above, this is required in order for schemata to enable inferences, but it is also what one expects from all we know about learning. We do not apparently encode concepts such as SHARK, FISH, FINS, DIVER without encoding at the same time information about how these concepts are connected with each other – and presumably with other concepts as well. For example, that sharks have fins – and markedly, that between sharks and fins there is a part-whole relation – is something that we come to represent as a simple result of their experiential co-occurrence. In fact, one could go even further and observe that not only do we encode SHARK and FINS as involved in a part-whole relation, but we also represent this as a specific spatial relation such that fins are located on sharks in certain positions. It is not difficult to see that this allows much more specific inferences than that from SHARK to (HAS) FINS alone.

In the second place, the "(x)" in Frege's notation is a very poor instrument for representing the variability within concepts. It just stands for possible arguments without providing any specific representation of the range of values within which the arguments may lie. However, in the history of the notion of schema stemming from Bartlett (1932) (and including Mandler 1979; Rumelhart and Ortony 1977; Schank and Abelson 1977; Smith 1989), there is a different approach which allows for a more concrete representation of variability. In practice, psychology and artificial intelligence have described schemata as containing specification of the possible values for any of their slots. This specification may include defaults for the most typical values but also other possible values, whose relative probability can be itself specified. To be sure, these values, just as any other component of schemata, have been traditionally represented by means of amodal symbols (propositional labels). However, one can legitimately presume that sensorimotor representations might also account for variability within schemata. For example, since sharks differ from one another to some extent, in order to apply their concept to actual instances of the species, this representation must specify not one single shape but instead a range of variability for possible shapes. And the same holds for fins and other parts. Thus, the schema SHARK HAS FINS can be thought to contain a sensorimotor representation of sharks and a sensorimotor representation of fins with their respective ranges of variability.

It should be noted that in this tradition the notion of schema is used to specify the representation of a single concept, rather than the relation between concepts. The difference, however, is not very important. If a concept has a schematic structure, its parts can in turn be concepts. This allows the construction of representational hierarchies such that, at any level, the same entities are concepts with respect to higher-level schemata and schemata with respect to lower-level concepts.[22] It is also possible that schemata have an entirely abstract nature. For instance, a variety of concepts appear to be structured in accordance with a part-whole schema that can itself be considered a concept.

To sum up, in the last sections I have defended the idea that the basic processes responsible for encoding and recovery of information in memory are associative processes in the implementation sense, that is, processes based on networks of nodes and their schematic configurations. Such configurations guarantee that transitions between representational contents are motivated: they allow the implementation of inferences whose basic structure is that of a generalized modus ponens. Furthermore, I analysed the notion of schema and

---

22 This does not imply that any component of a concept must be a concept in turn. It is possible that components at the lowest levels of the hierarchy do not have some of the features considered constitutive of being concepts: for instance, they might not be accessible to consciousness (the view that concepts must be consciously accessible is adopted in § 5.3). Analogously, it must not always be the case that schemata are concepts.

proposed that it is key to the hierarchical organization of our representations – of our memory, in the end. Schemata are in fact structures constituted by components, which in turn can recursively be schemata at a lower level. Finally, I have noted the similarity between the dynamic of activation described by Barsalou for concepts and by Recanati for the construction of explicit meaning, due to a common notion of schema/pattern: the activation of a schema's component causes the schema to be activated, which in turn causes the activation of its other components. This produces a double movement – with a bottom-up (from items at the lower level to items at the higher level) and a top-down direction (vice versa) – that starting from any component of a schema allows predictions on what else must be expected. As we are going to see, a similar dynamic is also invoked in other domains of cognition, specifically in linguistic processing and intentional action processing. Later, I will focus on how these considerations apply to pragmatics.

2.8 Hierarchies and schemata in language

As a matter of fact, a mechanism very similar to the one just described is invoked by Ray Jackendoff (2007a) in his proposal of a parallel architecture in language processing. The main idea is that the generative engine at work in language production and comprehension is not exclusively based on syntax.[23] On the contrary, syntax is just one of the layers involved – thanks to their respective principles of organization – in the generative arrangement of linguistic materials. Crucially, Jackendoff abandons the assumption of a radical distinction between grammar and lexicon, which was based on the idea that while lexicon is constituted by *representations*, syntactic rules are implemented instead by specific *processes*, with the former being inert entities processed by the latter. His alternative proposal is that linguistic entities at any layer, including syntactic structures, are bits of information stored in long-term memory and organized hierarchically, with higher levels prescribing the way in which items at lower levels must be arranged together. For any layer (syntax, semantics, phonology), the very same process of

23 The model questioned by Jackendoff, even if in a spirit of continuity, is obviously the theory of syntax proposed by Noam Chomsky. This is named Generative Grammar after the fact that its core is a set of syntactic rules, which are able to *generate* all and only the well-formed sentences of languages. In Chomsky's proposal, syntax is the only responsible for the generative processes through which sentences are produced and understood.

"unification" is held responsible for assembling specific items in accordance with the respective hierarchical organization.

For instance, in order to produce (or to parse) a nominal phrase (NP) we do not need a procedural rule such as

$$NP \rightarrow Det - N$$

which can be translated in words as "a noun phrase consists of a determiner followed by a noun". It is enough to have a stored pattern delivering the same information. Now, it is easy to see that such a stored pattern is a schema in the sense we proposed above: a configuration that prescribes how items at the lower level are combined together so as to form items at the higher level in a regulated manner.

Interestingly, Jackendoff's proposal is just the most prominent representative of a general trend within syntactic theory, of which even the recent Chomskyan "minimalism" is an example: that is, the trend towards the substitution of representations for procedural rules. In other words, the weight of explanation for language processing is nowadays mostly placed upon the organization of (linguistic) memory, and much less upon specialized processes.

On this background, Jackendoff describes the syntactic generation of a sentence as the result of a double bottom-up/top-down movement: first, an initial word sets up "grammatical expectations" about the possible sentence structures, based on the syntactic patterns associated to that word at higher levels of the hierarchy; then, "further words in the sentence may be attached on the basis of the [previously activated] top-down structure" (Jackendoff 2007a: 8). This amounts to the dynamic of bottom-up activation of schemata and top-down activation of their other components that is by now familiar to us. It is not a surprise, then, that Jackendoff characterizes the process as non-directional, such that it may work "from the bottom up or from top down or from anywhere in the middle" (idem: 8), and as based on competition between (and mutual inhibition of) alternative hypotheses. Competition and parallel activation, with no privileged starting point or direction, are characteristic features of associative processes, and as such we find them in the explanation of all the phenomena we are dealing with: from pragmatics (recall the associative hypothesis of Recanati, but also the notion of parallel mutual adjustment in RT) to theory of action, as we are going to see in a moment.

2.9 Hierarchies in action

Jackendoff's "theory of parallel architecture" shows very convincingly how, as far as language is concerned, hierarchical organization of representations is able to explain generative processing. But hierarchical representations have been taken to explain the generative nature of action as well.

The similarity between language and action with regard to their common generative nature is explicitly addressed in Jackendoff (2007b) and is largely recognized in psychological and neuroscientific theories of action (see Mazzone 2014b, for a review). For one example, Baars and Gage (2010) observe that making plans for the future requires the ability to reconfigure elements of prior experiences in a way that does not exactly copy past experiences. This ability, they claim, is apparent in tool-making, one of the fundamental features of primate cognition, but "the generative power of language to create new ideas depends on this ability as well" (Baars and Gage 2010: 402). According to the authors, "the ability to manipulate and recombine internal representations depends critically on the PFC [prefrontal cortex], which probably made it critical for the development of language" (idem: 402). We will turn below to this suggestion about PFC.

There is much research, in particular, on the relationship between hierarchical representations and generative processing in action understanding. Baldwin and Baird (2001: 171), for instance, claim that a "generative knowledge system underlies our skill at discerning intentions, enabling us to comprehend intentions even when action is novel and unfolds in complex ways over time" and suggest that this system "is probably just as rich and complex as the generative system underlying language" (idem: 171). They cite evidence that children can parse continuous actions along intention boundaries. However, they claim, the ability to parse and process hierarchically organized actions applies more generally:

> Adults also appear to process continuous action streams in terms of hierarchical relations that link smaller-level intentions (e.g., in a kitchen cleaning-up scenario: intending to grasp a dish, turn on the water, pass the dish under the water) with intentions at higher levels (intending to wash a dish or clean a kitchen). (Baldwin and Baird 2001: 172)

The idea of a strict analogy (together with common neurological bases) between hierarchical structures in language and action is further developed by Pastra and Aloimonos (2012), which offer some detailed examples of how actions can be analysed in terms of parse trees, within the framework of "a biologically inspired generative grammar of action, which employs the structure-building operations and principles of Chomsky's Minimalist Programme as a reference model" (Pastra and Aloimonos 2012: 103).

Moreover, Glenberg and Gallese (2012) show how a mechanism that is firmly grounded in the study of motor control might have "been exploited for language learning, comprehension and production" (idem: 905). Their proposal is based on HMOSAIC (Haruno et al. 2003), which is a hierarchical version of MOSAIC, a model-based theory of motor control developed by Wolpert and colleagues (e.g., Wolpert et al. 2003). Haruno et al. (2003) have demonstrated that, within such a hierarchical architecture, higher-level layers "can learn to select the basic motor acts and learn the appropriate temporal orderings of those acts" (Glenberg and Gallese 2012: 910). The whole mechanism is explicitly described as associative, but the hierarchical structure allows nonetheless for abstract representations, standing as a whole for intentions of the agent: in practice, while at the lowest level in the model motor acts are simply chained with each other so that any of them triggers the next one, higher-level representations provide abstract patterns that capture action structure and timing more explicitly.

Let me summarize. In all of these approaches to action, flexible and generative processing is explained by means of hierarchical representations, in which patterns at higher levels prescribe predictable arrangements at lower levels. As it should be clear, those accounts place the explanatory weight on the organization of memory, not on specialized processes; in some case, simple associative processing is explicitly mentioned as the appropriate mechanism for memory acquisition and exploitation. This picture is entirely compatible with the above considerations on concepts (Barsalou; semantic network models) and language processing (Jackendoff): the schematic, hierarchical organization of information is able to guide associative mechanisms in a way that is far from haphazard or accidental. In order to complete the picture and refer it back to our considerations on comprehension as goal recognition, it is opportune to briefly analyse the notions of goals and intentions in this perspective.

2.10 Schemata and goals

It is reasonable to think that goals and intentions are complex entities, whose representation involves a number of components of different nature (see Mazzone 2011a). Moreover, for certain theoretical purposes it is useful to distinguish between goals and intentions, based on the assumption that the latter but not the former require controlled processing. However, for the present purposes we can confine our attention to a simplified notion of goal/intention, along the lines of the above considerations on action. The idea – implicit in Baldwin and Baird (2001), Pastra and Aloimonos (2012), and Glenberg and Gallese (2012) – is that the goal underlying an action is the end-point of that action, with more complex actions being constituted by a sequence of smaller actions each of which is a means to (and a sub-goal of) the overarching goal, while actions at the bottom of the hierarchy are constituted by simple motor acts.

There are two points to this idea. The first concerns the existence of goal-directed patterns in memory, and we are going to address it in this section; the second concerns the thesis of a hierarchical structure of goals in the cortex, and we will turn to it in the next section.

As to the first point, Glenberg and Gallese (2012) argue, as we saw, that higher layers in HMOSAIC contain abstract patterns capturing the structure of actions. Based on our previous definition of schemata as the higher-level representations responsible for the organization of items at lower levels, such patterns can be legitimately considered as schemata. In the psychological, computational and neuroscientific literature on action, the existence of goal-directed patterns of this sort is commonplace. The most explicit defence of this claim – actually expressed in terms of the existence of "hierarchical schemas and goals in the control of sequential behavior"[24] – is provided by Cooper and Shallice (2006), mostly on the basis of computational considerations.[25] They adopt the notion of schema proposed by Bartlett (1932) and further developed by Rumelhart and Ortony (1977) among others, according to which a schema is a self-contained memory structure with a variable number of component parts. In their words, as far as action control is concerned,

> a schema may be seen as a means of achieving a goal or subgoal. More generally, recent computational accounts [...] take schemas to be goal-directed structures, with goals serving to mediate schema–subschema relationships. Thus, schemas achieve goals and, apart from at the lowest level of the schema hierarchy, consist of partially ordered sets of subgoals (which may themselves be achieved by other schemas). (Cooper and Shallice 2006: 888)

Consistently, the authors describe the role that schemata play in action control in terms of the bottom-up/top-down dynamic we considered above: "Schemas are

---

24 This is in fact the title of the paper.

25 The defence of goal-directed schemata in Cooper and Shallice (2006) is part of a larger debate, markedly with Botvinick and Plaut, about symbolic and connectionist models of action representation. Interestingly, in their reply to Cooper and Shallice (2006), Botvinick and Plaut (2006) admit that schemata and goals need to be represented somehow, they only object that "it is too strong to say [that their own model] is eliminativist with respect to task and subtask representations (i.e., schemas), it is true that the relevant patterns of activation may be more difficult to isolate within [their model than in the one proposed by Cooper and Shallice]" (Botvinick and Plaut 2006: 921). Moreover, they argue for a "quasi-hierarchical structure" of action representation (idem: 922), that is, a structure in which there is a balance between hierarchy and context sensitivity – I will say in a moment something more on context sensitivity in hierarchical representations. In sum, none of the claims we report here from Cooper and Shallice (2006) is really disputed by Botvinick and Plaut (2006).

explicit and play a causal role in determining behaviour: Excitation and subsequent selection of a schema cause excitation and then selection of subschemas or actions" (idem: 892).

The hierarchical organization of schema and goal representations is claimed to account for flexibility of sequential behaviour (idem: 887) – an issue to which I will return in a moment. However, Cooper and Shallice also explain contextual flexibility by appealing to optional elements in schema representations. This would allow schemata to be highly context-sensitive, since optional subgoals can either be activated or not on any particular occasion as a function of the context in which the schema is performed (idem: 897). In order for this to be possible, schemata should also contain representations of the contextual cues whose excitation causes the activation of optional subgoals. The representation of contexts is explicitly mentioned by Badre (2013) as a component of what, in the literature on reinforcement learning of actions, is called a "policy", that is, a rule that relates an action, a desired outcome and *a state in which the rule has to be applied*. Based on these considerations, we can describe a goal-directed schema as constituted by a final goal, a number of subgoals (or actions that are means to that goal), and some specification of the conditions in which both the final goal and the subgoals apply.

It should be clear that we are dealing, once more, with a "rich" conception of memory and concepts, in line with the notion of situated conceptualizations described by Barsalou.

2.11 Goals and the architecture of the brain

Another important question is whether the hierarchies of goals described above are actually represented in our brain, a question that needs to be addressed in the context of a more general understanding of the brain architecture.

As recently recalled by Badre (2013), Fuster (2001; 2003; 2014) was the first to associate a concept of abstraction in action control with the functional organization of frontal cortex. There is today some evidence that the hierarchical structure of goal-directed motor actions correlates with specific neurological regions (Badre 2008, 2013; Botvinick, 2008; Botvinick, Niv and Barto 2009; Hamilton and Grafton 2006; Grafton and Hamilton 2007; Koechlin and Jubault 2006; Koechlin and Summerfield 2007; O'Reilly 2010). This suggests, in Botvinick's (2008: 205) words, that "a topographical organization might exist within the frontal cortex and the DLPFC [dorsolateral prefrontal cortex], according to which progressively higher levels of behavioral structure are represented as one moves rostrally", that is, from back to front. For one example of these studies, Koechlin and Jubault

(2006: 936) reports evidence from magnetic resonance imaging showing “phasic activation at the boundaries of action segments that constitute a hierarchical action plan”; on this basis, they propose that Broca’s area and its homolog in the right hemisphere might “implement a specialized executive system governing action selection in hierarchically structured action plans”.

Although the focus of those studies is on hierarchical representations of action in the frontal/prefrontal cortex, it should be noticed that on Fuster’s account hierarchical organization is a general phenomenon concerning the entire brain:

> The physiology of the cerebral cortex is organized in hierarchical manner. At the bottom of the cortical organization, sensory and motor areas support specific sensory and motor functions. Progressively higher areas – of later phylogenetic and ontogenetic development – support functions that are progressively more integrative. The prefrontal cortex constitutes the highest level of the cortical hierarchy dedicated to the representation and execution of actions. (Fuster 2001: 319)

More specifically, Fuster proposes that the brain is organized along two distinct – though highly interconnected – pathways, respectively constituting a sensory and a motor hierarchy of cortical maps, which together form a perception-action cycle. The prefrontal cortex (PFC) lies at the top of the motor hierarchy and it seems to contain neuronal networks that, both in monkeys and in humans, represent abstract programs or plans of action (Fuster 2003: 76).

Two considerations are worth noting.

First, the above literature on action control emphasizes the role that hierarchies may play in flexibly dealing with large spaces of options. As Badre (2013) specifically notes, hierarchies permit a divide-and-conquer approach such that, on the one hand, choices about which actions to take can be made at multiple levels of abstraction, while, on the other hand, choices at the higher levels tend to constrain the space of possible actions at lower levels. Compare this with a situation in which an inflexible routine has to be performed, and a single set of criteria for its application has to be coded and then assessed against the factual context. On the contrary, on the hierarchical account each component at lower levels has its own set of application criteria, and the selection of goals at the higher levels is also the result of parallel activation of (and competition between) components at lower levels, with substantial gain in contextual flexibility. But this applies not only to goal selection in the frontal cortex: if Fuster – and our whole picture of concepts, language and motor control – is right, the mechanism of bottom-up/top-down activations along hierarchical representations extends to the entire cortex, thus accounting for contextual flexibility in a wide range of cognitive processes.

Second, since we described the prefrontal cortex as the seat of hierarchical representations, one might wonder whether this is compatible with the well-established view according to which this area has a crucial role to play in executive processes. As a matter of fact, a "representational" versus "processing" approach to PFC has gained consensus in the last fifteen years (Huey, Krueger and Grafman 2006; Miller, Freedman and Wallis 2002; Wood and Grafman 2003), in line with the influential model of executive functions proposed by Miller and Cohen (2001). As they observe, "one of the most fundamental aspects of cognitive control and goal-directed behavior [is] the ability to select a weaker, task-relevant response (or source of information) in the face of competition from an otherwise stronger, but task-irrelevant one" (Miller and Cohen 2001: 170). Now, Miller and Cohen's suggestion is that the PFC contains patterns of activity that map onto configurations in more posterior cortical areas. When such a pattern within the PFC is activated, this increases the activation of the posterior configuration it is connected to and allows that configuration to overcome task-irrelevant competing ones. In other words, plans of action in the PFC are here conceived as schemata, whose activation is transmitted to their components distributed in different cortical areas. This does not necessarily mean that the *automatic* spreading of activation up and down the hierarchy is all there is to executive functions. An influential proposal made by Dehaene et al. (2006) is that self-sustaining loops play a crucial role in the neural dynamic, to the extent that they prevent the rapid decaying of spreading activation; more specifically, Dehaene and colleagues claim that consciousness depends on the establishing of such loops between strongly activated sensory-motor representations and higher association cortices.[26] This might explain how prefrontal activation ensures stability of processing in accordance with current goals and tasks of the agent: thanks to recurrent loops, plans of action within the PFC might sustain the activation of the related sensory-motor representations for the time needed to attain the goals. Under this account, there is no inconsistency between the suggestion that the PFC is the top of the hierarchy of representations in the cortex and the widespread opinion that it is key to conscious processing.

We will turn back to automatic and controlled processes in chapter 3. It is now time to draw some conclusion with regard to associative-I processes – that is, processes based on transmission of activation through associative networks in our brain – and on how these processes are constrained and guided by the schematic and hierarchical organization of memory. In particular, we will focus on how the above considerations dovetail with the previous analysis of RT.

26 The model proposed by Dehaene et al. (2006) is actually more complex than this, and predicts a more gradual transition between automatic and controlled processes. We will say something more on this in § 3.5.

2.12 Explicit meaning, encyclopaedic assumptions, implicit meaning: some examples

In the last pages I provided a long argument in support of the claim that associative memory has a schematic and hierarchical organization. In other words, it has been proposed that associative links between concepts do not only capture the frequency of their co-occurrence in experience, without any information on their specific relations. On the contrary, concepts have a schematic structure: they are linked by schemata specifying their relations, and they are in turn schemata prescribing the organization of other concepts. The common idea that associative relations are too poor to account for most cognitive processes seems to depend on a confusion between different senses of "associative"[27]: it is one thing to observe that there are processes characterized by local activation with rapid decay, which can only account for encoding and recall of very simple co-occurrences; it is quite another to conclude that this representational poverty – so to speak – affects the whole model based on connections between nodes in an associative network.

I tried to show that a schematic and hierarchical view of associative memory is adopted in domains as different as language processing (with specific regard to Jackendoff's model), theory of concepts (semantic network models; Barsalou), theory of action and motor control (and here many references were given). I also mentioned the influential hierarchical model of the brain proposed by Fuster, and cited empirical research apparently showing the existence of such representational hierarchies in the cortex. Finally, I observed that, under a computational perspective, the schematic-hierarchical view of associative memory is able to account for contextual flexibility and generativity in cognition without invoking specialized processes. In sum, the schematic organization of memory appears sufficient to guide *motivated* processes of associative activation, and specifically, it allows drawing inferences.

If our previous considerations were convincing, as I hope, what would they imply for our analysis of RT? They would contradict Wilson and Carston's (2007) argument against associative accounts in pragmatics, insofar as this is based on a reductive view of associations and their power. On the other hand, I intend to show now that the inferential mechanism invoked by relevance theorists can be thought of as a high-level description of associative processes – coherently with occasional suggestions they provide. In the next section, based on these considerations, I will

27 And possibly also by a misleading identification of associationism with behaviourism: see Smith (2000).

draw more general conclusions on RT, specifically on the contrast between what I respectively called the standard and the non-standard view.

To start with, in the discussion of associative mechanisms in RT I already mentioned Wilson and Carston's (2007) example that I repeat here for convenience

(1) Peter: Will Sally look after the children if we get ill?
Mary: Sally is an angel.

As we saw above (§ 2.3), Wilson and Carston (2007) account for the modulation of "angel" in this context in clearly associative terms. I want to turn now to the other side of the issue: this example can be reconstructed, as is usual for RT, in terms of an inference having the explicit meaning and some encyclopaedic assumptions as premises. The implicit meaning of Mary's utterance is presumably an affirmative answer to Peter's question. This meaning can be considered as the conclusion of an inference having as a premise something like the proposition SALLY IS EXCEPTIONALLY GOOD (the explicit meaning), while another premise might be the proposition ONE WHO IS EXCEPTIONALLY GOOD HELPS PEOPLE WHEN THEY NEED IT. Based on such premises, one can conclude that Sally will be ready to help people when they need it.

In sum, the same considerations expressed in associative terms can be naturally rephrased in inferential terms. In particular, when Wilson and Carston (2007: 247) observe that properties such as EXCEPTIONALLY GOOD may receive further activation from the context, and specifically from Peter's question, they are implicitly making an appeal to a schema like ONE WHO IS (EXCEPTIONALLY) GOOD HELPS PEOPLE WHEN THEY NEED IT: this schema is presumably activated by Peter's mention of needy people (children whose parents are ill) and, in turn, contribute to enhance the activation of the property EXCEPTIONALLY GOOD – already activated as a property of the stereotypical angel. But this associative schema is also the premise that, in an inferential account, allows inferring the conclusion SALLY WILL HELP US IF WE NEED IT (or something similar).

The theoretical point is that Wilson and Carston consider the above schema as a component of the associative dynamic, on the one hand, and as a step of the inferential structure, on the other. This is occasionally described as a division of labour between the dynamic of accessibility and the process of inferential derivation, with schemata lying at the conjunction between the two:

> The appropriateness of different sets of encyclopaedic assumptions depends, on the one hand, on their degree of accessibility in the particular discourse context, and, on the other, on the potential contextual implications they yield. (Wilson and Carston 2007: 249)

In other words, the idea seems to be that an encyclopaedic assumption is delivered to the inferential procedure thanks to associative activation, but as soon as it is part of the inferential structure, the assumption is recruited in a process of a different kind: specifically, its appropriateness is evaluated at this stage (also) as a function of the conclusions it is able to produce (compared to expectations of relevance). What does this mean exactly? Let us outline, with some simplification, the inferential structure at issue, constituted by the following two premises and one conclusion:

a) SALLY IS EXCEPTIONALLY GOOD
b) ONE WHO IS EXCEPTIONALLY GOOD HELPS PEOPLE WHEN THEY NEED IT

---

c) SALLY HELPS PEOPLE WHEN THEY NEED IT

The previous quotation from Wilson and Carston (2007) suggests that the appropriateness of the encyclopaedic assumption b) depends, on the one hand, by its associative accessibility and, on the other, on the conclusion(s) it contributes to produce. However, at the same time they admit that b) can contribute to enhance backwards the activation of the property EXCEPTIONALLY GOOD, contained in the first premise – this seems to be meant when they say that this property receives "additional activation from other items in the context". Now, it is hard to see why b) should not contribute equally to the activation of the property HELPS PEOPLE WHEN THEY NEED IT, contained in the conclusion c). Let us note that the propositions forming this inferential structure can be rephrased, in Recanati's (2004) notation, in the following way:

a) EXCEPTIONALLY GOOD (SALLY)
b) EXCEPTIONALLY GOOD (x) → HELPS PEOPLE WHEN THEY NEED IT (x)

---

c) HELPS PEOPLE WHEN THEY NEED IT (SALLY)

Here the encyclopaedic assumption in b) is a schema in the sense of Recanati (2004), with variables that are substituted for by a proper name in a) and c). Such schemata, we argued in line with Barsalou, can yield inferences through associative activations. And, let me repeat, I see no reason why this might occur backwards between b) and a), as Wilson and Carston appear to acknowledge, but not forwards between b) and c). In sum, it seems that – instead of a division of labour between processes of different nature (associative activation and a process of inferential derivation) – descriptions at different levels are at play here: the same facts that are described as inferential derivations of conclusions at a certain level, can be accounted for by means of an associative dynamic at another level.

As a matter of fact, as we already saw, Wilson and Carston (2006: 429; my emphasis) acknowledge that associative links may alter "accessibility of contextual assumptions and *implications*". In sum, the division of labour should not be drawn, as it seemed from Wilson and Carston's (2007) quotation above, between activation of encyclopaedic assumptions and the inferential ability to draw conclusions, but instead between the entire inferential structure and its ability to satisfy expectations of relevance. To put it differently, it seems that what exceeds the simple mechanism of associative activation is not the inferential structure in itself, but instead its assessment described by the second step of the comprehension procedure.

I will turn to this point in the next section (see also § 4.9 below). My purpose in this section was only to show that the inferential structure admits of an explanation in associative terms. In this perspective, there is another issue that is worth addressing, that is, the case of extreme contextual modulation of concepts for the construction of explicit meaning. RT has referred to this phenomenon as the selection of "emergent properties", considering it as a special case of the selection of "ad hoc concepts".

Ad hoc concepts can been defined as temporary concepts constructed spontaneously in order to achieve a goal that is relevant in the current situation (Barsalou 2010). The notion has been introduced in psychology by Barsalou (1983) in the context of a discussion of the dynamic nature of concepts and it has recently been the focus of some research in cognitive pragmatics, under the assumption that utterance understanding requires that concepts are not simply activated but rather modulated and adjusted in order to fit specific linguistic and non-linguistic contexts. In some cases, this does not appear problematic, insofar as the contextually relevant properties are directly associated to the words requiring modulation, or to the concept conventionally associated to those words. In these cases, as Carston (2007) observes, a simple account in terms of activation and deactivation of already encoded concepts (or their parts) seems sufficient. In other cases, however, genuinely "constructive" processes seem to be involved, in the sense that conceptual modulations give rise to novel properties, which are not directly accessible from the initial concepts – as in the case of fresh metaphors. These non-directly accessible properties are called in fact "emergent".[28]

For instance, Carston observes that the utterance

(3) Mary is a bulldozer

requires the construction of the ad hoc concept[29] BULLDOZER* which can be paraphrased as being "obstinate, insensitive, uninterested in other people's opinions

---

28 The nature of the processes by which emergent properties are activated will be further analysed in chapter 3. See also fn. 31.

29 It is conventional to mark with a star the fact that a given concept is not the linguistically encoded one, but a contextual modulation of it.

and feelings", a concept which is not going to be found in the encyclopaedic entry or the schemata attached to the linguistically encoded concept BULLDOZER.[30] Therefore, she concludes, "some process or mechanism other than, or additional to, the activation (and deactivation) of existing concepts or parts of schemas is required" (Carston 2007: 29).

But is it really the case that emergent properties require more than associative activation? I want to suggest, on the contrary, that even in the absence of a direct connection with the appropriate ad hoc concept (or property), we can nevertheless have an associative explanation on condition that that there is a chain of schemata providing an indirect connection with it. The psychological literature on concept combination gives a hint on how this may occur. Hampton and Jönsson (2012), specifically, raise the issue of how, when the concepts BIRD and PET are combined together in the complex concept PET BIRD, the emergent property LIVES IN CAGES – which is not present in either of the constituent concepts – can be formed. They propose two different possible routes. One route is what they call extensional feedback: "The attribute is clearly made available by people recalling visits to pet shops or to friends' homes where they have seen pet birds" (Hampton and Jönsson 2012: 395). This amounts to the inductive justification for inferences we spoke of above (§ 2.6). Through experience a schema is formed such as PET BIRD LIVES IN CAGES, which then justifies the inference from the complex concept PET BIRD to the property LIVES IN CAGES. But Hampton and Jönsson also mention another possibility: "Alternatively people might use their 'background theories' to guess that if a bird was not kept in a cage, it would not remain a pet for very long" (ibidem). The question is, what does it mean that people use background theories and how do these theories provide non-inductive justification for inferences such as that from PET BIRD to LIVES IN CAGES?

In my view, the answer can be found in the notion of schema. This is the direction suggested by Hampton himself when he describes how background theories could be incorporated into prototype representations (Hampton 2006: 4, my emphasis):

> The crucial difference is that similarity to prototype is not a simple function of matching attributes, but involves deeper causal information. One way to think of this is to suppose that in addition to having a set of features, a theory-based prototype has a set of information about the *relations between those features*. If an item has the features, but does not have them in the right relations to each other [...], then its similarity to the prototype will be poor.

30 I am here assuming that the metaphor is actually new and BULLDOZER* is not a lexicalised concept. If this is not the case, one should apply instead these consideration to a different example in which the metaphor is new.

As in the notion of schema we considered earlier, the crucial idea is that the conceptual system must encode the relations between its components. We have already seen that this is essential in order to have inferences conceived as pattern completions. In addition, Hampton and Jönsson suggest that background theories – and therefore, according to Hampton (2006), relations between features – are key to the explanation of emergent properties. My proposal is that this might occur as a form of complex pattern completion based on chains of patterns.[31]

An interesting indication of how this mechanism could work is found again in semantic network models, an important feature of which was inheritance of properties from superordinate to subordinate categories. For one example, if BIRD is a superordinate category with respect to ROBIN and if (HAS) WINGS is encoded as a property of BIRD, then the network licences the conclusion that that property applies to ROBIN as well. In such a case, there is no encoded pattern directly connecting ROBIN and (HAS) WINGS and therefore no pattern completion in the sense we considered earlier. Nevertheless, there is a chain of two patterns – ROBIN ISA BIRD and BIRD HAS WINGS – such that ROBIN is indirectly connected to HAS WINGS thanks to that chain: this can be called a case of *complex pattern completion*.

With all this in mind, we can sketch an explanation of how the emergent property LIVES IN CAGES can be inferred starting from the combination of the concepts PET and BIRD. Let me emphasise that what follows is just a sketch, intended to give a general idea of how complex pattern completion might work in a case like this. For the sake of simplicity I will use the sketchy notation adopted by Recanati (2004), in which there is no explicit representation of the relations between concepts – generally speaking, it is reasonable to assume that any attempt to represent explicitly our conceptual system suffers from a certain number of arbitrary simplifications. I propose to consider two chains of schemata, one starting from the concept BIRD, the other from the concept PET:

(a) (i) BIRD (x) → FLY (x)
(ii) FLY (x) → FREE TO GO AWAY (x)

31 It is crucial here to keep in mind our previous distinction between two senses of "associative". By proposing an account of emergent properties in terms of associative activation, I do not intend to claim that automatic (versus controlled) activation is sufficient. On the contrary, as I will argue below in § 3.10, the phenomenon of emergent properties, as any other cognitive capacity involving the interaction of non-directly associated contents, is expected to require sustained activation and therefore (partially) controlled processing.

(b) (i) PET (x) → PEOPLE WANT TO PREVENT (FREE TO GO AWAY (x))
(ii) PEOPLE WANT TO PREVENT (FREE TO GO AWAY (x)) → PEOPLE KEEP (PRISONER (x))
(iii) PRISONER (x) → IN CAGE (x)

By way of complex pattern completion, the concept BIRD allows one to infer FREE TO GO AWAY, which is also a component of the property PEOPLE WANT TO PREVENT (FREE TO GO AWAY (x)) associated to the concept PET. Thus, the activation of both PET and BIRD can be expected to cause strong activation of this property, which in turn activates the sequence ending with the concept IN CAGE.

This necessarily sketchy account shows nevertheless how even emergent properties can be explained in terms of associative pattern completion, provided that the system contains appropriate chains of schemata. One important simplification we made was to only consider the schemata that are required to obtain the desired conclusion, while, as a result of the activation of the concepts PET and BIRD, other properties than (LIVES) IN CAGES may be activated as well. But, let me repeat, the overgeneration would be overcome by the plurality of inputs in context and the coherence-inducing effect of schemata. In our last example, the key point is that the same property is jointly activated by two different concepts, so that their activation sum and make that property contextually more relevant than others. In the next section I will focus on how such convergences of activations provide an alternative answer to the question that the second step of the comprehension procedure is intended to answer in RT, that is: How is the relevance of pragmatic interpretations assessed?

2.13 Taking stock: RT between standard and non-standard view

In this chapter we have outlined the following theoretical picture. Conceptual memory is organized in schemata endowing it with a hierarchical structure. Thanks to that structure, any input produces a double dynamic of activation: bottom-up, towards the schemata of which the input is a component; top-down, from these schemata to other components. A crucial point is that, given the plurality of the inputs, and the plurality of the schemata associated to any of them, the dynamic described above causes effects both of competition and convergence: the activation of any schema is – so to speak – a hypothesis that may receive support from other inputs, and that competes with alternative hypotheses.

This is without doubt a low-level account of cognitive abilities. It is not presumed to be an alternative to the idea that certain processes can be described, at a different level, as inferential. Rather, the aim is to show how inferences can be implemented in a biological substrate constituted by an associative network through which waves of activation travel. Insofar as this is a low-level account concerning the basic functioning of our cortex, it is candidate to explain high-level processes of various kinds, and to do so exhaustively: that is, with no need to appeal to other kinds of processes.

This picture is easily applied to pragmatic inferential processes, in a way that is coherent with what I called the non-standard view of RT, and in particular with the notions of parallel mutual adjustment and expectations about the type (versus the amount) of cognitive effects. In practice, an interpretation is conceived as an inferential structure produced by a bidirectional process: inferences can proceed both forward, from explicit meaning to contextual conclusions, and backward, from conclusions suggested by the context to explicit meaning. In sum, in this picture contextual assumptions and conclusions licensed by forward inferences are indeed subject to a sort of assessment, but this is ensured by the backward side of the same associative dynamic, not by a different kind of process. That is, forward and backward inferences constrain each other – they are *assessed* against each other. Expectations of relevance about the type of cognitive effects (the intended contextual conclusions) would be nothing but activations of schemata due to contextual inputs and apt to constrain backward the activations caused by linguistic inputs. The assessment of interpretations would be one and the same process as their construction, and it would be performed through competition between the activated schemata.

In a recent paper, Sperber and Wilson (2015) provide further considerations at least compatible with such an associative account of inferences. The key idea is that many inferences cannot be described in terms of standard logical derivations, constituted by successive steps in a linear sequence. Rather, what we form is an "impression", based on changes in the manifestness of a number of propositions, none of which needs to be distinctly and explicitly entertained, but that together activate a certain conclusion. In practice, the process can be described as a competition between alternative conclusions, whose result is determined by a large, or anyway hardly determinable, number of changes in the system's pattern of activation. "The winner of such competitions is determined by activation or inhibition caused by brain states that represent information in all kind of ways (from consciously entertained propositions to unconscious weightings of features [...])" (Sperber and Wilson 2015: 137). Although the process "is quite different from a sequence of good old syllogisms", it would nonetheless count as genuinely inferential to the extent that the mechanisms determining the final outcome "tend to favour warranted conclusions" (ibidem).

As in other cases considered previously, the terminology adopted here by relevance theorists is clearly associative. Inferential processes of belief formation are described in terms of spreading activation and associative competition between representations. Nonetheless, this mechanism is taken to be inferential to the extent that its outcomes can be re-described, at a different level, as warranted conclusions.

Interestingly, Sperber and Wilson (2015) take a very cautious stance toward this associative view. If, on the one hand, they claim that arguably "the vast majority of inferences made by humans and other animals" (ibidem) are better accounted for in terms of such associative competitions, not of standard logical derivations, on the other hand they make it clear that their aim is not to argue for an associative account of inferences, but only to avoid any commitment towards a "narrow and questionable view" of what inferences are like (idem: 138). This caution is understandable, in the light of the doubts expressed by relevance theorists toward associative accounts.

To repeat, the key point is the second step of the comprehension procedure, which predicts a further mechanism, distinct from simple accessibility, for the assessment of interpretations. Relevance theorists appeal to the opposition between associative and inferential as a demarcation criterion, apt to capture what is specific of RT with respect to cognitive linguistics (see Wilson and Carston 2006) and to Recanati's theory of pragmatics (see Carston 2007). Let me quote again Wilson and Carston's (2006: 429) claim according to which "associative links may affect the outcome of the mutual adjustment process by altering the accessibility of contextual assumptions and implications, but the resulting overall interpretation will only be accepted as the speaker's intended meaning if it satisfies the hearer's expectations of relevance". Apparently, here the dynamic of associative activations is taken to be only the first stage of the process; a further stage, which is not based on associations, must then follow. It seems, thus, that Mazzarella (2014: 77) has actually grasped the spirit of RT by claiming that "what makes a pragmatic account genuinely inferential is that it maintains a distinction between [the following] two stages" (the distinction is taken from Wilson and Matsui 1998: 2–3):

a. Candidate interpretations differ in their accessibility, and are therefore entertained in a certain order.
b. They are evaluated in terms of some criterion or standard of pragmatic acceptability that the resulting overall interpretation is supposed to meet.

This idea – that what essentially characterizes RT is a mechanism not reducible to simple associations – may explain why it is important for relevance theorists to provide arguments against associative accounts. We analysed, specifically, Wilson and Carston's (2007) argument according to which associative processes "will vastly overgenerate, and some method of filtering out unwanted associations will be required" (Wilson and Carston 2007: 252) In the same vein, Carston (2007) has provided an argument against Recanati, based on the alleged difficulty that associative models would have in accounting for emergent properties: to that effect, she concludes, "some process or mechanism other than, or additional to, the activation (and deactivation) of existing concepts or parts of schemas is required" (Carston 2007: 29).

RT's arguments against Recanati concern, in fact, two different points. As we saw, Recanati (2004) distinguishes two stages of pragmatic processing: a first associative stage, and a stage based on conscious inferencing. On the contrary, according to RT (at least in its standard version), neither consciousness nor associative processes play a significant role in pragmatics: there would be a single pragmatic process that is automatic but genuinely inferential (i.e., not reducible to associative processes). In this chapter, I analysed RT's argument against associative accounts in pragmatics and I found it untenable. In the next, I am going to analyse in greater depth the other aspect of the theoretical contrast between RT and Recanati: the role of conscious processing in pragmatics.

3 Automatic and controlled processes

3.1 Introduction

In this chapter we will first address the issue (briefly touched upon in § 2.11) of what automatic and controlled processes are; then we will analyse the way in which those processes divide cognitive labour in general and, in particular, how they interact in pragmatic comprehension.

In this specific domain, the issue arises naturally: pragmatic processing seems to be at the same time an automatic and a personal-level affair. On the one hand, humans produce and understand utterances in context quite rapidly and effortlessly, just as it is expected to occur in automatic processing. On the other hand, verbal communication is thought to require an intentional involvement on the part of the speaker, and a recognition of the speaker's intention – possibly requiring rational capacities – on the part of the addressee. This duality is, in a way, already intrinsic to Grice's model, which describes pragmatic processing as a form of personal-level reasoning, but considers this description as a rational reconstruction of cognitive mechanisms that might turn out to be much less under control of the subject than that reconstruction suggests.

The tension between automatic and controlled processing in pragmatics is made apparent by the debate between Recanati (2004) and relevance theorists on this issue (see Recanati 2007; Carston 2007; Mazzarella 2011, 2013a; Rubio-Fernández 2013). Participants on both sides of the debate try, though in different ways, to solve the tension, but in my opinion both fail. Recanati stays closer to the letter of the Gricean model, by claiming that pragmatic inferences (Gricean implicatures) are practical arguments of which the addressee is consciously aware, but then he must weaken the notion of consciousness involved to the point that it is made irrelevant. On the other hand, relevance theorists postulate a mechanism that is automatic, thus denying that consciousness has a role to play in it, but at the same time insisting on its genuinely inferential – versus associative – nature. However, as we saw in the previous chapter, this is problematic: in psychology, inferential and associative processes (at the behavioural level of description) are opposed to each other based on the fact that the former but not the latter are characterized by conscious attention and sustained activation. Therefore, there appear to be no clear grounds for positing the notion of automatic inferential processes.

My suggestion is that the complementary problems of Recanati and RT are caused by the lack of an intermediate notion between conscious reasoning

https://doi.org/10.1515/9781501507731-004

and purely automatic processing, notion that I will refer to with the expression "conscious attention". By this I mean a process that is largely automatic but in which some of the representations activated are nevertheless consciously focussed. In other words, this kind of processing is not purely automatic but, on the other hand, the inferences involved are not such that all the steps, and the transitions between them, are entirely in the focus of consciousness. In the absence of such an intermediate notion, when facing with processes that are neither purely automatic nor entirely conscious, one is forced to choose one pole of the dichotomy, but without finding rest in it. In practice, Recanati puts his bet on conscious reasoning, but then he waters down the notion by describing it as merely dispositional; while RT opts instead for the notion of automatic, though genuinely inferential, processes, but this notion is hard to make sense of, in the light of the standard distinction between associative and inferential in psychology – based on which "inferential" means controlled and therefore *non*-automatic.

To be sure, it is possible to intend the notion of "inferential" in a different sense that is not, however, in opposition to "associative". In the previous chapter we saw that pragmatic processes can be said inferential in Grice's sense provided that they admit of a rational reconstruction, irrespective of the actual processes by which they are implemented. This notion is apparently accepted by Sperber and Wilson (2015), too: in that paper we are told that associative processes can be considered inferential to the extent that they tend to favour warranted conclusions. One might go even further and observe that, in the account proposed here, processes can be described as inferential in the sense that the organization of memory is based on schemata enabling motivated transitions from content to content. This means that associative processes not only produce the same results that could have been obtained through inferences, but also they *actually* perform inferences, that is, transitions between contents ensured by the same schemata that enable their rational reconstructions.[32] In other words, both automatic and controlled associative-I processes are governed by the same rational structure: the fact that automatic (or better, as I will specify below, partially automatic) processes can be rationally reconstructed is not an accident; it depends on the fact that those processes have a rational structure themselves.

But, as I will argue in this chapter, it is also possible to claim that pragmatic processes are inferential in the other sense considered above (but not embraced

32 Recall our previous considerations on associative pattern completion as a generalized form of modus ponens, in § 2.6.

by RT), for which I preferred the term "controlled": pragmatic processes come together with conscious attention, and therefore they are not *entirely* automatic without being, for this reason, instances of conscious reasoning. In this chapter I will analyse two aspects of utterance understanding with regard to which conscious attention appears to play a role.

The first example concerns the prominence of information related to the speaker. In the debate between Recanati and relevance theorists, an issue is whether in utterance understanding the addressee takes into consideration the mental states of the speaker. Recanati, given his distinction between primary and secondary pragmatic processes, seems committed to the thesis that explicit meaning is constructed without consideration of mental states. Relevance theorists argue against that assumption, and in fact force Recanati to amend his theory, though in a direction that is itself questionable. I will argue that RT makes a crucial point here: information about the speaker's mental states has special prominence in every stage of the comprehension process. But at the same time I will argue that the theory does not possess the theoretical resources to account for this phenomenon, which is instead naturally accounted for in terms of conscious attention.

The second example concerns the construction of emergent properties, a phenomenon I already discussed in the previous chapter with regard to its associative implementation. Rubio-Fernández (2013) provides further empirical evidence on this issue, which she interprets as supporting RT's view of pragmatic inferential processes more than Recanati's. But, as I will try to show, the entire argument tacitly presupposes the notion of inferential that involves conscious attention. And this is problematic for RT, whose account of pragmatic inferences does not assign any explicit role to consciousness.

In the light of this chapter and the previous one, my overall proposal is then the following. Pragmatic processes are at the same time automatic and controlled (i.e., associative and inferential in the behavioural sense), as incidentally is the case for any cognitive process of some importance. Moreover, both automatic and controlled processes have inferential nature in the sense that both involve motivated transitions, based on schemata, between conceptual contents; while, on the other hand, both are implemented by associative processes, in the sense of their implementation in associative neural networks. Neural networks are in fact able to implement both automatic and controlled processes: what changes is the dynamic of activation, which is characterized by rapid decay on a local scale for the former, and long-distance sustained activation for the latter.

Let us now consider in turn the respective views of Recanati and RT with regard to the role of consciousness in pragmatics.

3.2 The role of consciousness in Recanati and RT

As already said in chapter 2, Recanati distinguishes between primary pragmatic processes, conceived as associative and local (i.e., concerning the assignment of concepts and referents to word forms in the utterance), and secondary pragmatic processes, which are genuinely inferential and conscious, and concern the relation between complete propositions – specifically, they concern the way in which the addressee derives the implicit meaning from the explicit proposition conveyed by the utterance. In practice, Recanati conceives of secondary pragmatic processes as "transparently or consciously inferential" in that they are presumed to satisfy the "availability condition" (Recanati 2004: 44): they are accessible to consciousness, that is, the subject is aware of what is said, of the implicature, and of the inferential transition from the former to the latter.

For an example, let us consider the following question–answer pair:

(4) (a) Could you pay back the money you owe me?
(b) I'm going to the bank now to get some cash.

In this context, the implicit meaning of (b) is presumably a positive answer to the yes–no question (a). As to the explicit meaning, an important point is that there are two possible meanings for the word "bank", FINANCIAL INSTITUTION and RIVER SIDE, the former of which is to be preferred in the context. Recanati's assumption is that both the explicit and the implicit content are available to consciousness, in that the former conforms "to the intuitions shared by those who fully understand the utterance" (idem: 14), and the latter follows inferentially from the former insofar as the expectation for a yes–no answer raised by the previous question is taken into consideration.

It is important to emphasize that the conscious availability here appealed to is qualified by Recanati as tacit rather than fully explicit – or, to put it differently, dispositional rather than occurrent. He recognizes that conscious processes are typically effortful, slow and under voluntary control, while comprehension processes normally are not. However, although the inferences involved in comprehension cannot be conceived of as conscious in this explicit, occurrent sense, according to Recanati they are not even the sort of sub-personal inferences that are merely ascribed to a cognitive system on the grounds that the system behaves in the same way as someone who performed the relevant inferences in an explicit form (Recanati 2004: 49). There would be an intermediate condition between the two: an inference can also be considered consciously available in a tacit dispositional sense when "the cognitive agent to which it is ascribed […] is itself capable of making the inference explicitly and of rationally justifying whatever methods it spontaneously uses in arriving at the 'conclusion'" (idem: 50). Therefore, in Recanati's opinion, some inferences are merely sub-personal (so, strictly speaking, they are not inferences at all, but can only be reconstructed as such); some are conscious in the prototypical sense (they are explicit, slow and effortful); some others are personal-level and yet only dispositionally conscious.

This view, however, raises a serious problem for a cognitive account of comprehension. Such a *dispositional but not actual* process is not a cognitive process proper, it is just the possibility that a process occurs in substitution for the one that is actually occurring. Thus, when Recanati tells us that a cognitive agent is capable of providing a conscious justification of "whatever methods it spontaneously uses in arriving at the 'conclusion'", what is certain is only that the spontaneous process employed by the agent *is not* actually a conscious justification. Therefore, Recanati leaves us in the dark as to the actual process involved.

A further problem pointed out by Carston concerns the thesis that primary and secondary pragmatic processes behave differently with respect to conscious availability. She makes various examples of cases in which people seems to be aware of how explicit content may depart from linguistic meaning as a function of contextual factors. Let us consider the following example:

(5)	Mother to young child just before bedtime:	Have you brushed your teeth?
	Child (grinning):	Yes I have – [pause] – last night.

The answer clearly shows that the child is well aware of the normal pragmatic enrichment by which the relevant time is assigned to the temporal parameter of the question: in fact, the child openly violates the expectations raised by that normal enrichment. But in Recanati's view that sort of enrichment is a case of primary pragmatic process for the determination of explicit content. Therefore, conscious availability seems not to be an exclusive property of secondary pragmatic processes.

On their part, relevance theorists have always considered pragmatic understanding as an inferential process, "albeit a spontaneous, intuitive rather than a conscious, reflective one" (Wilson and Sperber 2002: 278) and, starting from Sperber and Wilson (1995, which is the second edition of *Relevance*), they have also characterized it as modular. The paper just quoted (Wilson and Sperber 2002) is a synopsis of RT, thus it is significant that the adjective "conscious" is present in it only once, in the above quotation, with the aim of specifying what inferential pragmatic processes are *not* (while the noun "consciousness" is never used). On the other hand, Carston (2007) is perfectly right when she claims that the "capacity for explicit reflective reasoning" (idem: 39) may play a role in communication and comprehension only with regard to post hoc rational reconstruction of spontaneous pragmatic processes: "this is not an exercise that people perform much off their own bat. Its most likely role is as a backup mechanism when something goes wrong with the automatic intuitive mechanisms of utterance understanding" (idem: 44). One may object that the dispositional conscious accessibility required by Recanati is not the same as the "explicit reflective reasoning" that Carston addresses here. But it is Recanati himself who speaks in terms of explicit reflective reasoning in the first place (even if then he feels the urge to weaken the notion by characterizing it as dispositional), since he lacks the conceptual resources to distinguish this from less demanding forms of conscious access. Thus, neither is Recanati able to grasp correctly this intermediate notion, nor are relevance theorists in the position to appreciate his efforts to do this, though in a contradictory way.

It is this sort of less demanding conscious access that we are going to describe now, after having analysed the distinction between automatic and controlled processes.

3.3 Definitions of automatic and controlled

The view that human cognition involves two different types of processing, automatic and controlled, is a well-established theme in psychology at least since the writings of William James (1890). The issue has received renewed attention in the last decades after the seminal studies of Shiffrin and Schneider (1977) and Schneider and Shiffrin (1977) – see Schneider and Chein (2003) for a more recent overview. Schneider and Shiffrin (1977: 2, 3) define an automatic process as the activation of a sequence of nodes in our knowledge representation that "nearly always become active in response to a particular input configuration" and that "is activated automatically without the necessity for active control or attention by the subject" (idem: 2). In contrast, a controlled process is defined as "a temporary sequence of nodes activated under control of, and through attention by, the subject" (idem: 2–3).

The standard tests employed to assess whether a process of interest is automatic or controlled are subliminal presentation and techniques based on cognitive load (see Satpute and Lieberman 2006: 91). The fact that an input is processed subliminally, that is, outside awareness, is treated as the most distinctive feature of automaticity. On the other hand, it is also expected that whenever the process of interest is automatic, it will not be influenced by load manipulations. This is because automatic processes are thought to occur in parallel, in contrast with controlled processes that operate serially, resulting in task-switching costs. Another important manifestation of the automatic-controlled distinction is that "extended consistent training is required in order to develop automatic processing, while controlled processes can be established in a few trials and under varied mapping conditions" (Schneider and Chein 2003: 528). As a consequence of extended training and parallel processing, automatic processes are fast and accurate. On the contrary, controlled processes are typically slow and inaccurate.

3.4 Some variants of the distinction

In the last decades, the basic distinction just outlined has been framed in largely similar ways by different scholars (Carver and Scheier 2009): intuitive versus conscious in Smolensky (1988), associative versus rule based in Sloman (1996), reflexive versus reflective in Shastri and Ajjanagadde (1993). Moreover, two-mode, or dual-process models of functioning have emerged in personality psychology (experiential versus rational system: Epstein 1973), and in social psychology (reflexive versus reflective: Lieberman et al. 2002; impulsive versus reflective: Strack and Deutsch 2004; Strack et al. 2009).

In some of those developments of the distinction, the emphasis is on the fact that the second kind of process operates on "symbolic, or propositional structures" (Satpute and Lieberman 2006: 88), enables symbolic logic (Lieberman et al. 2002), can be simulated by symbolic architectures allowing the binding of variables (Schneider and Chein 2003: 532) – in contrast to automatic processes which can be simulated by simple connectionist networks. This shift towards the sub-symbolic/symbolic distinction is pushed to the point that in some cases consciousness is no more considered distinctive of controlled processes.

As useful as it can be for some theoretical purposes, this way to recast the automatic/controlled distinction is probably misleading for various reasons. First, it is hardly coherent with the most accepted way to assess automaticity, that is, by means of tests based on subliminal processing: these tests precisely aim to ascertain whether a cognitive process occurs outside consciousness. Second, at least for a crucial class of cognitive phenomena, by claiming that a process is controlled (versus automatic) scholars mostly intend to emphasize its conscious and voluntary nature, irrespective of whether it is a symbolic (propositional) process or not. This is the case with a large amount of research in neurophysiology, where the issue is at which conditions bodily movements become actions, that is, they are under conscious control (versus merely automatic: for instance, see Jeannerod 2006; Pacherie 2006). Third, by downplaying the importance of the conscious/unconscious distinction one loses the crucial theoretical connection between the automatic/controlled issue on the one hand, and the notion of executive functions on the other. This latter notion is used in psychology and neuroscience to describe a loosely defined set of capacities having to do with guidance of behaviour: planning, initiating and maintaining appropriate actions while inhibiting inappropriate ones, cognitive flexibility etc. Executive functions appear as prototypical examples of controlled processes: but this is so because of the fact that executive functions involve consciousness and selective attention, not propositionality.

For all these reasons, I will rest on the most widely accepted view of the automatic/controlled distinction, that is, the one that takes consciousness as the main line of demarcation and emphasizes the connections with theories of intentional action and executive functions. Against this background, there are three points that need to be further analysed. One is the observation that "automatic" and "controlled" presumably are not all-or-none notions; instead, they appear to come in degrees. A second point is that, although consciousness and controlled processes have a crucial role to play in goal-directed behaviour, it is partially possible to have goal-directed behaviour outside consciousness. Finally, the emphasis in recent research is less on how automatic and controlled processes may be detected and analysed in isolation than on how they factually cooperate for most of our cognitive activities. Let us now briefly address each of these points in turn; this will prepare the ground for an updated view of the automatic/controlled issue, according to which intentional actions and most superior cognitive abilities can be explained in terms of a largely automatic dynamic of activation, with conscious attention shifting from one component to the other as a function of the circumstances. Mazzone and Campisi (2013) have spoken in this sense of "distributed intentionality". Then I will turn back to the domain of pragmatics, and to how these considerations may answer to some questions in that domain.

3.5 All-or-none notions?

The traditional view according to which there is a sharp boundary between automatic and controlled processes has been challenged in the last decades, either because automaticity has been explained in terms of properties which vary gradually, or because automaticity has been analysed in components which can, but need not, be present together (Garrod and Pickering 2007). The latter line of thought has been pursued by Bargh (1994): in his view, a process is automatic to the extent that it is unaware, mandatory, efficient, non-interruptible.[33] However, since those features do not always co-vary together, there may be different degrees of automaticity as a function of the number of features involved.

As to the former line of thought, it is well exemplified by Cohen et al. (1990). They propose that automaticity is a function of what they call "strength of processing", which in turn is defined in relation to processing pathways within a connectionist network. A strong connection leads to fast and accurate transmission of information along the pathway; moreover, the strength of processing may determine the extent to which processes are open to interference from other processes.

A more complete and refined hypothesis with regard to the neural basis of consciousness has been put forth by Dehaene and colleagues (see especially Dehaene et al. 2006; Dehaene 2014). In the model they propose, the distinction between conscious and unconscious processing is not all-or-none, for two reasons. First, they assume that besides conscious and purely subliminal processing there can be intermediate conditions. Second, in their model consciousness is also a function of the strength of activation in the interested brain areas. To be more precise, Dehaene et al. (2006) distinguish four conditions of un/consciousness, depending on the degree of activation that is found respectively in posterior sensory-motor representations and higher association cortices. *Pure* (i.e., unattended) *subliminal processing* occurs when there is weak and rapidly decaying activation in posterior sensory-motor areas, without any significant interacting activation in anterior cortices. In certain cases, however, attention (with the related frontal activation) may occasionally interact with such weak posterior activations, thus resulting in *attended subliminal processing*. Moreover, an intense activation which is yet confined to sensory-motor processes is thought to cause occipito-temporal loops and local synchrony, and therefore a condition of *preconscious processing*: processes are virtually accessible to consciousness, although attention is actually oriented away from the stimulus, so that activation is blocked from accessing higher parieto-frontal areas and establishing long-distance synchrony. Finally, *conscious* controlled processes require the establishing of long-distance loops between strongly activated sensory-motor representations and higher association cortices.

In sum, not only do considerations from both psychology of learning (Bargh 1994) and neurobiology of consciousness (Cohen et al. 1990; Dehaene et al. 2006)

---

33 In Bargh's (1994) own terms, the four parameters are awareness, intentionality, efficiency, and controllability. However, Garrod and Pickering suggest that "non-interruptibility" is a more proper label for what Bargh calls "controllability". Similarly, Mazzone and Campisi (2013) observe that by the term "intentionality" Bargh properly means that a process is not mandatory.

suggest that the automatic/controlled distinction admits of degrees, instead of being an all-or-none affair.[34] But also, in line with what we saw in the previous chapter, we can count on influential hypotheses about how the two components are implemented in associative networks. In particular, according to Dehaene and colleagues' proposal, automatic and controlled processes simply correspond to different dynamics of activation within such networks. But there is a further aspect for which the distinction between automatic and controlled appears less dramatic than is thought. To the extent that the distinction concerns different modes of activation through the *same representational structures*, we can expect the two processes to have important features in common. This thesis has been actually argued for, as we are going to see, by models of action developed in social psychology.

3.6 Automatic goal pursuit

Traditionally, goal pursuit has been conceived of as a typical case of conscious and effortful processing. In the last decades this view has been challenged especially by John Bargh (starting from Bargh 1989; 1990). His notion of automatic or non-conscious goal pursuit has witnessed in the meantime a number of empirical demonstrations (for recent reviews see Hassin et al. 2009; Ferguson et al. 2007). The thesis of non-conscious goal pursuit is based on the notion of habit, with habits conceived of as

> associative networks that include contexts, goals that are regularly pursued in these contexts, and means that one usually uses to attain these goals [...]. These networks are shaped by one's history, and they allow for goal pursuit via spreading of activation. (Hassin et al. 2009: 550–551)[35]

34 To be sure, Sergent and Dehaene (2004) address the hypothesis that the transition from unconscious to conscious perception is gradual, and they provide instead empirical support to the conclusion that consciousness requires "all-or-none changes in neural activity" (idem: 720). However, the paper says nothing against the distinctions drawn by Dehaene et al. (2006). It focuses on the existence of a threshold in the perception of a single stimulus. This does not preclude the possibility that more complex patterns of stimuli may admit of degrees, as is explicitly acknowledged by the authors: "One possible explanation of the observed gradual increase in subjective visibility is that, as target duration increases, the bottom-up wave of activity gains strength and increasingly deeper processing stages are activated. Thus, the information that enters consciousness is increasingly richer" (idem: 727).

35 Incidentally, this description of habits as constituted by goals, context in which they are pursued, and means to pursue them, is entirely coherent with the definition of goal-directed schema provided at the end of § 2.10.

Given this conception of habits as associative networks, it seems an obvious consequence that the activation of a component may spread to other components of the network, and this has been largely confirmed by experiments based on priming.[36] In particular, priming of goals appears to affect subsequent representations and behaviours in many ways. For instance, when an action is regularly selected and performed in order to obtain a goal (for instance, taking the bicycle instead of the bus to go to the university), "priming these goals automatically activates behavior representation and resultant action according to an 'if-then' rule, enabling the goal-directed behavior to occur directly and independent of conscious intentions" (Dijksterhuis et al. 2007: 105). Of particular interest is the fact that similar results have also been obtained through unobtrusive or unconscious priming. For instance, Bargh et al. (2001) unobtrusively exposed subjects to words such as "strive" and "succeed" to prime the achievement goal, and then tested their performances in an anagram puzzle task. Participants primed with the achievement goal outperformed those who were not primed with the goal. Similar effects may also be obtained in more indirect ways: for instance, priming the names of significant others may lead to the automatic adoption of the goals associated with them; or for another example, thinking to a good friend may enhance the disposition to participate in a subsequent task as a possible means to help (Dijksterhuis et al. 2007: 101–102).

What these observations apparently show is that automatic processing may go deep into the guidance of behaviours that are thought of as typically intentional and controlled. That this must be the case is also shown by the fact that most of our intentional actions are nonetheless rapid and effortless. This has led to models of intentional actions where the most part of cognitive processing is thought to occur automatically. However, such models often tend to assume that automaticity does only concern the mere execution of intentions: conscious representations of the goals to be pursued are held to be required for action control, while the specific behavioural means by which the goals are pursued would be activated automatically. For example, Levelt (1989) has proposed a model of this sort with regard to language production. On the contrary, the evidence concerning non-conscious goal pursuit invites us to believe that even high-level goals may drive action without becoming conscious, that is, they can operate in an entirely automatic way.

---

36 See also Gollwitzer et al. (2009: 605), where they suggest that goals may behave in accordance with simple associative (hebbian) principles: "Under the assumption that goals, too, are represented mentally and become automatically activated by the same [hebbian] principles, goal representations should also be capable of automatic activation through contact with features of the contexts in which those goals have been pursued often and consistently in the past".

This has an important implication. Huang and Bargh (2014) have recently insisted on the striking similarities between conscious and unconscious goal operations, including the production of similar effects upon individual judgment and behaviour. Specifically, "people who are unaware that they are pursuing a goal respond to the world in a way that maximizes the likelihood of goal completion" (Huang and Bargh 2014: 123). In other words, automatic goal pursuit tends to be (in the appropriate circumstances) just as effectively goal-driven as controlled goal pursuit, which means in turn that the agent must be representing the very same coherent structure of goals, means and situational constraints that needs to be taken into account both in conscious decision making and in rational reconstructions of action.

This hypothesis can be generalized along the lines discussed in the previous chapter, when I proposed that inferential pragmatic processes – processes that can be described in terms of rational inferences – are implemented by associative networks. This is made possible by the fact that associative networks have a motivated structure, thanks to which simple processes of pattern completion yield results that are rationally justified. This conclusion, it should be noted, does not depend on whether the processes at issue are automatic or controlled. In fact, there is no reason why the mechanism of competitive activation should not operate, by and large, in the same way in both cases: what changes is only the dynamic of activation, respectively local and with rapid decay versus distributed and sustained in time.[37]

The general picture is therefore the following: the representational structure of associative networks explains the ability to draw inferences, an ability that can be exercised both in automatic and controlled ways. The hypothesis of Bargh and colleagues about non-conscious goal pursuit appears to be nothing but a special case of this general picture, according to which controlled and automatic processes have quite similar effects. This is not surprising if, as I argued in the previous chapter, goal representation is only a special case of the organization of knowledge in hierarchically structured schemata.

3.7 How automatic and controlled processes cooperate

On the basis of our previous considerations, according to which automatic and controlled processes have largely similar outcomes, one might be tempted to

37 Nevertheless, I will examine below, in § 5.6, an important aspect for which automatic processes and their rational reconstructions behave differently.

think that consciousness does not play a significant role in human cognition. Our actions are mostly rapid and effortless, and this suggests a major role for automatic processing. In this direction, another relevant line of evidence is provided by the experiments of Libet (e.g., Libet 1992), which have shown that "consciousness of the goal of an action is not immediate, it takes time to appear" (Jeannerod 2006). More specifically,

> the first conscious awareness associated with the initiation of the movements [...] occurs well after the start of the neural activity that culminates in the movement. [...] This clearly suggests that whatever events one might reasonably consider to be the neural initiators of these movements, those events occur pre-consciously. (Pockett 2006: 18–19).

Based on this sort of evidence, some have drawn the conclusion that consciousness is essentially a post hoc phenomenon, which has little to do with initiation and guidance of action. It would rather be (part of) a mechanism "for the cognitive rearrangement after the action is completed" (Jeannerod 2006: 37), in the service of our sense of agency and the distinction between our own and others' actions (Pockett 2006; Jeannerod 2006; Choudhury and Blakemore 2006). However, there are reasons to believe that conscious and controlled processes should be accorded instead a significant role in active online processing and guidance of action. First, conscious control appears to be occasionally required in the course of action when smooth automatic processing fails (Gollwitzer et al. 2009: 610; Bongers and Dijksterhuis 2009; Jeannerod 2006: 30). Second, sometimes we make conscious plans of action, or we are explicitly required to accomplish a task, and so on. In such cases, but possibly also in cases where initiation of action is automatic, consciousness seems to play a key role in top-down maintenance of goals and top-down inhibition: the execution of plans that extend in time cannot be accounted for solely in terms of automatic spreading of activation. This suggests that not only have both automatic and conscious processes a role to play in human cognition; they are also expected to cooperate in most of our cognitive performances. There is nowadays growing acceptance that "conscious and nonconscious goal pursuit are two collaborative partners taking turns in working towards goal attainment" (Gollwitzer et al. 2009: 620–621).

This cooperative view of automatic/controlled processes is entirely coherent with the neurobiological model proposed by Dehaene et al. (2006): as we saw, that model proposes that both in attended subliminal processing and in conscious processing frontal and more specifically pre-frontal activations can affect automatic processes, by amplifying the independent activation of certain representations (and by causing the active inhibition of others) in posterior areas. An interesting way to frame attended subliminal processing is in terms of Neumann's (1990) theory of "direct parameter specification". According to this theory "[a] given attentional (or intentional) state might be necessary for unconscious stimuli to trigger further processes" (as Kiefer 2007: 293, puts it). More specifically:

> [Subjects] search for information in order to specify free parameters within the currently active intention/action plan. Unconsciously registered information that resembles this searched-for information is selected and processed to specify the free processing parameters. Therefore, unconsciously perceived information will translate into behavioural effects that are absent if the same information is sufficiently dissimilar from the searched-for features. (Kiefer 2007: 300)

In other words, top-down intentional processing would cause certain stimuli to affect behaviour even when they are not consciously perceived.

3.8 Distributed control

In the light of the sort of evidence we have reviewed so far, the distinction between automatic and controlled processes should be considered just the first step on the way to understanding their cooperation in most of our cognitive operations. Mazzone and Campisi (2013) have proposed a general approach to intentional actions – the "distributed intentionality model" – based on such a cooperative view of automatic and controlled processes. We propose that in order for actions to be intentional it is not required that action plans are consciously represented and then put into effect in a purely top-down manner. In the general case, actions are largely the result of automatic processes of activation, integration and competition between a huge number of goal-related representations. On the other hand, human behaviour is intuitively intentional in essence, in that it never seems to occur without agents consciously attending this or that component of the complex goal-directed representation involved. However, conscious attention is not necessarily directed towards one specific component of that representation, be it an overall goal or whatever: conscious intentions should rather be conceived of as beams of light temporarily directed towards this or that goal-related component of a largely automatic flow of processing. In a word, intentionality is better thought of as dynamically distributed along the complex goal-directed representation involved in any single action, than concentrated in (the representation of) one single purpose of the action.

In our model, the role played by automatisms is very large. This is in line with the view of Morsella (2009), according to which human behaviour is based on a "stream of action [...] driven by a continuous series of activations stemming from various sources" (idem: 19). In other words, our perceptions would endlessly feed automatic processes impinging on motor representations, so that plans of action are activated automatically at each moment and then compete for behavioural expression (idem: 16).

However, this is far from implying that consciousness is either absent or purely epiphenomenal in most of our intentional actions.

First, even if consciousness takes time to appear, nonetheless it may emerge in the course of action and then play a crucial role as a mechanism for goal maintenance and shielding, for reorganization of habits, or for the management of unexpected difficulties (Mazzone and Campisi 2013).

Second, it should not be forgotten that for the most part of our lives "we live in a supraliminal world" (Satpute and Lieberman 2006: 91), that is, automatic responses to perceptual inputs occur while we are engaged in conscious monitoring of the environment and our own behaviour. In a sense, then, it might be true that there are conscious representations at the instigation of most of our actions, after all: humans often respond to situations they are conscious of, and these situations set the purposes of our forthcoming actions, even when the purposes are not themselves conscious (or they are not conscious from the beginning). For instance, in dialogue we normally attend to our interlocutor's utterances. Such a conscious representation of the utterances we intend to respond to can be thought to drive automatic processing by constraining the kind of information which is needed to accomplish the task – as predicted by the "direct parameter specification" theory considered above.

In sum, it seems that in principle any component of the complex goal-directed representation involved in action – including goals – can be processed automatically. Nonetheless, consciousness is far from being epiphenomenal since it may focus on this or that component when needed and, as a consequence, play a role in directing automatic processing: specifically, as in Dehaene et al.'s (2006) model, by amplifying or inhibiting representations in posterior areas of our brain.

3.9 A pragmatic issue: the prominence of speaker-related information

In the light of our previous discussion of automatic and controlled processes and their interaction, let us now turn back to pragmatic processes. As we said, Recanati adopts conscious verbal reasoning as the model of explanation for secondary pragmatic processes, and therefore in his view the explicit meaning of the utterance, its implicit meaning, and the transition from the former to the latter are entirely in the focus of consciousness. However, in order to avoid the anti-intuitive consequence that the process is slow and effortful, he speaks in terms of an activity that is only dispositionally (but not occurrently) conscious. On the other hand, RT does not assign to consciousness any explicit role and conceives instead of pragmatic processes as inferential but automatic; consciousness would rather intervene when something goes wrong in normal comprehension processes.

As it can be seen, both views tend to presuppose a polar opposition between automatic and controlled processes, and to disregard the possibility that those processes cooperate, with the consequence that both parties feel forced to choose one of the poles. An alternative possibility, which is more coherent with the current knowledge of the matter, is that extensive automatic activation coexists with the "distributed" presence of consciousness in the sense described above: in monitoring automatic processes, consciousness focuses on its components in changeable ways as a function of the circumstances (the task, the difficulties met in processing, the salience of the inputs, and so on), and affects processing in various manners (essentially, maintenance and enhancement of activations, inhibition of alternatives). I will analyse two phenomena – one in this section and the other in the next – that in my opinion are convincingly explained by this hypothesis.

The first concerns the issue of whether the speaker's mental states play a role in the construction of the explicit meaning of utterances. There has been a debate on this issue that has involved Carston (2007), Recanati (2007), Mazzone (2011b, 2013), Mazzarella (2011, 2013a, 2013b), and that I am going to briefly summarise. Incidentally, we should note that this discussion is directly related to the issue of mindreading: the point is precisely whether the construction of explicit content makes an appeal to *mental state attribution*.

In Recanati's (2004) model, primary pragmatic processes resulting in explicit meanings are conceived as local (involving the activation of concepts, not inferences from proposition to proposition), associative, and *non-metarepresentational* (in the sense that they do not require consideration of the speaker's mental states). This last point has been questioned by Carston (2007), based on the following example. Let us suppose that Robyn is a teacher of the linguistics department and that her student Sarah addresses her with the utterance in (6):

(6) Neil has broken his leg

Let us further suppose that Robyn knows two people called "Neil", her young son ($NEIL_1$) and a colleague working in the same department where she works ($NEIL_2$), and that Sarah knows $NEIL_2$ but not Robyn's son. Let us finally suppose that Robyn is constantly worried about her son, so that her $NEIL_1$ concept is candidate to become more active than $NEIL_2$, whatever the circumstances in which (6) is uttered. According to Carston, the simple associative dynamic of activation cannot account for the fact that presumably, in that scenario, Robyn's preferred interpretation will be instead $NEIL_2$.

In sum, the challenge raised by Carston (2007) is whether an associative model such as that proposed by Recanati can account for the role presumably played, in understanding (6), by the addressee's knowledge of what the speaker knows (in this example, by Robyn's knowledge of what Sarah knows). As we already know, RT's view is that a different automatic process is needed, which is inferential (not associative) and involves consideration of the speaker's mental states. But, I will argue below, it is questionable that an automatic inferential mechanism as the one described by RT can actually account for Carston's (2007) example. As an alternative, I will propose an account based on the contribution of conscious attention – precisely the ingredient that is lacking in RT's account.

But let us proceed in order. Recanati (2007) has partially conceded that Carston's example raises a problem for his account and has tried to solve it by granting an exception: in that sort of case, where one needs to take into account the contribution of speaker-related information, purely associative processes would be integrated with the intrusion of a metarepresentational step. In practice, in the course of associative processing a proposition of the form "the speaker [for instance: Sarah] says that ..." would be constructed, thanks to which the identity of the speaker would be explicitly taken into consideration. Mazzarella (2011) objects that this solution is not really viable: the problem is how, in that specific case, associative processes can establish that their own outcome is wrong in the first place, so that a metarepresentation is required in order to amend it. Alternatively, one might think that associative pragmatic processes are systematically subject to some *external* assessment, possibly involving metarepresentational mechanisms: but this is hardly compatible with Recanati's claim that, in the general case, construction of the explicit content requires nothing more than associative processing.

A different route has been explored by Mazzone (2011b). The key idea is that no metarepresentational step is needed, since speaker-related information can be activated because of the mere fact that the addressee perceives the speaker as a salient component of the current communicative interaction. In other words, the hypothesis is that speaker-related information can be associatively accessed just as other information is. In support of this view, one may quote Shintel and Keysar (2009: 264), who argue that "speaker-specific effects [on the addressee] emerge out of memory representations that incorporate episodic information, such as the identity of the speaker". Therefore, "the effect of the speaker's identity may result not from a consideration of the speaker's communicative intentions, but from salience and significance of information about the speaker during encoding, allowing the speaker's identity to act as a rather potent retrieval cue" (ibidem).

This hypothesis, too, is criticised by Mazzarella (2011) with good arguments. The question is: What ensures that information associated to the speaker has "the force to trigger the required accessibility shift" (idem: 17)? If, in the example above, Robyn's NEIL_1 concept has a significant advantage over her NEIL_2 concept as to their respective accessibility, then the additional activation of the latter due to its association with Robyn's SARAH concept might not be sufficient to overcome the activation of the former. In other words, there seems to be no guarantee that, as a consequence of simple associative activation, speaker-related information comes to have the power to yield the desired effects. A related issue concerns the time course of processing. Associative activation, to the extent that it occurs in a purely automatic fashion, is characterized by rapid decay. As a consequence there is no reason why, as a rule, the relevant speaker-related information should stay active until it can deliver the desired effects.

While conceding this point, Mazzone (2013a) observes that, with regard to this problem, RT is in no better position.

To be sure, relevance theorists have proposed notions that explicitly mention speaker-related information. Specifically, they claim that utterance understanding is guided by a presumption of optimal relevance, which is defined as follows:

a. The ostensive stimulus is relevant enough for it to be worth the addressee's effort to process it.
b. The ostensive stimulus is the most relevant one compatible with the communicator's abilities and preferences.

According to the second condition, the addressee, in his search for a relevant interpretation, has to take (and actually takes) into account the communicator's abilities and preferences. This is because the communicator may fail to be relevant for two reasons: because she lacks to know that something is (or is not) relevant for the addressee, or because she has occasionally no interest to provide information that would be relevant. As a consequence, the communicator may have a communicative intention that is less relevant than it might be otherwise, and the addressee has to be sensitive to this possibility.

Thus, relevance theorists are clear on the *necessity* that addressees take into account information about mental states of the speaker. But unfortunately, the mechanisms they actually describe say nothing about how that information may play a special role. To summarize, according to RT interpretations are constructed in order of accessibility and then they must be assessed against expectations of relevance. The constructed interpretations have the structure of inferences from premises (the explicit meaning and some contextual assumptions) to contextual conclusions. This inferential structure is key to their view, but the access to premises and conclusions is described essentially in associative terms (see chapters 1 and 2). In other words, with regard to the way in which information is conveyed to pragmatic inferences, the only explanation provided by RT is no different from an associative one. Thus, if associative explanations cannot account for the special role of speaker-related information, neither RT can.[38]

How, then, can one explain the special role of speaker-related information in cases such as (6)? My proposal is based on the idea that utterances have the power to draw conscious attention not only to themselves, but also to the people who utter them. Conscious attention can be described as directedness toward information that is actively maintained in working memory (Knudsen 2007). This active maintenance prevents the rapid decay of associative activation and shields information from distracting inputs. Moreover, it affects further processing by both active top-down control and automatic top-down recovery of related information (see § 3.7 above). What I suggest is that utterances draw our conscious attention to the speakers, so that the information related to them is prominently activated during utterance interpretation.

This is a further sense in which we can make sense of RT's intuition, according to which there must be a mechanism for the assessment of utterance interpretations over and above the simple dynamic of activation.[39] As we saw, relevance theorists concede that the formation of interpretative hypotheses may be largely associative, but they conceive of associative processes as insufficiently constrained and such to require a distinct component of assessment and selection. The overall view that I propose here breaks up this idea of a final assessment in three distinct components. First, the schematic organization of information in memory guarantees that associative activations are motivated, not accidental: bottom-up activations recall schemata that allow specific inferences. Second, I suggested a role for contexts: in any given context, different co-occurring inputs activate schemata that may either cohere or compete with each other, and this

38 Mazzarella (2013b) concedes this point, and tries to solve the problem by appealing to the mechanism of epistemic vigilance, that is, an extra-pragmatic mechanism. In fact, one might object to my argument that appeal to other modules (such as the ones for epistemic vigilance or mindreading) can explain the prominence of speaker-related information. Even assuming modularity – which I propose not to do for reasons I will give in § 4.7 – I do not think this is a viable option. The question is how, once the appropriate module has packed the required information, this is fed into the pragmatic inferential structure. Unless relevance theorists are able to specify a mechanism to this effect which is different from the associative one they themselves appeal to, the contribution of other modules will not help.

39 Mazzarella has recently insisted (see Mazzarella 2013b: 21, 2014: 77) on this specific stage of "hypothesis confirmation", beyond the simple "hypothesis formation", as a distinctive feature of RT. See also above, § 2.13.

mechanism favours the schemata providing the most coherent interpretations. What I am suggesting now is a third component that is apt to constrain the entire process. The first two mechanisms can in principle operate both in controlled and automatic ways; in other words, there can be competition/integration between schematically organized information both with and without consciousness – see § 3.6 above. But, as we also saw, most cognitive processes require interaction between automatic and controlled components. It is therefore worth analysing how conscious attention may change the picture.

That attention to others and their goals is crucial in communication has been made apparent by more than thirty years of research on shared attention (for one single influential example chosen from a huge literature, see the work of Michael Tomasello and colleagues: for instance, Tomasello 1999; Tomasello et al. 2005). In joint attentional frames, a subject selectively attends to other agents and what is in the focus of their attention. The reason why this is thought to be crucial for the emergence of communication is that a subject can exploit the others' attention to the focus of her attention in order to produce ostensive stimuli, that is, manifestations of her will to communicate. In other words, a subject A makes manifest her intention to attract the attention of a subject B towards an object C, so that B not only directs his attention to C but also becomes aware of A's intention that this occurs. The attention of both A and B is then focussed on each other and on aspects of the shared situation that are made "'mutually manifest' and so potentially 'relevant' for acts of interpersonal communication (Sperber and Wilson 1986)" (Tomasello et al. 2005: 683).

It is interesting that in this context Tomasello et al. (2005) quote Sperber and Wilson (1986). Indeed, RT has much insisted on the fact that utterances are ostensive stimuli produced in order to capture the addressee's attention, and that actually induce the addressee to form metarepresentations about the speaker's mental states. It may then appear questionable that RT lacks the resources to explain a case such as the one exemplified by (6) *in that* the theory assigns no role to conscious attention to the speaker. And yet, I suggest, there are good reasons for this claim. A cornerstone of that approach is that relevance is a basic feature of human cognition, since cognitive systems have to pick out from the mass of competing stimuli (i.e., *to attend*) what is worth being processed. As it should be clear, then, what is meant in the first place by saying that certain inputs are attended or attract attention is that they are selected to be processed by the cognitive system, *irrespective of whether this is actually accomplished by attention proper*. As a matter of fact, in RT attention (to ostensive stimuli and other inputs) is not appealed to as a specific mechanism for the explanation of cognitive processes (i.e., it is not an *explanans*); it is rather what the theory aims to explain by postulating automatic heuristics oriented to maximization of relevance. In Wilson and Carston's

(2006: 407; my emphasis) words: "According to the Cognitive Principle of Relevance, human cognition tends to be geared to the maximization of relevance, so that perceptual, memory retrieval and inferential processes are likely to include *automatic heuristics* for selecting potentially relevant inputs and processing them in the most relevance-enhancing way". The inferential comprehension heuristic by which relevance theorists explain utterance understanding would be nothing but one of those automatic, domain-specific mechanisms that they presume to account for selective processing of inputs. As such, this heuristic is meant to *get rid of conscious attention* in their explanation of comprehension.

In sum, on the one hand it seems clear that RT's overall picture does not assign a role to conscious attention – in spite of the apparent fact that utterances are literally produced in order to attract the addressee's attention, and actually able to attract it. On the other hand, as argued above in this section, RT frequently describes information recall in terms of generic mechanisms of associative accessibility.

If, however, we try to take seriously the idea that utterances attract the addressees' conscious attention on themselves and *on the speakers*, and that conscious attention can affect the subsequent processing of inputs even in an automatic fashion, then the example (6) can easily be explained in the following terms. The utterance uttered by Sarah draws attention on the identity of the speaker (i.e., on Sarah herself); as a consequence, the concept SARAH is present in Robyn's working memory and this causes strong activation of the associated information together with inhibition of potentially competing information.

In sum, the example seems easily explained within the general picture proposed here. If information is organized in memory in a motivated fashion, its recall yields, to some extent, rational outcomes irrespective of whether the processes are automatic or controlled: in this specific case, the association between the concepts SARAH and NEIL$_2$ allows in principle the co-activation of information that is likely to be simultaneously relevant . One limitation of automatic processing, however, is that the contextually relevant concepts might not have the prominence they deserve, in comparison to other potentially competing information. Conscious attention is crucial to ensure the stability and coherence of cognitive processes, due to its power to maintain and amplify the information that is actually related to the task at hand: in this specific case, the task of understanding the utterance *uttered by Sarah.*

3.10 Emergent properties and conscious attention

Another interesting example of the role played by conscious attention in pragmatic processing is provided by Rubio-Fernández (2013), which is a recent study on how emergent properties are processed (a wider discussion is in Mazzone 2016a). As a matter of fact, this study presents new empirical evidence on emergent properties and claims that these are compatible with RT but not with Recanati (2004). Thus, coherently with RT's approach, the article does not assign any role to conscious attention. Nevertheless, I will argue that this notion is in fact presupposed by the structure of the experiments and their consequent interpretation.

The study is based on the distinction between context-independent and context-dependent properties, introduced on experimental basis by Barsalou (1982). The former are the properties directly associated to a concept, which are consequently activated together with it whatever the context; the latter, since they are not directly associated to the concept, are only occasionally activated when required by the context – these are the properties that we earlier called "emergent". The new data presented by Rubio-Fernández (2013) essentially show that the recovery of emergent properties does not disrupt or delay the normal understanding of explicit meaning.

More specifically, Rubio-Fernández (2013) reports two studies. The first is a pre-test of the material used in the second one, with the purpose to confirm that the assessed concepts (for instance, BASKETBALL) can give access to properties that are presumably not associated to them (for BASKETBALL, the emergent property CAN BE USED TO STAY AFLOAT) if contexts are appropriate. In the second study, a context is provided with respect to which three concepts are tested: the previously tested one (BASKETBALL), which in context is unfamiliar but appropriate to the situation (which involves helping someone who is not able to swim) and is therefore expected to activate the emergent property; a concept that in the context is both familiar and appropriate (LIFEBOUY); and a concept that in the context is familiar but inappropriate (NEWSPAPER). This second study was a self-paced reading task, with measures of reading latencies. The crucial results were as follows: "Processing the segment following the critical targets was comparable in the two appropriate conditions, with only inappropriate targets showing longer reading latencies" (Rubio-Fernández 2013: 739). In other words, although the initial level of activation of familiar and appropriate targets (LIFEBOUY) was judged to be significantly higher than that of unfamiliar but appropriate targets (BASKETBALL), the context seemed to ensure the integration of the latter—via the activation of the relevant emergent property—without any perceptible delay.

It is important to understand why, according to Rubio-Fernández, these results would speak in favour of RT and raise problems for Recanati instead. In principle, Recanati conceives the activation of ad hoc concepts as a primary pragmatic process, without distinction between associated and emergent properties. As a consequence, the fact that the activation of emergent properties is as rapid and automatic as the activation of the properties associated to the concept seems in no way incompatible with his view. The problem arises from a specific assumption of Rubio-Fernández, that is, the assumption that while context-independent properties are accessed "by an automatic process of spreading activation of associates, context-dependent information or 'emergent properties' are accessed through local inferential processes" (idem: 724). Since Recanati conceives of inferential processes as reflective, not automatic, if emergent properties require inferential processes then he is committed to the following view: when an utterance contains emergent properties, the construction of its explicit meaning requires the intrusion of non-automatic processes into automatic ones. And this is in contrast with the data provided by Rubio-Fernández (2013). On the contrary, the problem would not affect RT: since this theory conceives of inferential processes as automatic, associative and inferential processes may be thought to cooperate with each other from the beginning, with no reason to presume that the latter disrupt or delay the former.

The advantage of relevance theorists over Recanati would then depend on the fact that the former, in contrast to the latter, conceive of inferential processes as automatic instead of reflective and conscious. However, this raises a problem I have already pointed out: in this perspective, RT lacks any clear specification of what inferential processes are. In fact, as widely discussed in chapter 2, in psychology the distinction between inferential and associative processes is essentially based on the presence/absence of consciousness. But this, I would add now, is also the demarcation criterion (between context-dependent and context-independent properties) adopted by Barsalou (1982) and presupposed by Rubio-Fernández' argument.

To be precise, Barsalou offers a more complex picture than the one outlined by Rubio-Fernández. According to Rubio-Fernández (2013), there are only two cases: context-independent properties for which automatic activation is sufficient, and context-dependent properties requiring instead inferential processes. Barsalou, on the other hand, distinguishes between three different cases. First, there are context-independent properties, that is, the case in which associations between concepts and properties are so strong/direct that activation of the former suffices to ensure activation of the latter. Another case is when associations are less strong/direct and, as a consequence, properties are automatically activated by the concept only if the context contributes further (automatic) activation. Finally, when associations are quite indirect, automatic spreading of activation is not sufficient to ensure that the concept activates the properties even when the context provides further activation: in these cases, activation must be inferential, that is, it must involve "conscious processes that are subject to capacity limitations" (Barsalou 1982: 87). Barsalou puts together the second and the third case under the label of context-dependent properties.

But he also draws a sharp distinction between the second case, in which activation is automatic, and the third, the only one for which he proposes that activation is *inferential*, that is, *sustained by consciousness*.

Rubio-Fernández (2013) assumes instead, without making this difference explicit, that activation of emergent properties is inferential in RT's sense: that is, it is automatic, not conscious. Thus, she uses "inferential" in a different way than the standard use in psychology, which is also the one adopted by Barsalou (1982). As a consequence, it is hard to specify the real nature of such "inferential processes": they are said to be automatic although they are not simple associative activations, and at the same time they are called inferential although they are not presumed to be conscious. In sum, while Barsalou makes reference to a clear and well-established notion of "inference" (the notion of associative processes sustained and amplified by consciousness, that is, by long-distance recurrent activations) Rubio-Fernández (2013) in line with RT wants us to take seriously a notion (that of automatic inferential processes, which are neither associative nor conscious), which appears rather obscure and ad hoc.

On the other hand, we do not need to opt instead for Recanati's view of inferential processes. We had better escape the false choice between conceiving inferential processes either as a form of conscious reasoning or as entirely non-conscious. The proposal is, again, that conscious attention interacts with largely automatic processes, in a way that implies relatively little cognitive effort and that, in the appropriate contexts, does not cause significant delay in reaction times. This may be enough, nonetheless, to guarantee long-distance activations, which flow through (even long) sequences of nodes in the conceptual network. In other words, conscious attention can explain how activation is enhanced so as to reach mental contents that would not be activated in a purely automatic fashion, not even if different inputs in context contributed to their activation. In particular, in § 2.11, I explained the activation of emergent properties in terms of complex pattern completion, involving chains of schemata. In the light of Barsalou's distinctions, these chains presumably require more than either simple or contextually reinforced automatic activation: they may require what we have referred to as activation *sustained by conscious attention*.

3.11 Conclusions

Let me summarize where we stand now.

RT explains utterance understanding in context as guided by relevance. Moreover, the processes at issue are conceived as automatic and inferential (not associative) at the same time.

In chapter 1 I challenged the view that the notion of relevance explicitly defined by RT – as well as the mechanism based on it – is actually able to account for comprehension. That notion is essentially based on the amount of cognitive effects, and brings with it the problem of providing a plausible account of the second step of the comprehension procedure, that is, the assessment of the amount of cognitive effects against expectations of relevance. However, in relevance theorists' writings, an alternative hypothesis is that comprehension depends crucially on the organization of memory and its recovery by means of simple mechanisms of accessibility. The overall interpretation – including contextual conclusions – might be the result of a competitive activation that is sufficient, by itself, to ensure relevance. This hypothesis allows giving renewed importance to the Gricean intuition that comprehension is strictly related to goal recognition, thanks to the notion of a mutual adjustment involving forward and backward inferences. In practice, the recognition of non-communicative goals may affect comprehension through backward inferences, able to determine expectations on the type of cognitive effects intended by the speaker.

In chapter 2 we analysed the debate between associative and inferential accounts of pragmatic processes, and discussed at length the possibility that accessibility-based mechanisms provide an exhaustive explanation of comprehension. To this effect, we considered the distinction between two senses of "associative", as a description of psychological processes – characterized (in contrast to inferential ones) by the absence of conscious attention – and as a mechanism for the implementation of those processes. Both inferential and associative processes in the former sense can be conceived as associative in the latter sense – that is, as implemented by different dynamics of activation in associative networks. In order to avoid misunderstandings, I used the terms "controlled"/"automatic" for the distinction between psychological processes. Given the above distinctions, it is possible to claim that the processes described by RT as inferential are implemented by associative mechanisms. A crucial aspect is the schematic and hierarchical organization of memory: it guarantees that simple associative processes are sufficient to produce rationally motivated transitions between mental contents. Pragmatic processing, but also syntactic processing and action, have been described in terms of bottom-up activation of schemata and top-down activation of their (further) components. Goals can be considered as high-level schemata in the overall organization of our memory.

Based on the model just described, we claimed, it is possible to provide an associative account of what RT describes as inferential processes. Unfortunately, this notion of inferential in RT is far from clear. In particular, RT describes inferential processes as automatic, not conscious, and therefore the use of the term is not the one that is standard in psychology. To be sure, in order to determine what it means for a process to be inferential one can count on the criterion adopted by Grice, based on the fact that processes can be *reconstructed* in terms of inferential derivations. This, however, leaves indeterminate the real nature of the cognitive mechanisms at issue. My proposal is that pragmatic processes are inferential not only in the sense of being driven by the schematic organization of memory, but also in the sense that is standard in psychology: that is, they have conscious attention as a constitutive component. The latter idea was defended in this chapter, especially through the introduction of a notion that is intermediate between purely automatic processing and conscious reasoning. The point is that most cognitive processes consist in largely automatic activations that are monitored, and to some extent guided, by conscious attention.

What emerges here is a unified picture, in which recovery of lexical (and, more generally, linguistic) information, pragmatic inferences, and goal understanding, can all be described as processes of the same kind: that is, processes of associative activation based on the schematic organization of memory, with automatic and controlled components that, in most cases, are both present and interact with each other. In such a picture, one might ask, is the specificity of goal understanding sufficiently preserved? In other words, to what extent the organization of memory and the associative recovery of schemata are sufficient to account for the complex set of phenomena that go under the name of mindreading? And what the above picture suggests about the relations between pragmatics and mindreading? How deep is the cooperation between these two abilities? In the next chapter, I will try to answer these questions, while also addressing the related issue of how modular those processes can be.

4 Mindreading, pragmatics, and modularity

4.1 Introduction

A key assumption in pragmatics is that language is a special case of action, and therefore an activity driven by intentions and apt to be described in terms of practical reasoning. A main thesis of this book is that we should take that idea very seriously, and that there is a substantial continuity between language production and comprehension on the one hand, and action execution and comprehension on the other.

I described the goal representations involved in human action as high-level schemata, situated at the top of the hierarchies in which our world knowledge (and the linguistic information as well) is organized. The way in which those high-level representations take part in cognitive processing has been described, in turn, as part of a bottom-up/top-down dynamic of associative activation travelling through the entire representational network. Furthermore, such dynamic of activation can take either an automatic or a controlled form (although the distinction between the two is not sharp), and most of the times the two forms are present together and cooperate with each other.

As a further support for this picture of continuity, in the present chapter I will analyse an important feature that seems to be common to non-linguistic action control and linguistic processes: it is what, in chapter 2, we described in terms of co-presence, and collaboration between, forward and backward inferences. But, at a closer look, not only do we have here similarity between two processes; but also these processes dovetail with each other, as we suggested in chapters 1 and 2. Utterances convey communicative intentions that are subgoals within (individual or collective) actions that are, in turn, directed to goals. In sum, human verbal communication seems to presuppose the ability to construct chains of goals that cross the boundary between language and action. With the help of some experimental evidence, in this chapter I will argue for a generalization of this idea, that is, I will claim that we are able to construct chains of goals that cross the boundaries not only between language and action, but also between action and perception, and between representations of our and others' goals.

In practice, the understanding of goals, whether communicative or not, is here conceived as a unitary process of associative activation of the appropriate schematic representations. In the present chapter I will analyse the idea that not only intentions but also all kind of mental notions can be accounted for as generalizations from past regularities, associatively recalled in the appropriate

https://doi.org/10.1515/9781501507731-005

circumstances. Through a rapid glance at the overwhelming literature on mindreading, I will consider two possible objections to this approach. The first is that mental state understanding necessarily requires innate notions, instead of mere generalization over behavioural regularities. The second is that simple associative mechanisms are as such insufficient, and that higher-level processes are required: in particular, the ability to construct and put to use mental models of the observed situations. I will answer to the first objection by analysing what is involved in the re-identification of mental states, and I will draw the conclusion that nativism about mental states is much more demanding and less plausible than is often realized. The second objection will be answered by considering, once again, the complex relation between the pairs of notions associative/inferential and automatic/controlled. Explanations of mindreading tasks that make an appeal to mental models aim in fact to draw our attention to the role played by working memory. This concerns the distinction automatic/controlled: the point is not that the processes of interest cannot be associative at the implementation level; rather, the suggestion is that they cannot be purely *automatic*, since the relevant information must be kept active by conscious attention.

Then, I will discuss the issue of modularity. As for mindreading, this is a huge problem that can be touched upon only briefly here. My proposal that utterance understanding is a special case of goal understanding implies that domain-specific processes play no role in pragmatics. This line of thought can be generalized. That is, if it is true that cognitive processes in different domains are, in the end, implemented by the associative dynamic described in the previous chapters, then one can argue – and this I will do – that the modularity thesis can only be right in a sense that is quite trivial, while it is untenable in the sense in which it is usually understood.

4.2 Forward and backward inferences in action

RT has proposed that an important component of utterance understanding is the parallel process characterized by inferences that proceed in two directions: forward, from explicit meaning to contextual conclusions, and backward, from the context to the explicit meaning. This is the process called "parallel mutual adjustment" that we described in chapter 1. Now, I intend to show that a similar double movement has been conjectured by recent accounts of action execution and comprehension.

To start with, the Event Coding Theory of Bernhard Hommel (2003; Hommel et al. 2001) claims that action goals are represented as perceptual effects associated to the motor act representations which have proved apt to pursue those effects in the past. Thanks to association between motor acts and perceptual effects, it is possible both for the observer to make forward inferences from the observed movements to the intended effects, and for the agent to make backward inferences from the intended effects to the required movements. However, such a distinction between forward inferences in action observation and backward inferences in action execution might be just a first approximation. Both the inferential directions have been suggested to play a role both in execution and observation of action.

Let us start from action execution. Wolpert and colleagues (e.g., Wolpert et al. 2003) have proposed a computational theory of motor control based on the now widespread hypothesis that action execution involves a dynamic of prediction and control, making an appeal to both inverse (controller) and forward (predictor) models. In practice, while Hommel focuses on the fact that backward and forward inferencing are respectively crucial for planning and interpreting action, Wolpert and colleagues have importantly insisted that the dynamic between forward and backward models imbues action control itself. In their view not only does action execution require that a motor program is inversely computed, on the basis of information about intended outputs and the actual situation, but also forward models are computed in order to predict the motor and sensory effects of actions, thanks to an offline simulation which flows parallel to – though more rapid than – the actual implementation of motor programs. Prediction is crucial, amongst other things, for fast correction of movement before feedback can be obtained (Glenberg and Gallese 2012: 908).

While these studies suggest that both forward and backward models are required for action execution, a similar conclusion can be drawn with regard to action observation. For one example, it is well known that Rizzolatti's group, and especially Vittorio Gallese, has explained intention reading in terms of a form of prediction. At least in the simplest cases, the goal of an action would be the motor act in which the action culminates. In practice, on the basis of statistical chaining of motor acts we can make a forward inference to the likely intended goal of a given motor act, and thus to the underlying intention:

> Determining why a given act (e.g. grasping a cup) was executed can be equivalent to detecting the goal of the still not executed and impending subsequent act (e.g. bringing the cup to the mouth). (Gallese 2007: 662)

However, other studies conducted by this group seem to show that there is more to perceptual recognition of intentions than forward inferences. In particular, Iacoboni et al. (2005) tested observers with actions (such as grasping a cup) both out of context and in contexts suggesting different intentions (drinking tea, cleaning up). In the latter condition (presence of context) there was increased activation of premotor mirror neuron area, a result strongly suggesting – in the author's words – that "this mirror neuron area actively participates in understanding the intentions behind the observed actions" (Iacoboni et al. 2005: 532). Since in those experiments the manipulated factor is the presence/absence of a context, it follows that, in order to recognize the underlying intention of an observed motor act, mirror areas may be sensitive not only to subsequent motor acts but also to statistically relevant contexts. In other words, in the described circumstances it is the context that suggests the intended goal (in the example, respectively the intention either to drink the tea or to clean up) independently from any forward inference starting from the observed action. The analogy with RT's proposal according to which communicative intentions may be suggested backwards from contexts should be apparent.

In sum, in research on both execution and comprehension of action there is a widespread belief that goal-directed processes imply the construction of both forward and backward inferences.

4.3 Shared intentional contexts

As noted above, both motor and sensory information play a role in goal representation. In Hommel's (2003) model, a goal is typically the sensory outcome of a motor act. As to Gallese (2007), he emphasises the role that the final motor act of a sequence may play in understanding observed action. But we also saw that, in that theoretical framework, perceived contextual information can be crucial as well: for instance, the contextual information provided in the experiment of Iacoboni et al. (2005). Analogously, in the model proposed by Wolpert and colleagues, action control requires that not only motor representations, but also perceptual representations of the outcomes play a role in feedback mechanisms.

In sum, goal representation requires information structures that cross the boundary between perception and action. But this is not the only boundary that is crossed in execution and understanding of action. If action involves cooperation between agents, representations must cross the boundary between the self and others as well. This undoubtedly occurs in linguistic action. Language is not only a kind of action; it is more specifically a kind of joint action (e.g., Clark 1996; Tomasello 2008). In fact, as many scholars have emphasized (e.g., Brennan et al. 2010; Garrod and Pickering 2004; Kecskes 2010; Pickering and Garrod 2013), spoken language is mostly used in dialogue, and we should refrain from conceiving of dialogue as mere "'serial monologue', in which interlocutors alternate between production and comprehension" (Pickering and Garrod 2013: 330). On the contrary, in dialogue – insofar as it is a specific case of joint action – interlocutors can be thought of as co-agents participating in a common coordinated event that they jointly co-produce.

One way to frame this conception of interlocutors as co-agents is in terms of the philosophical analysis of shared cooperative activities (SCA) proposed by Bratman (1992). According to Bratman, in order for there to be SCA, agents must have – amongst other things – the intention to accomplish a given activity in accordance with, and because of, meshing subplans aimed at the accomplishment of that activity. In other words, each agent should have a representation of the other agents as participating in the joint action, and a representation of her own plans of action as just a component of that wider (joint) action.

There is some evidence that this is the case. In experimental settings, individuals engaged in joint tasks are shown to share task representations and integrate each other's task in their own action planning (Sebanz et al. 2003). The evidence comes from cooperative versions of interference tasks (like the Simon task or the Erikson flanker task), in which the task at issue is split between two participants. In traditional interference tasks, conflicts between simultaneously activated representations of responses arise within a single agent – in terms of errors and delayed response times – when irrelevant stimuli are presented together with a target stimulus that requires a different response by the agent. In research on joint action the tasks at issue are divided between two co-actors and, as a result, there appears to be conflict between self- and other-generated responses in a way that resembles conflict between two self-generated responses (Atmaca et al. 2011; see also Milanese et al. 2010; Wenke et al. 2011). Thus, it seems rather safe to conclude that "when people perform different parts of a task they tend to represent the whole task at hand rather than just their own part in the task" (Atmaca et al. 2008: 418).

On similar grounds, Jordan (2009) has argued that humans construct shared intentional contexts that make joint action and communication possible in the first place. More specifically, on the basis of evidence that "actions are planned in terms of the distal effects they are to produce" and that "planning and perception share common neural resources" (Jordan 2009: 127), Jordan argues that "perception actually takes place in terms of what one plans to do". In practice,

> a component of one's observing [actions] is the activation of the plan for that same event in the observer. As a result, as humans observe each other generating events [. . .] they find themselves directly linked with each other at the level of plans (i.e., goals or intentions). (Jordan 2009: 129)

In sum, the idea is that, thanks to the strict relationship between sensory and motor representations described in the previous section, observed actions can be directly compared with, and translated into, motor representations. As a consequence, our and others' plans of action can be meshed with each other so as to form a shared intentional context linking perception and execution of actions. In this perspective, a reasonable hypothesis is that the double movement of forward and backward inferences we described above can cross the boundary between executed and observed actions, so that pursued and observed goals can be combined and even assessed together in a wholly automatic fashion. This hypothesis seems reasonable in the light of the previously mentioned evidence that the forward-backward dynamic seems to be present both in execution and observation of action, and that agents automatically represent the others' goals as if they were their own.

Dialogue gives us simple behavioural examples of such intersubjective goal nesting. Let us consider the following example from Pickering and Garrod (2013):

(7) (a) A: I'm afraid I burnt the kitchen ceiling.
(b) B: But have you
(c) A: burned myself? Fortunately not.

In this dialogue, specifically in (7c), A anticipates and completes what B is going to ask. Thus, the first part of her linguistic production ("burned myself?") does not pursue an independent communicative goal of A, it pursues instead a (presumed) communicative goal of B (though described from A's point of view: "myself" instead of "yourself"). In practice, based on context and previous experience of social interactions, A predicts the likely completion of B's utterance and therefore his communicative goal.

Such an example makes apparent that our and others' communicative goals can be meshed together within the same linguistic act. But even when our and others' goals are not so apparently meshed in a single individual act, planning utterances requires nonetheless that we incorporate the others' goals into our plans. Let us consider another example (from Wilson and Carston 2006, modified):

(8) (a) A: Will Caroline help us clear up the flood damage?
(b) B: Caroline is a princess.
(c) A: Too bad!

On its face value, A's last utterance only makes sense on the assumption that the intended meaning of (8b) is that Caroline will not help them to clear up the flood damage. Thus, A's decision to utter (8c) depends on the fact that the communicative intention expressed by B in (8b) is promptly integrated into the shared intentional context. In turn, this implicit meaning of (8b) – that Caroline does not intend to help – can only be inferred in the light of (the communicative purpose of) A's previous utterance: in the absence of (8a), the statement that Caroline is a princess would not convey this communicative intention.

In sum, dialogue seems to be a form of joint action in which each interlocutor has to integrate the other's communicative goals into her own action planning, to the point that within the same utterance the speaker can easily shift from the other's to her own goals (as in 7c). More generally, cooperative action seems to depend on the ability to construct shared intentional contexts, in which the others' action plans are meshed with our own plans in a single intentional context.

4.4 Intentions and other mental states

Let us take stock. In chapter 2 I explored the general idea of a hierarchical organization of associative memory. I have thus developed the hypothesis, already introduced in chapter 1, according to which the schematic organization of memory could explain pragmatic comprehension, but also syntactic abilities and action, in terms of simple associative processes of bottom-up and top-down activation. Such a picture implies a substantial continuity between different cognitive abilities. In § 4.2 we considered in fact theoretical models that focus on important similarities between pragmatic processing and action understanding. Specifically, those models propose that action planning and understanding display the same double dynamic of forward and backward inferences as the one posited by RT for utterance understanding. This similarity is far from unexpected. On the contrary, it is entirely coherent with the hypothesis that there is at play a single mechanism operating through the whole associative memory. This, in turn, would naturally explain the fact that, in episodes of utterance understanding, that dynamic can smoothly cross the boundary between action and language.

In § 4.2, we argued that the described dynamic seems to cross the boundary between perception and motor action as well, while in § 4.3 we analysed a fact that is, in a sense, a consequence of that: the fact that we are able to construct shared plans of action, in which the boundary between our and others' actions is travelled across, too.

In short, there are reasons to believe that human beings have the ability to construct chains of means and ends, thanks to processes of associative activation operating through both sensory and motor representations, relative to both our and others' communicative and non-communicative actions.

This picture raises two issues that I cannot entirely ignore. First of all, it presupposes that goals and intentions can be represented as associative schemata stored in memory.[40] Is this assumption compatible with the huge literature on mindreading? Specifically, is it in accordance with the most common views of mental states attribution? In the second place, it is worth analysing how the above hypotheses affect the issue of modularity, with specific regard to modularity of pragmatic processes but also in more general terms. We are going to address now the first question; in § 4.7 we will examine the second one.

The thesis that goals are represented as high-level schemata, and that these schemata also explain our ability to attribute intentions to others, can assume a generalized form according to which mental state attribution in general is based on representations abstracted from behavioural regularities. Such a view has been suggested by Whiten's (1996) notion of "intervening variable". Whiten takes the notion from the late behaviourist literature (specifically by Tolman), where it is used to refer to unobservable entities that one is forced to interpose between stimuli and responses in the study of behaviour. Whiten's idea is that, in understanding behaviours, the observer who attributes mental states spontaneously makes something similar: she postulates an unobservable intermediate entity between stimuli and behaviours, which accounts for their correlation. A crucial point of Whiten's proposal is that this intermediate entity is a generalization over classes of stimuli and responses. In practice, a certain internal state can be expressed in the external state of the agent by a variety of manifestations, and it can be the response to a variety of environmental conditions.

The idea that mental concepts – meaning by this our representations of mental states – are such generalizations has played an important role in the recent debate opposing nativist and empiricist views of mindreading. In particular, there has been wide discussion about whether non-human primates and infants have genuine mindreading abilities, or generic abilities to capture behavioural regularities, or even simple perceptual predispositions (Heyes 2014). Now, as we will see in a moment, there is wide consensus that a sufficient degree of generalization over stimuli and responses would count as evidence of genuine

40 Mazzone (2011a) proposes that goals can be analysed in terms of a) motoric and perceptual representations of end-states; b) attributions of value to those representations by the reward system; c) representation of means apt to pursue those ends together with appropriate contexts (including an appreciation of the fact that, for a given end-state, different means are needed in different contexts). Moreover, intentions are usually thought of as consciously attended goals. In the present context, I adopt a simplified approach, also in the sense of using the terms "goals" and "intentions" as equivalent. Furthermore, I do not explicitly consider the internal complexity described in points b) and c). The implicit assumption is that the notion of schema is sufficient to capture such complexity. The last point, that is, the role of consciousness, will be discussed below.

mindreading abilities: in this sense, Whiten's notion of intervening variable can be considered a well-established characterization of mental concepts.

For instance Onishi and Baillargeon (2005: 257), in a study that has been a forerunner of the recent literature in favour of mindreading abilities in infants, draw the following conclusion:

> it is more parsimonious to assume that infants attribute to others beliefs that can be shaped and updated by multiple sources of information than to assume that infants form an extensive series of superficial expectations linking different perceptions to different actions. (Onishi and Baillargeon 2005: 257)

In other words, according to the authors it would be more parsimonious to assume that infants apply the *mental concept of belief* than to assume that they are recalling one of a great number of independent correlations between perceived stimuli and actions. In fact, in the latter case a plurality of representations is needed, while, in the former, one single representation is supposed to subsume that plurality.

It should be noted that the argument from explanatory parsimony has been applied in the opposite direction by the critics of the mindreading interpretation. This distinct argument has been put forth by Penn and Povinelli (2007) in the context of the debate about mindreading in non-human primates, and then extended by Perner (2010) to the debate on infants. The point is that, if mental concepts refer to unobservable entities mediating between environmental clues and behaviours, then for any explanation in which behaviours are indirectly inferred from clues by means of unobservable mental states, there is always a more parsimonious explanation connecting clues and behaviours directly. However, as Perner (2010) acknowledges, although it is true that any mental explanation of single cases can be substituted for by a more parsimonious behavioural one, this strategy becomes less and less plausible and attracting as the number and variety of cases that are subject to experimental scrutiny grows, since one needs to postulate a new behavioural rule for each case instead of a limited number of general explanations based on mental states attribution. In particular, according to Perner we should test whether subjects are able to transfer what they have learned about a correlation to other more or less similar correlations: "If such transfer occurs, we have evidence against the use of behaviour rules, and failure of transfer speaks against the use of mentalism" (Perner 2010: 249).

In sum, there seems to be wide consensus that if subjects exhibit the ability to generalize over stimulus-response correlations, then it means that they apply (a very limited number of) mental concepts, instead of (a huge number of) behavioural rules (for a more detailed analysis, see Mazzone 2014b, 2015a). Thus, mental concepts are characterized as entities of the same nature as the schemata described in chapter 2: higher-level entities prescribing the organization of lower-level entities, as an alternative to direct correlations between the latter.

4.5 Mental concepts and nativism

The view of mental concepts as intervening variables, as we saw, is implicitly accepted also by scholars with nativist inclinations such as Baillargeon. Nevertheless, since intervening variables are conceived as generalizations over correlations between stimuli and behavioural responses, that view seems more naturally suited to an empiricist framework, based on experience, than to a nativist one.

However, as noted by Ruffman (2014), the literature on the topic shows some scepticism towards the possibility that infants learn the appropriate correlations between stimuli and responses from experience, and this fuels the idea that mental concepts have to be innate instead. Ruffman quotes to this effect Surian et al. (2007: 585), who claim: "evidence of where people last saw an object is not easily tracked in everyday experience". And most of all, scepticism is expressed by Baillargeon and colleagues: "as more and more belief-inducing situations are examined, more and more behavioral rules must be posited to explain positive results, and the claim that infants and toddlers come to the laboratory equipped with the same extensive list of ordered rules becomes less and less plausible" (He et al. 2011: 302). This is essentially the argument from parsimony we already considered, but Ruffman is concerned here with an implicit assumption, that is, the suggestion that the ability to extract regularities from the environment is not sufficient to guarantee the complex performances of infants.

In sum, the scepticism towards the infants' ability to generalize significantly complex stimulus-behaviour correlations from experience is used as an argument in favour of nativism about mental concepts. Against this argument, Ruffman (2014: 276) objects that the conclusion is entirely self-defeating for the nativist perspective, "because if infants really do understand false belief, then they must also understand how the exact same perceptual conditions are causes of beliefs (rather than behavior)".[41] What Ruffman means by this is that, if infants were not able indeed to capture the correlations between observed stimuli and behaviours, it is hard to understand how they might capture the correlations between stimuli and the *unobservables mental states* that cause behaviours, in the first place.

41 Mindreading abilities are tested through the so-called "false belief task", originally proposed by Wimmer and Perner (1983). The key idea is that an observer can be credited with a genuine belief attribution only when the agent's belief is false.

The argument is rather hasty, as it seems to disregard the fact that innate mental concepts are appealed to precisely in order to solve the problem of learning: the intuition is that innate concepts do not require subjects to learn any correlations. However, in my opinion Ruffman has a point here, which can be developed in a robust argument showing that nativism about mental concepts is committed to a much more demanding – and therefore problematic – view than is generally thought (for a more detailed discussion, see Mazzone 2015a).

A concise way to express the issue is this: if mental concepts have to explain our sophisticated abilities to understand behaviours – abilities that are already apparent in infancy – then they cannot be Fodorian atomic concepts. Fodor (1975; 1987) has notoriously proposed that concepts are indecomposable and semantically unstructured mental labels, which do not contain any information on their own application. Of course, there have to be neurophysiological mechanisms (or sensorimotor representations) responsible for concept application, but those mechanisms (and representations) must not be considered as constitutive of concepts. In other words, Fodor assumes a sharp distinction between concepts and the criteria for their application. However, this does not seem to be possible in the case of mental concepts. In particular, if these concepts have to explain how a subject can predict the others' behaviours on the basis of environmental clues, then the information regarding the correlations between stimuli and behaviours *must be constitutive* of them. If, in fact, something over and beyond concepts – conceived as mere labels – were required in order to recognize the stimulus-behaviour correlations to which they apply, then this "something", and not concepts, would be what actually explains mindreading. Thus, nativists about mental concepts have a dilemma: either they commit themselves to the claim that what is innate are precisely the generalizations (over classes of stimuli and responses) that are said to be too complex to be learned, but this is not an easy claim to make, and in fact it is not what nativists seem to claim; or they claim that what is innate are Fodorian concepts, but then nativists must acknowledge that the correlations between stimuli and behaviours can (and have to) be learned, while innate concepts do not play a significant role in mindreading, after all.

Onishi and Baillargeon (2005: 257) seem to choose the second horn of the dilemma, when they claim that "development involves primarily learning which states underlie which actions and not coming to understand that such states exist at all". In other words, they try to disjoin the understanding that mental states exist, which is presumed to be guaranteed by innate concepts, from the ability to apply them to actions, which would depend instead on experience. But this move condemns innate mental concepts to irrelevance, since they lack precisely the information that would ensure their application to actions. In particular – as suggested by Ruffman – if one wants to claim that infants apply mental concepts to stimulus-response correlations too complex to be learned, then what has to be innate (not learned, as Onishi and Baillargeon suggest instead) are indeed the correlations at issue.

In sum, once it is assumed that mental concepts are intervening variables in the sense of Whiten (1996), and therefore generalizations over behavioural rules correlating classes of stimuli and responses, to conceive of them as innate appears not less, and probably more, problematic than the thesis that those concepts are learned from experiential regularities.

This does not mean that mental concepts are simple sets of correlations between stimuli and behaviours, in other words, that they are what are called (collections of) "behavioural rules". The suggestion is instead, based on our considerations in § 4.4, that infants are able to generalize over such sets, and that mental concepts are nothing but such generalizations.

4.6 Mental concepts and world models

In a reply to Ruffman (2014), Perner (2014: 294) has cautioned against the "claim that all infants need is to understand that people act depending on what they perceive". Perner's suggestion is rather that the information about what the agent has witnessed "must be used to define a model of the world for the agent, within which the infant can reason about what the agent should do" (idem: 295). In a similar vein, Christensen and Michael (2016) have invoked the necessity to go beyond mere statistical learning: in their opinion, a satisfactory account should include the ability to encode causal schemas and construct situation models.

Do these objections really threaten the picture that I have presented so far? Specifically, should we revise the thesis that mental concepts enabling action understanding are schemata extracted by generalization from experience? Rather, my claim is that the appeal to world models, within which infants can reason about actions in typical false belief tasks, amounts to saying that there are at play two different abilities. While one can indeed be described as the ability to generalize over stimulus-response correlations, encode such generalizations in long-term memory, and re-activate them from memory when needed, the other can be described as the ability to keep active in working memory, during the task, the information that is actually relevant. A world (or situation) model of this kind can therefore be thought of as an information structure kept active in working memory. Let us consider a specific example.

In a study of Song and Baillargeon (2008), in the course of the familiarization stage, infants come to attribute to an agent a preference for one of two visible objects. In practice, there are two toys, a doll with blue pigtails and a skunk, and infants see an agent repeatedly reaching for the doll; as a consequence, they are presumed to attribute a mental state to the agent, specifically, a preference for the doll. This would be revealed, in the test phase, by looking times, which are considered a standard measure of expectations: subjects look longer at events that they do not expect. In our example, in the test phase infants appear to look longer when the agent reaches the skunk instead of the doll for which she has previously (during the familiarization) shown a preference. Baillargeon et al. (2010) observe that such an expectation is not formed if, in the familiarization phase, only one object (let us say, object A) is visible and repeatedly reached by the agent. In this case, the infant does not show any surprise if, in the test phase, the agent is faced with both the old object A and a new object B, and she reaches the latter. From this, Baillargeon and colleagues infer that when infants exhibit the expectation that the agent will reach again the doll instead of the skunk they are using a genuine mental concept, instead of a simple association (idem: 115). In fact, if it were a simple association between an agent and an object A, then this should be formed even if only A is present in familiarization, and consequently infants should be equally surprised when the agent, in the test phase, reaches the new object B.

What do Baillargeon and colleagues mean by saying that infants form a genuine mental concept instead of a simple association? As we saw, the notion of association is used in potentially ambiguous ways in psychology. In some cases, it is used to refer to the representation of mere statistical co-occurrences without any specification of the relations involved (see § 2.6 above). In this vein, Christensen and Michael (2016) oppose statistical and causal learning, suggesting that the former cannot capture some properties that are required by genuinely causal descriptions of the world. However, as already observed when we spoke of the ambiguity of "associative", one should not presume that associative-I networks cannot in principle capture relations of different kinds, whether spatial, temporal, causal, final or whatever: our cortex is such an associative network, and for sure it captures relations of those kinds. And one should not, similarly, presume that those connections cannot be extracted from experience. At the very least, as far as mental concepts are concerned, it is far from evident that nativism is a cheaper solution (see above, § 4.5).

For one example, let us turn back to the mental concept PREFERENCE in the experimental task described above. It implies that an agent has a privileged relation with an object over others. This relation, however, must be manifest in experience for us to apply the concept (we can see the agent reaching and grasping that object rather than others etc.). But, if this relation is manifest in experience, then it can also be associatively learned (in the double sense that it can be learned from experience, and that it can be encoded by associative networks).

As a matter of fact, the two distinct cases of familiarization – the one in which the subject S repeatedly grasps A in the presence of A alone, and the one in which S grasps A when both A and B are present – are clearly different with respect to the stimulus-behaviour correlation involved. From the former it is not appropriate to infer that S will choose A *instead of B* in the future, since the observer had no occasion to learn such a correlation between stimuli and responses. Thus, what can be learned by observation in the two cases appears sufficient to account for the different expectations of the infants.

The argument from Song and Baillargeon (2008), however, hits the mark if used against the view that experiments on infants do not show genuine mindreading, but only low-level forms of associative behaviour-reading. In particular, what Song and Baillargeon draw our attention to is the fact that infants' abilities cannot be described in terms of simple agent-object associations preserving no information about the nature of the relation. On the contrary, infants appear able to detect complex stimulus-behaviour patterns, such as the fact that S repeatedly grasps A even in presence of another object B, and to represent this situation as different from one in which there is no such object B competing with A for S's attention. This only shows, however, that we need to account for a sophisticated ability to represent stimulus-behaviour patterns – one that is better described in terms of mindreading. It does not show that infants cannot extract those patterns from experience, and represent them in associative networks.

On the other hand, given the picture outlined in chapters 2 and 3, the thesis that mindreading is explained by the encoding of experiential regularities in associative networks does not commit us to the claim that the involved mechanisms are purely automatic (associative in the behavioural sense). Conscious attention may play a role even in the detection and encoding of statistical regularities, especially in the light of our considerations in chapter 3, according to which cooperation between automatic and controlled processes is rather the rule than the exception. In his review on associative and cognitive processes in learning, Shanks (2010: 275) observes that modern associative theories do not deny the pervasive role of attentional controlled processing in most (and possibly all) cases of learning; but they find reasons to think that attentional processing emerges itself from basic associative mechanisms – in line with the view defended here that both automatic and controlled processes are implemented by associative networks. With specific regard to mental concepts such as PREFERENCE, the hypothesis that they require conscious attention and sustained activation is quite reasonable. In order to form the concept PREFERENCE the observer needs to track through time – and compare with each other – different behaviours of the agent with respect to different objects (S grasps A but not B). But, to say the least, it is not always the case that the objects (and the related behaviours) are simultaneously present, so that they can be directly compared: S might meet B and ignore it, and after a while she might meet A and grasp it. But then, the observer needs to keep track of the entire sequence – to *keep it active in working memory* – in order to appreciate the fact that S prefers A to B.

For this reasons, it can be conceded that mental concepts (as claimed by Baillargeon and colleagues) and causal relations (as claimed by Christensen and Michael 2016) are more than simple associations *in the behavioural sense*: that is, more than relations that can be detected in the here and now by means of purely automatic processes. This means that conscious processing can be expected to creep even into our generalizations from experience, including the ones in which – I suggest – mental concepts consist.

But conscious attention is especially required in the test phase of mindreading tasks. For one example, let us consider again the experiment of Song and Baillargeon (2008) whose familiarization phase I described above. In the test phase the agent can see in one condition, while she does not see in the other, that the toys are moved in two opaque boxes: the skunk is displaced in a box whose lid has a tuft of blue hair (similar to the doll's) attached to it, the doll in a box that is identical to the first but without the tuft – let us call them, respectively, the hair and the plain box. The result is that infants look longer when the informed agent (the agent that has seen where the toys have been placed) reaches the hair box, while they look longer when the non-informed agent reaches the plain box. Apparently, infants understand that the informed agent should reach the plain box, since she knows that her preferred toy is located there, and they are surprised when she reaches the hair box instead. On the contrary, infants expect the non-informed agent to reach the hair box, based on its appearance and the agent's preference.

Now, to have the mental concept PREFERENCE, and more specifically the information that the agent prefers the doll to the skunk, is clearly only one component of what is required to account for those performances. That information must also interact with other in appropriate ways. Specifically, in the case of the informed agent, infants must know where the toys are placed and that the agent has seen their displacement. Moreover, the knowledge of these facts must be assembled so as to produce, at the right moment, the expectation that the agent will reach the box in which the preferred toy actually is. But – as we saw in § 3.9 with regard to speaker-related information in pragmatics – one cannot explain in purely automatic terms a robust ability to combine pieces of knowledge that are not immediately accessible to each other. Simple spreading of activation, in fact, does not guarantee that information is made available whenever required for cognitive tasks. In our example, observers must keep active the knowledge regarding the agent's preference at the moment when they see that the toys are displaced; they must combine this information with the fact that the agent is able either to see the displacement or not; finally, they must recall the consequent expectations when the agent reaches one of the boxes. If working memory does not intervene, by maintaining active the required information at each step of the task, there is no guarantee that information can interact in the relatively systematic way shown by the experiments.

Thus, when Perner (2014) and Christensen and Michael (2016) invoke, beyond the simple encoding of perceptual regularities, the ability to construct online models of the observed situations, they are likely to be right. This ability is related to conscious attention as a way to sustain activation, and to working memory as a "mental space" in which information can be combined. Even the formation of mental concepts, as we saw, may require controlled processing in order to keep active the complex information over which the relevant generalizations are made. But none of this implies that mental concepts cannot be generalization from experience, and therefore schemata correlating environmental stimuli and behavioural responses.

4.7 The modularity issue

What I propose in this book is not a reductionist model of cognition, that is, I do not intend to show that seemingly complex cognitive processes can be reduced to simpler ones. Rather, my purpose is to show that the variety of cognitive processes, whether simple or complex, manifested at the behavioural level can be explained as emerging from a single mechanism of implementation. To be sure, this implies a certain displacement of the explanatory weight from processes to the organization of knowledge: associative processes are governed by our previous knowledge, whose schematic organization prescribes how inputs must be combined together into coherent interpretations.

Since the approach adopted here is not intended to deny both the complexity and the variety of cognitive processes at the behavioural level, we need to account – among other things – for the existence of cognitive domains operating with relative autonomy from each other. In conclusion, I intend to briefly discuss whether this autonomy justifies claims of modularity.

The notion of module has become established in cognitive science mainly due to Fodor (1983), according to which a process is defined as modular when it has some (but not necessarily all) of the following features: it is fast, mandatory, automatic, specialized for certain kinds of input, not internally accessible to other processes, innate, localized in specific cerebral areas, subject to selective damage. Since then, the notion has generated a huge literature and a lively debate, across a variety of fields in cognitive science. One of the issues is whether some features, among the ones listed by Fodor, are more important than others, and whether it is really useful to employ a notion that can be weakened at will, simply by deleting one or the other of those features.

Coltheart (1999), in particular, has proposed that a very important feature of modular processes is specificity for domain (or, in brief, domain-specificity), in his opinion the only "necessary condition for the applicability of the term 'modular'" (idem: 118). Within the limits of the present investigation, I will adopt this view without argument. Suffice it to say that, as far as I can tell, it captures the essential intuition of modularity, that is, the idea of different domains of cognition each with its own specialized processes and mechanisms. This is, in any case, the feature that is the most relevant for our purposes. Let us analyse this claim in some more detail.

A crucial component of Coltheart's argument is the distinction between a *knowledge module*, that is, a body of knowledge that is independent of other bodies of knowledge, and a *processing module*, which is instead defined as a mental information-processing system. His thesis about domain-specificity as a necessary condition for modularity is intended to apply to processing (not knowledge) modules. In this perspective, the modularist's commitment to the existence of a plurality of modules amounts to saying that there are different processes for different domains, and therefore a plurality of specialized processes. For instance, as far as syntax is concerned, Coltheart (1999: 118) claims that the kind of domain-specificity he is interested in is not relative to syntactic knowledge but to the "syntactic processing module", although this module can be expected to "have, as part of its internal structure, a body of knowledge about syntax".

My claim is that this distinction is crucial for establishing a view of modularity that is not trivial. To see why, let us consider the following definition of "domain-specific" provided by Coltheart: "not responding to inputs except those of a particular class" (idem: 119). Unfortunately, this characterization of the notion is too weak to be controversial. Let us suppose that there is one single basic process operating on a variety of bodies of knowledge, so that when the system receives inputs of the type A, the body of knowledge A' is mobilized, when inputs are of the type B, the body of knowledge B' is mobilized, and so on. In this case, we can distinguish a variety of processes (A", B", etc.) that differ from each other not for the mechanism employed (by hypothesis, there is one single mechanism at play), but for the bodies of knowledge they operate on. Nevertheless, they would satisfy the above definition of domain-specific process: each responds to inputs of a specific domain. But, if this were enough to claim that domain-specificity exists, the claim would be entirely *un*controversial. There is no opponent of modularity who wants to deny that knowledge tends to organize in (relatively) independent bodies, and that new inputs are recognized and processed based on such previous knowledge about the respective domains. If modularity has to be a non-trivial thesis, it needs to appeal to processes that differ from each other *in themselves*, not relative to the bodies of knowledge they operate on.

To be sure, this does not mean that it is trivial to discover which processes are modular in the above sense. For one example proposed by Coltheart, suppose we found a double dissociation between face-recognition and object-recognition (i.e., patients with impaired face-recognition but intact object-recognition and patients with intact face-recognition and impaired object-recognition). One could plausibly infer from these data that the two systems work independently from each other, which is a substantial (non trivial) claim about the cognitive architecture of visual recognition (at least two distinct modules). However, my point is that there would be little reason to resist both to the premise (the double dissociation) and the conclusion (domain-specificity of face- and object-recognition) even in case you are anti-modularist in the standard sense: the conclusion is, in fact, compatible with the idea that there are two physically distinct bodies of knowledge but one single process, which operates on one or the other of them as a function of the inputs it is exposed to.

It is interesting to consider again the case of syntax. Coltheart observes that what is required in order to vindicate the modularity thesis in this domain, is a specialized system for syntactic processing, not a body of syntactic knowledge. As we said in § 2.8, this is precisely the main point on which Jackendoff distances himself from Chomsky: while the latter conceives of syntactic rules as specialized procedures, Jackendoff conceives of them instead as specific representations on which a domain-general process operates. In other words, according to Jackendoff a set of representations (a specific body of knowledge) is sufficient to specify the input-output transformation rules in which syntactic processing consists. Now, the general intuition is that Chomsky's model counts as modular while Jackendoff's does not (except in a trivial sense). In sum, in syntax and elsewhere the standard modularity thesis appears to require that each domain have its own specialized *process (or processes)*.

However, while conceiving of domain-specificity in terms of distinct bodies of knowledge trivializes the modularity thesis, conceiving of it instead in terms of distinct processes is, I submit, untenable. The reason is that the processes at issue should differ from one another at the implementation level. If, in fact, they only differed at the behavioural level, the possibility would remain open that this difference is explained in the trivial way: that is, in terms of different bodies of knowledge apt to process different categories of inputs *via the same mechanism of associative activation*. Thus, domain-specificity is non-trivial only if there are a variety of processes *at the implementation level*. But the claim that there are a variety of processes at the implementation level is untenable: as far as neural implementation is concerned, there is no other process than the mechanism of associative activation and inhibition.

Based on these considerations, let us consider again the case of pragmatics in some more detail.

4.8 Modularity and consciousness in RT

Relevance theorists have a general modularist approach. This is probably part of the reasons why they oppose associative processing as an explanation of pragmatic comprehension (see above, § 2.4). Associative processing is, in fact, a paradigmatic example of domain-general process. Thus relevance theorists presumably think, correctly in my opinion: if pragmatic processes are implemented by associative mechanisms, then they cannot be considered as domain-specific (and therefore as modular) in any non-trivial sense. In this conditional proposition, they find reason to reject the premise due to their rejection of the conclusion; my proposal is, instead, to accept both premise and conclusion. Modularism is probably also one reason why RT conceives of pragmatic processing as automatic, in the specific sense that consciousness plays no role in it. Let me first address these issues in the reverse order (consciousness in this section, associations in the next). Then I will turn to a couple of specific problems raised by RT's view about modularity in pragmatics.

When Wilson (2003) addresses the issue of modularity, she also provides as usual a summary of RT. Her use of the term "attention" in this context is well exemplified by the following quotation: "overt communication involves the use of an ostensive stimulus, designed to attract an audience's *attention* and focus it on the communicator's meaning" (idem: 315; emphasis mine). This and similar expressions might suggest that relevance theorists assign a role to (conscious) attention, after all: in their opinion, utterances are designed for, and actually capable of, attracting the addressees attention, and this can be expected to affect the way in which meaning is processed. As a matter of fact, relevance theorists make regular mention of attention, in ways that are similar to the previous quotation. Besides, it is apparent that conscious attention is pervasive in our cognitive life, and has well-established effects. Furthermore, there is a huge literature on the role of attention in communication.

I already presented these facts in § 3.9. But I also observed that the use of "attention" in RT is not in accordance with the psychological notion of *conscious* attention. This is justified because, in psychology, attention is conceived as something that can be set apart from consciousness, in a sense that is very close to what RT intends: the point is that, among the myriad of inputs, only some are actually processed at any moment, whether in a conscious fashion or not.[42] But, although this use of "attention" is legitimate, utterances seem to prompt *conscious* attention proper. And it is conscious attention, again, that is pervasive in our mental life and has well-known effects on the maintenance of information. Thus, RT makes here a disputable theoretical move. It neglects the notion of conscious attention, which is able to play the role of *explanans* in pragmatic explanations (see §§ 3.9, 3.10). And it conceives instead attention in the minimal sense of "preferential processing of certain inputs", in accordance to which the notion is only an *explanandum*. In practice, RT explains attention in this minimal sense by an appeal to modular, domain-specific heuristics.

As Wilson (2003) makes clear, such heuristics are conceived as automatic mechanisms, not involving conscious attention:

> It follows from the Cognitive Principle of Relevance that human *attention and processing resources* tend to be automatically allocated to information that seems relevant enough to be worth processing. This is not because we have a choice in the matter, but because of the way our cognitive systems have evolved. As a result of constant selection pressure towards increasing efficiency, the human cognitive system has developed in such a way that our perceptual mechanisms tend *automatically* to pick out potentially relevant stimuli, our memory retrieval mechanisms tend *automatically* to activate potentially relevant contextual assumptions, and our inferential mechanisms tend *spontaneously* to process them in the most productive way. (Wilson 2003: 315; my emphases)

Wilson traces back to Grice this opposition between, on the one hand, "reflective reasoning" (idem: 307), "complex discursive reasoning process[es]" (ibidem), "conscious, reflective process[es]" (idem: 310) and, on the other, "spontaneous, intuitive process[es] which takes place below the level of consciousness" (ibidem). The fact is that there is in Grice a tension (which will be addressed in more detail in chapter 5). His reconstructions of how conversational implicatures are derived suggest that the hearer has "to go through a complex discursive reasoning process" (idem: 307). But, actually, "Grice himself might not have been opposed to the idea of an intuitive mind-reading ability. What mattered to

42 This use of "attention" matches the notion of "attended subliminal processing" we presented in § 3.5 (based on Dehaene et al. 2006) and, in a looser sense, the notion of "subliminal processing", too.

him was that this ability – whether intuitive or reflective – was not code-like but properly inferential" (idem: 311).

What is of particular interest to us is that both Grice and the subsequent discussion on his model have adopted this dichotomy ("whether intuitive or reflective") as a satisfactory inventory of the theoretical options at stake. But even more importantly, the same dichotomy is somehow suggested by Fodor's modularity thesis. This is crucial for relevance theorists, because, after all, they want to go beyond Grice in the direction of a more realistic cognitive account of comprehension. And Fodor's modularity provides precisely the framework for this enterprise. Now, key to Fodor's view of cognition is the distinction between modular and central processes. Reflective reasoning is a typical central process, with no principled limit on the contextual information it may resort to. "Modular processes, by contrast, are 'local', 'encapsulated', and heavily restricted in the type or source of contextual information they may draw" (Wilson 2003: 304). The crucial point is that Fodor's modularity encourages the idea of a sharp distinction between processes that are fast, automatic and unconscious and others that are instead modelled on verbal reasoning. To be sure, it is far from clear that Fodor conceives of central processes as essentially conscious. As a matter of fact, he has never attributed great importance to consciousness, occasionally suggesting an epiphenomenal approach to it.[43] In *The Modularity of Mind*, what he says of central processes is that they "are, of course, largely unconscious, and very little is known about their operation" (Fodor 1983: 104).

In general, whether epiphenomenal or not, conscious awareness is seen as characterizing a small set of sophisticated and effortful cognitive processes, while most cognitive processes, and for sure the modular ones, are presumed to occur unconsciously. In this way, Fodor's modular view encourages RT to conceive of pragmatic processing as entirely automatic, in opposition to conscious discursive reasoning. A serious fault of modularism is precisely this rigid opposition between automatic processing and conscious reflective reasoning. We already mentioned some reasons to call this opposition into question. First of all, to repeat, there are intermediate conditions between effortful conscious processing

---

43 Consider the following quotation from Fodor (1975: 52, fn. 19): in order to characterize the conscious states of the organism, we should ask "whether there are generalizations which hold (just) for conscious mental states, and that depends in turn on whether the conscious states of an organism have more in common with one another than with the unconscious states of the nervous system of the organism. It is, in this sense, an open question whether conscious psychological states provide a natural domain for a theory [...]. I should have thought that, since Freud, the burden of proof has shifted to those who maintain that the conscious states (of human beings) do form a theoretical domain".

and purely automatic processing: specifically, there is the "low-effort mode" of consciousness (Kahneman 2011: 24) that we called conscious attention. Second, conscious attention seems to be present in most cognitive activities, and it has a special role to play in active maintenance, amplification, and inhibition of information for the task at hand. Third, modularism tends to conceal the fact that most automatic processing is the result of automatization of cognitive steps, which are not impervious to conscious access anyway. Interestingly, as we saw above (in § 3.2), Carston (2007) observes that pragmatic processing, and specifically the construction of explicit meaning, can in fact be penetrated by consciousness. This notwithstanding, she limits herself to oppose "the automatic intuitive mechanisms of utterance understanding'' (idem: 44) proposed by RT to the "capacity for explicit reflective reasoning" (idem: 39) that, according to Recanati, accounts for secondary pragmatic processes. The theoretical framework provided by Fodor (1983) suggests no reason to consider any other option.

4.9 Modularity and associationism in RT

Another aspect for which, I submit, Fodor's modularism has led relevance theorists astray is their position regarding associative processes. As I argued above, if a process is associative, then it cannot be modular in any strong sense.[44] Thus relevance theorists – to the extent that they aim to a modularist view of pragmatics – need to reject associative accounts of comprehension. But this position, I argue, is hardly tenable. Let me summarize the issue.

First of all, the opposition between modular and associative approaches lies at the very foundations of Fodor (1983). In the first introductory chapter of the book, Fodor contrasts his "faculty psychology" – the idea that cognition is based on a number of distinct modular faculties – with associationism. In fact, his target is the traditional notion of associations between ideas that traces back to Hume. But there is a clear logical relationship between this associationism and the "implementation" version I defend here: ideas can be thought as represented by neural patterns, their relations equates to strength of connection in neural networks, and the recall of ideas equates to associative spreading of activation through the network.[45] As a matter of fact, advocates of modularity have also

44 Recall the case of face- and object-recognition (§ 4.7): a double dissociation between them might be explained in associative terms, thus implying only a weak notion of modularity, which is acceptable by standard anti-modularists as well.
45 More on associationism will be said in the next chapter.

attacked the implementation version, under the name of "connectionism". One case in point is Pinker (2002) that is essentially a defence of nativism, which is of course a cornerstone of the modularity thesis. Traditional associationism and modern connectionism share the idea that cognition is based on detection and encoding of experiential regularities, and encoded representations guide the processing of new information. But if this is the case, then there is little room left for innate domain-specific processes.

Although this point cannot be addressed in detail here, I must be clear on this point: I am not committed to a radical anti-nativism. But nativism must be reconciled with the basic structure of the brain and specifically with its being constituted by neural networks through which activation spreads, and that are plastically shaped by this activation. Significantly, Pinker (2002: 82; emphasis mine) writes: "It's not that neural networks are incapable of handling the meanings of sentences or the task of grammatical conjugation. They had better not be, since *the very idea that thinking is a form of neural computation requires that some kind of neural network duplicate whatever the mind can do.* The problem lies in the credo that one can do everything with a generic model as long as it is sufficiently trained". In other words, Pinker acknowledges that any cognitive process must ultimately be implemented by associative activation in neural networks, but he nevertheless insists that something more than the training of "a generic [connectionist] model" is required. He specifically suggests that complex cognitive abilities such as grammatical combination need to be accounted "by different systems in the brain rather than by *a single associative network*" (Pinker 2002: 82; my emphasis). I agree that a single connectionist network cannot account for complex cognitive abilities. In Plebe and Mazzone (2016) the suggestion is made that what is required is a plurality of distinct, hierarchically organized, neural maps (instead of "a single associative network"), and a number of morphological constraints on their reciprocal connectivity (which maps are directly connected with each other). Such morphological features and constraints are the bit of nativism for which current neuroscience provides evidence (the argument for this is in Plebe and Mazzone 2016). However, none of this calls into question the general point that any cognitive process has to be implemented by associative activations that spread through patterns in neural networks, and shape these patterns in turn.

The case of RT shows how problematic it can be to defend the modularity thesis for a given domain, in the face of the previous argument from associative implementation. First of all, it is hard to deny the contribution of associative recall to processes of different sorts, including pragmatic ones. And in fact, as we repeatedly said, relevance theorists acknowledge such contribution, but they aim to delimit its scope: the idea is that associative processes have to stop at a certain point and then leave room for processes of a different kind.

Now, one possibility is that this demarcation is drawn at the behavioural level. But, as we saw, at this level the distinction between inferential and associative processes is standardly based on the presence/absence of consciousness. This option is therefore not available to RT, since consciousness is not part of its theoretical apparatus. More importantly, even if one were to draw the distinction at the behavioural level, this would not harm the argument for associative implementation. In fact, difference of processing at the behavioural level does not prevent the possibility that there is only one process at the implementation level, so that the modularity thesis is trivialized anyway.

Thus, the distinction between associative and inferential needs to be drawn at the implementation level. But this sounds implausible. Can we really imagine that the flow of associative activation through neural networks stops somewhere and is substituted for by something different? The only alternative model ever proposed is not really viable: it is what I called the inferential-I model, based on the notions of symbol and symbolic rule. As observed in § 2.5, this model seems to lie at a different explanatory level than the associative-I one, so it is really hard to imagine a coherent system in which one process starts where the other stops.

The difficulty to draw boundaries around associative processes is made apparent by RT's hesitation between three different ways to do it.

First of all, on some occasions the theory suggests that what is provided by associative activation is merely the raw materials, so to speak, of inferential structures: the premises (explicit meaning, contextual assumptions) and possibly the contextual conclusions that are fed into the derivation. Let me repeat once again the following passage from Wilson and Carston (2006: 429; emphasis mine):

> associative links may affect the outcome of the mutual adjustment process *by altering the accessibility of contextual assumptions and implications*, but the resulting overall interpretation will only be accepted as the speaker's intended meaning if it satisfies the hearer's expectations of relevance and is properly warranted by the inferential comprehension heuristic.

To be precise, this quotation is ambiguous between two possible interpretations. The first is the one we already introduced: associative links are responsible for which components are accessed and then fed into the derivation, but not for the validity of the derivation as such. In other words, in this interpretation there is no guarantee that associative activation produces correct inferences, in which premises and conclusions are related appropriately. In favour of this interpretation we can mention the fact that, after all, what is contrasted with associative processing is *inferential* processing, so one expects inferential structures to be beyond the power of associations. This interpretation is also encouraged by the line of reasoning pursued by Wilson and Carston (2007; see also Sperber and

Wilson 2008) against associative explanations. Their general argument is that not all associations are inferential, and therefore some method of filtering out unwanted associations is required. But then, the suggestion seems to be that associations give no guarantees that valid inferential structures obtain.

While on this interpretation inferential processes may be held responsible for assessing the *validity* of inferences (they have to assess which associations are also valid inferences), another possibility is that they are responsible instead for assessing whether the valid inferences produced by associations are *sufficiently relevant*. In this case, we must presume that associative processes suffice to construct valid inferential structures (i.e., internally sound interpretations of utterances), but then something more is required: those interpretations must be submitted to the second step of the comprehension procedure (as said in the final part of the above quotation, they must be assessed against "the hearer's expectations of relevance" and must be "properly warranted by the inferential comprehension heuristic").

In favour of this interpretation, apart from the final part of the quotation, there is also my argument in § 2.12. As I said relevance theorists, in their explanations of specific cases, make an appeal to contextual assumptions that are in fact equivalent to schemata in my sense: they are sufficient to ensure *motivated* transitions between premises and conclusions thanks to simple pattern completion. But then, the logical validity of pragmatic inferences can be guaranteed by associative activation alone. If this is the case, the power of associations extends beyond the mere access to premises and conclusions: it also accounts for the validity of the resulting inferential structures.

This option receives further support from RT's proposal of a mutual adjustment process, according to which pragmatic inferential structures are accommodated incrementally and in parallel, via both forward and backward inferences. As a consequence, derivations cannot be thought as blind applications of inference rules to premises. Rather, a monitoring-and-adjusting process is required, such that changes in any step of the derivation are detected and then cause the appropriate changes in the other steps. Now, this is most naturally explained in terms of associative activation: changes in the activation of certain representations affect the activation of other representations, provided that the appropriate schemata are encoded. It is not easy to imagine a different, non-associative, mechanism apt to ensure such a bidirectional process of monitoring and adjustment between the steps of inferential derivations. In sum, in this second view, associative processes have a wider role than simple access to premises and conclusions: they grant *motivated* transitions between premises and conclusions, although the amount of conclusions (cognitive effects) must then be assessed against expectations of relevance.

However, the mutual adjustment process (together with other suggestions reviewed in chapter 1) also suggests a third possibility. Let us repeat: the second step of the comprehension procedure prescribes that the amount of conclusions is assessed against quantitative expectations of relevance. But, as we saw in chapter 1, a way to think of the mutual adjustment process is in terms of backward inferences based on expectations about the type (not the amount) of cognitive effects. As I showed in § 2.13, this implies a different picture than suggested by the second step of the comprehension procedure. It is not that contextual conclusions, licensed by forward inferences, are then assessed by a wholly different mechanism. Rather, the assessment is ensured by the backward side of the same dynamic. In practice, forward and backward inferences are assessed against each other. And this dynamic is plausibly associative. This conclusion is supported by my previous considerations about the role of schemata in mutual adjustment. Specifically, as observed in § 2.11, expectations about types of cognitive effects can naturally be explained as backward inferences from contexts to conclusions. Thus, if forward and backward inferences involving premises and conclusions can be performed associatively, then backward inferences from contexts to conclusions can plausibly be performed associatively as well. Moreover, this is consistent with a couple of suggestions of RT: specifically, Sperber and Wilson's (1996) suggestion that the organization of memory is sufficient to account for relevance; and the suggestion that the assessment of interpretations might be comparative rather than absolute, which suggests that the most accessible interpretations are ipso facto the most relevant. Both these ideas seem to imply that, in order to assess the conclusions of pragmatic inferences, there is no need for the second step of the comprehension procedure. In practice, there is no need for a distinct process, beyond the associative activation of premises and conclusions via forward and backward inferences.

To summarize, RT suggests three different ways of drawing boundaries around associative processes in pragmatics. First, associative processes may be held responsible for which premises and conclusions are fed into pragmatic inferences, but then the validity of the resulting inferential structures must be assessed independently. Second, associative processes may suffice to ensure that valid inferential structures are formed, but these structures must then be assessed with regard to their relevance. Third, associative processes may account not only for the validity of inferential structures, but also for their contextual relevance, in which case no other process is required.

If my considerations in §§ 4.7 and 4.8 are correct, this irresolution is no surprise. On the one hand, the commitment to the modularity thesis, and in particular to domain-specificity of pragmatics, requires relevance theorists to deny that genuine pragmatic processes can be associative at the implementation level.

Therefore, they need to circumscribe the scope of associative processes in one way or another. But, on the other hand, there is no sensible way to draw this boundary: at the implementation level, associative activation is the only viable model of explanation. Thus, RT explores both a stronger way to draw the boundary (associative formation of inferences on the one hand, non-associative assessment of their validity on the other), and also a weaker one (associative formation of valid inferences on the one hand, non-associative assessment of their relevance on the other), but in the end it comes very close to the idea that there is no boundary to draw: mutual adjustment (and the related associative competition between interpretations) seems sufficient to assess both validity and relevance of pragmatic inferences.

I find it of some significance that, in a paper devoted to pragmatics and modularity, Wilson (2003) writes: "The mutual adjustment of explicit content and implicatures, constrained by expectations of relevance, is *the central feature of relevance-theoretic pragmatics*" (idem: 316; my emphasis). If one considers that the notion of mutual adjustment was not even present in *Relevance*,[46] this is a sign that, indeed, the theory has shifted its centre of gravity. This change can hardly leave the rest of the theory untouched, and in this sense I spoke in chapter 1 of a non-standard version of it. This shift, as I argued here, especially calls into question the modularity thesis.

4.10 Mindreading and RT: some conclusions

Let us take stock. This book is mainly concerned with the relation between cognitive pragmatics and mindreading, with special attention to the way in which RT has framed the issue. I started from the Gricean thesis that "pragmatic interpretation is ultimately an exercise in mind-reading" (Sperber and Wilson 2002: 3). In § 1.11, in particular, I summarized ideas from Grice himself, from relevance theorists and from Levinson, all contributing to the view that utterance understanding is based on inferential recognition of the speakers' communicative goals, and that this process may be affected backwards by expectations about contextually relevant goals. Since these latter goals may also pertain to non-communicative actions, it follows that (the kind of mindreading involved in) utterance understanding must somehow interact with the ability to attribute non-communicative goals.

46 Wilson (2004: 352, fn. 14) attributes its introduction to Sperber and Wilson (1998), Wilson and Sperber (2002, 2004).

From a cognitive point of view, a crucial issue is how this cooperation between mindreading and comprehension specifically occurs. I will first summarize the general approach pursued here; then I will consider RT's view in more detail.

In this chapter I provided reasons to think that communicative and non-communicative mindreading might be characterized by a similar bi-directional mechanism, with inferences drawn both from means to ends and from ends to means. Although the above considerations are far from conclusive, the observation of such similarity is of some interest in itself: if the same ability to construe means-ends chains were responsible for the understanding of both utterances *and* non-communicative actions, this might explain how communicative means and non-communicative ends can be combined with each other as well.

Specifically, in § 4.3, I suggested that the process by which we manage means-ends chains does automatically mesh ours and others' goals, so as to construe shared intentional contexts that are crucial for both cooperative and competitive social actions. Again, although more research is needed to clarify the issue, these reasons are further support for the claim that the construction of means-ends chains is driven by information from different sources: perceptual and sensorimotor information concerning both communicative and non-communicative, ours and others' actions.

In chapter 2 I tried to show that this construction of means-ends chains can be accounted for in terms of a bottom-up/top-down mechanism of associative activation, thanks to the schematic and hierarchical organization of memory: intentions, in particular, are conceived as high-level schemata linking perception and action. Since intentions are a special case of mental states, in §§ 4.4 to 4.6 I compared my approach with the current literature on mindreading, and defended the former from arguments provided by the latter against associative accounts. Finally, in §§ 4.7 to 4.9, I proposed that modularism is one reason why RT rejects associative accounts of comprehension, but I also argued that it is (standard) modularism that is indeed in trouble when contrasted with associative explanations. The former presupposes a variety of domain-specific processes at the implementation level, a claim that is hardly tenable in the light of what we know about the basic associative functioning of the brain.

Given all these considerations, the conclusion I tend to draw is the following: pragmatic comprehension and mindreading are very close components of a unitary dynamic based on associative activation. In contrast with this view, RT adopts a modular approach according to which there are two distinct processes at play. Before addressing this proposal in more detail, let me make some general considerations.

Strictly speaking, relevance theorists do not provide an explicit account of the interaction between general mindreading abilities and utterance understanding.

This is coherent with RT's aim of providing a cognitive explanation of what is *specific* to utterance understanding. In this perspective, general mindreading abilities are external to the relevance-theoretic comprehension procedure, although information on mental states may possibly be handed to, and then processed by, the comprehension procedure. This silence, however, might have a deeper reason in their sympathy for a modular strategy of explanation. As Perner (2010) has noted, nativism-with-modularism is an explanatory strategy by which many have exempted themselves from the necessity to provide actual explanations of cognitive processes. While, if you claim that a capacity is accounted for by domain-general processes, you are held responsible for explaining how this may occur, who makes an appeal to modular, innate capacities is not expected to be specific about the actual mechanisms to any comparable extent. In this sense, according to Perner (2010), nativism-with-modularism as a default explanatory strategy is a potential treason to the cognitive turn: instead of looking into the "black box" of behaviourists and disclosing its internal functioning, it tends to provide us with an entire system of black boxes. Be it as it may, as a matter of fact relevance theorists seem to have little interest in the details of the interaction between general mindreading and pragmatic processing. In their papers dedicated to the issue, the focus is rather on what makes these processes different from each other. So, in a strict sense, RT does not provide an explanation of that interaction to be contrasted with the one that I propose.

One might go even further and argue that the explanation of the interaction is out of the reach of modular approaches. According to RT, consideration of the speaker's mental state affects pragmatic processing at any step – including reference assignment (see above § 3.9) – and in ways that change flexibly and unpredictably with contexts. Now, in the approach I propose this is not hard to account for. To be sure, I acknowledged that information is organized in (relatively) autonomous bodies of knowledge – that is, portions of the associative network characterized by strong internal connections. But this leaves room for flexible interaction between domains. We detect and store in memory regular patterns of covariation, both within and *between* domains, and consequently the recall and integration of information based on associative activation is not confined within domain boundaries.[47] The within-domain organization of information is sufficient to ensure a relative autonomy of processing, but, since between-domain relationships are also coded, the resulting pattern of activation is far from being one of rigid encapsulation. In sum, my approach naturally accounts for flexible interaction between relatively autonomous bodies of knowledge. The modularity

47 This argument is presented in some more detail in Mazzone (2016b).

thesis conceives instead modular processes as encapsulated: that is, they do not exchange information except in ways that are rigidly constrained by design.

One might of course weaken modularity for this respect, and in fact the idea of non-encapsulated modules has had some currency in the debate. Specifically, as Mazzarella (2016) observes, RT has actually explored the idea that informational encapsulation of modules is a matter of degrees. She quotes the following passage from Carston (1997: 20):

> it may be that we have to rethink the concept of module and allow for a kind of continuum, from peripheral perceptual systems, which are rigidly encapsulated [. . .], through a hierarchy of conceptual modules, with the property of encapsulation diminishing progressively at each level as the interconnections among domain-specific processors increase.

However, this weakened notion of non-Fodorian modules is an attempt to have it both ways: to acknowledge the need for flexible (non-encapsulated) interaction between processes, without abandoning the commitment to modular, specialized processes. As a matter of fact, Mazzarella (2016: 184) concludes her argument for non-Fodorian modularity by adopting RT's view that pragmatic communication is a very special case of mindreading, which therefore requires "its own dedicated comprehension procedure". But then, one has to face all the by now well-known problems: the difficulty to make sense of the standard RT's view based on quantitative expectations of relevance and the second step of the comprehension procedure (as opposed to the view based on the organization of memory: see chapter 1); the difficulty to make sense of the notion of specialized processes at the implementation level and in particular of a "dedicated comprehension procedure" (as opposed to the notion of one single associative process of implementation: § 4.7); and also the difficulty to spell out the details of how flexible interaction between modules is possible without ending up in something like the generalized spreading of activation in associative networks I described.

Is there a way to interpret RT so as to overcome those problems? Yes, but there are costs to be paid. First, we should be ready to abandon any literal commitment to the relevance-based comprehension procedure. The assessment of interpretations would be comparative instead: it would be one and the same thing as their construction, and implemented by forward and backward associative activations based on the organization of memory. Second, we should be ready to abandon the argument against associative processing: there would be no way to draw a boundary around associative processes, in order to make room for specialized pragmatic processes. Third, we should be ready to abandon the idea that consciousness has no special role to play in utterance understanding – that is, the idea that utterances attract our attention only in the sense that there is a domain-specific heuristic dedicated to communication. And finally, we should be ready to abandon the commitment to modularity in any non-trivial sense. This is the pruning of RT that actually I suggest to do.

All this said, let us see how RT addresses the issue of mindreading. A first assumption is that presumably mindreading "is not a single, homogeneous module but a set of special-purpose mechanisms or sub-modules attuned to regularities in narrower domains" (Wilson 2003: 314). Against this background, relevance theorists propose the existence of "a dedicated comprehension mechanism, an evolved 'mental organ' with its own special-purpose inferential principles or procedures" (ibidem). In sum, the idea is that there is in humans a mechanism specifically evolved for utterance comprehension, "a sub-module of the mindreading module, an automatic application of a *relevance-based procedure* to ostensive stimuli" (Sperber and Wilson 2002: 20; emphasis mine). The emphasized phrase suggests that the modular mechanism at issue is (or at least mainly consists in) the relevance-theoretic comprehension procedure. Wilson (2000) is entirely explicit on the matter. After having described the procedure, she writes: "In this section, I have outlined a comprehension procedure which might form the basis for a modularized metacommunicative ability, itself a sub-part of the more general metapsychological ability, or 'theory of mind'" (Wilson 2000: 140).

It should be noted that, in a strict sense, the comprehension procedure has nothing metarepresentational in it. It simply prescribes that interpretations are selected in order of accessibility, and then assessed against expectations of relevance. Information about the speaker's mental states must be introduced from the outside of the procedure, specifically from the modules responsible for general mindreading abilities. Wilson (2000: 148, fn. 2; my emphasis) in fact speaks of clear "cases in which the mindreading ability makes a direct contribution to communicated content, by *providing access to information about the speaker's mental states which may then be picked out by the relevance-theoretic comprehension procedure*". To my knowledge, however, nothing is said about *how* this mindreading ability would feed into the procedure information about the speaker's mental states. And nothing is said about how this mechanism might cohere and integrate with associative activation. In principle, if associative activation provided contextual assumptions and conclusions to pragmatic inferences, and if pragmatic comprehension and mindreading were modular (non-associative) abilities, then boundaries should be drawn around associative activation: this process should stop where the comprehension procedure on the one hand, and mindreading mechanisms on the other, start. As we saw, this is not easy to imagine.

An interesting question is why, if the comprehension procedure is not in itself metarepresentational, we must consider it a sub-module of the *mindreading* module. Not only because it makes use of mental information, but also with regard to its outcome which is the representation of a communicative intention – a mental state – of the speaker. It is important to note a potential ambiguity of the phrase "communicative intention" in Gricean pragmatics. In one sense, it is used to refer to the fact that, by an utterance in a context, the speaker intends to convey a certain proposition *P*, and therefore, in order to understand the utterance, the addressee has to represent that intention. This is the representation of a speaker's representation, and therefore a metarepresentation, that we can roughly express as "the speaker intends to communicate that *P*". However, in line with Grice, RT assumes that communicative intentions are quite complex and layered phenomena. A speaker not only has the intention to convey the information that *P*, she also intends the addressee to be informed that *P* by recognizing her intention to inform him. In other words, the communicative intention is the intention that another intention – the informative intention, that is, the intention to inform the interlocutor of something – is recognized by the interlocutor. The reason is the following: cases in which a sender intends to inform the addressee that *P without the intention that he recognizes this intention* seem better described as cases in which the sender provides clues than as genuine cases of communication. But then, communicative intentions are metarepresentations of a complex sort. In Wilson's (2000: 140) words, "the attribution of a full-fledged speaker's meaning involves a fourth-order metarepresentation [. . .]: she intends me to believe that she intends me to believe. This is complex enough to suggest a modularised meta-communicative ability".

I do not intend to say much about levels of metarepresentation, except that this speculation of fourth-order metarepresentations[48] is disputable and possibly incoherent with other claims of relevance theorists, and it may be in fact a vestige of a Grice-like rational reconstruction of the structure of comprehension. First of all, it is common sense in the mindreading literature that children pass the standard false-belief task – which is thought to address *first order* mindreading abilities – at the age of four years, well beyond their first understanding of verbal communication. And second order belief tasks are passed only a couple of years later. For one example, Perner et al. (2015: 77) speak of a "curious window in child development, which opens when a child first passes verbal false belief tasks around 4 years and closes 2 years later when she passes second order belief tasks".[49]

---

48 The speculation can be found in Wilson (2000), and in Sperber (2000). In the same vein, Sperber and Wilson (2002: 12) say: "there are always several level of metarepresentation involved in inferential comprehension".

49 The emphasis here is on the qualification "*verbal*" (false belief tasks): starting from Onishi and Baillargeon (2005), there is ample evidence that non-verbal false belief tasks are passed earlier. However, in this context verbal abilities are what matter.

Relevance theorists are, of course, well aware of the gap between their proposal of fourth order metarepresentations and what the research on mindreading shows. But in their view this provides one main reason for thinking that comprehension is special, and requires – in Wilson's (2003: 314) words – "its own special-purpose inferential principles or procedures". The general argument is that comprehension has special difficulties compared to proper mindreading, and this is why a specific sub-module would be required. However, apart from the fact that there is little evidence of this up to now,[50] it is not even clear that RT is always coherent on this point.

To see why, let us consider Sperber's (1994) thesis that metacommunication has a developmental history. In early childhood – he maintains – there is no awareness that, as a consequence of incompetence or malevolence of the sender, the correct interpretation of ostensive stimuli might not be the most relevant. Therefore, the addressee follows the strategy called "naïve optimism" which is exclusively based on the assessment of relevance. Later on, children gain awareness that the sender might not be competent about what is most relevant to the addressee, and so they apply the strategy of "cautious optimism", that is, they ask themselves which interpretation the speaker would have thought is the most relevant. At last, children come to acknowledge that the sender may have reasons for not being as relevant as she could; at this point they are ready to apply the strategy called "sophisticated understanding".

When adopting cautious optimism and sophisticated understanding, addressees are clearly engaged in some sort of mindreading. But according to relevance theorists a metarepresentation is always needed, even when the addressee is applying naïve optimism. In this case the addressee is content with the most relevant interpretation, which is the output of the procedure. Nonetheless, he has furthermore to attribute this interpretation to the sender as her communicative intention, and this is a metarepresentational affair (recall the first meaning of "communicative intention" we picked out above, according to which the addressee has to form the metarepresentation "the speaker intends to communicate that *P*"). In Wilson's (2000: 137) words,

> A Naively Optimistic hearer has no need to think about the speaker's thoughts in identifying the speaker's meaning: the only time he needs to metarepresent the speaker's thoughts is when, having found an acceptable interpretation, he concludes that it is the intended one.

50 The only piece of evidence that relevance theorists cite is Happé and Loth (2002), who seem to have shown that children are better at understanding intentions in communicative than in non-communicative tasks.

The question is whether this minimal form of metarepresentation is the same as the fourth-order (or anyway, multi-layered) metapresentation that elsewhere RT claims to be essential to communication. This seems at odds with the following passage:

> Sperber (1994) discusses three increasingly sophisticated strategies, each requiring *an extra layer of metarepresentation*, which might correspond to stages in pragmatic development. (Wilson 2000: 137; my emphasis)

As far as I can tell, the suggestion is that naïve optimism is a less sophisticated strategy of comprehension also with regard to the layers of metarepresentation involved. In the same vein, Sperber (2000: 133) speaks of the "relatively unsophisticated" metarepresentational abilities of children in a passage where he contrasts the Gricean view of communication, involving complex metarepresentations, with the interpretation process described by RT. Thus, one is tempted to conclude that RT is exploring a weaker view of communicative intentions, which does not imply fourth-order metarepresentations.

Let me summarize. Relevance theorists focus their attention on what makes comprehension special – and therefore in need of domain-specific mechanisms – with respect to general mindreading. In their arguments to this effect, a modular strategy of explanation is presupposed. However the modularity thesis, if I am right, has to face the problem of implementation: given the basic associative functioning of the brain, it is not clear that domain-specificity can be defended except in a trivial sense. Moreover, the modular strategy of explanation encourages RT to leave unaddressed the issue of how comprehension and mindreading interact, and specifically how their operations are segregated from associative activation. Finally, one main argument intended to show that comprehension is special – the argument from metarepresentationl complexity – is itself disputable: there is little evidence in its favour, and it is not even clear that relevance theorists are coherent on that issue.

These conclusions are essentially confirmed if we consider another argument that relevance theorists provide for the claim that comprehension is special (see Wilson 2000; Sperber and Wilson 2002). According to them, a specific module for communication would be needed since communicative intentions are especially difficult to identify, for two related reasons: they are not directly accessible in the environment, and they are hard to predict. In fact, the argument goes, while many (non-communicative) actions have a goal which is directly accessible through perception, the goal of a communicative act is instead the modification of the addressee's mental state, therefore something that cannot be seen and does not even exist until comprehension occurs. Besides, non-communicative actions are rather easy to re-identify and comprehend, since they are quite regular and practically constrained, which would not be the case with communicative actions:

> Leaving stereotypical utterances aside, the prior probability of most utterances ever occurring is close to zero, as Chomsky pointed out long ago. Semantically, the complexity of ordinary intentions is limited by the range of possible actions, which is in turn constrained by many practicalities. There are no such limitations on the semantic complexity of speakers' meanings. Quite simply, we can say so much more than we can do. (Sperber and Wilson 2002: 11)

As in many other occasions, what relevance theorists provide here is a very interesting high-level description of certain aspects of cognition. The issue is whether such high-level descriptions can be directly translated into hypotheses about concrete mechanisms of implementation. Specifically, I maintain, there is a quantum leap from the above considerations to the conclusion that there exists a module for comprehension which is distinct from other modules for general mindreading. As far as I can tell, the main lesson to be drawn from the above considerations is, rather, that comprehension is a complex cognitive activity, which depends on the one hand on goal recognition and, on the other, on linguistic knowledge.

Significantly, the authors distinguish comprehension and general mindreading due to their respective "*semantic* complexity". And most of all, their argument is a reformulation of Chomsky's argument for syntactic unpredictability of utterances. And in fact, one obvious reason why speaker's meanings are so difficult to predict is because of the combinability of linguistic items, and their respective concepts, into an indefinite number of sentences and propositions. Zufferey (2010: 23) summarizes this special difficulty for mindreading in communication by saying that "the hearer should have a very precise idea beforehand of what the speaker might have wanted to communicate", since mindreading requires the attribution of such an intention to the speaker. But the point is that, luckily, in communication the speaker may provide very rich evidence about her communicative intention, thanks to the production of appropriately complex utterances. On the other hand, the context usually provides information about the goals in which the speaker's communicative intention is embedded as a sub-goal: for example (see above § 1.11), a fire may suggest that the agent intends to ask for a hydrant, and a yes/no question may suggest that the speaker intends to provide an affirmative or a negative answer to it. So there is a sense, after all, in which communicative intentions can be perceived in, and thus predicted by, contexts. Also, there is a variety of general expectations about the possible communicative goals, be they related to specific speakers, to categories of them, or to social scenarios (for one trivial example, consider small talk on the train).

To repeat, Sperber and Wilsons's considerations call our attention to the fact that comprehension is a complex affair, which depends both on linguistic processing and on intention understanding. In itself, this is far from implying modularism. On the contrary, what is suggested by the flexible exchange of information between language processing and intention understanding is the need for some non-encapsulated mechanism. I proposed that this mechanism is, in brief, associative activation of information which is schematically and hierarchically organized, both within and between domains. And I also proposed that, if this is the case, then modularism is either trivial (if one is content with the idea that domain-specific bodies of knowledge are processed by one single basic mechanism) or untenable (if one sticks to the idea that there is a variety of domain-specific processes at the implementation level).

As it should be clear, my general view is that RT is not entirely convincing in its attempt at distancing from Grice and, in general, from high-level descriptions of comprehension. In my opinion, in order to specify the actual cognitive mechanisms at play, a close consideration of the associative dynamic of our brain is a better guide than modularism.

This notwithstanding, relevance theorists and I share a couple of important presuppositions. First of all, since they do not deny the rational, personal-level dimension of comprehension, but only propose to account for it in cognitive terms, the presupposition is made that there must be some structural correspondence between the two domains. This is not entirely uncontroversial, and in fact the idea of a correspondence has been questioned either by the normative side ("no cognitive explanation can account for pragmatics as a rational domain") or by the cognitive one ("rational descriptions set an implausibly high standard"). We may call this view – according to which the rational-normative level of description is outside the reach of cognitive explanations – the "divorce view" of pragmatics and cognition.

On the other hand, both relevance theorists and I think that, although the correspondence between rational-normative and cognitive levels is not entirely lacking, it is not perfect either. There is something right in the claim that high-level descriptions in the style of Grice may lead us astray in cognitive explanations. In this respect, however, my view is perhaps more radical than RT, insofar as I think it advisable to go deep into the basic mechanisms of the brain.

In sum, I definitely agree with RT about the inferential nature of comprehension – which is, to that extent, a rational capacity. And I also agree that this capacity must be accounted for in plausible cognitive terms, which probably imply largely automatic processing, and mutual adjustment via both forward and backward inferences. I do not think, however, that the processing is *entirely* automatic, and I think that it is basically associative. This raises the issue of clarifying how an associative account of comprehension can accommodate rationality. I already provided this clarification, at least in part, by proposing that encoded schemata ensure motivated – and nevertheless, associative – transitions between representations. But much more can, and must, be said about this issue, if not for other reasons because my proposal needs to be more closely compared to (and defended from) alternative approaches in pragmatics.

This issue – that is, the relation between the rational-normative and the cognitive levels of explanation in pragmatics – is the main focus of the next, final chapter.

5 Rational and cognitive: an opposition?

5.1 Introduction

Does speaking involve rational abilities? We began this book by saying that Grice has laid the foundations of an inferential – and in this sense, rationality-based – theory of communication. According to this view, speakers have communicative intentions that normally exceed the meanings conventionally conveyed by utterances, and addressees have to recover those meanings by means of inferential derivations. Such inferential derivations by which a speaker means or implies one thing by saying something else – and that the addressee has to recover – are called by Grice "implicatures".

As every student of pragmatics knows, Grice has proposed a very analytic "working-out" schema for the derivation of conversational implicatures:

> He said that P; he could not have done this unless he thought that Q; he knows (and knows that I know that he knows) that I will realise that it is necessary to suppose that Q; he has done nothing to stop me thinking that Q; so he intends me to think, or is at least willing for me to think, that Q. (Grice 1989: 30–31)

The schema suggests that conversational implicatures are indeed quite complex arguments. As opposed to conventional implicatures, they are in fact the *prototypical* implicatures, that is, the ones in which what is meant by the speaker is presumed to be not just decoded, or somehow recalled, but properly inferred or "calculated".[51] Or, more precisely, according to Grice what is meant is "calculable": Saul (2010) has appropriately called "Calculability Criterion" the following characterization of how conversational implicatures are to be distinguished from conventional ones.

---

51 As a matter of fact, as noted by Sbisà (2006: 234), Grice never provided an explicit definition for implicatures in general, he only gave the following definition for *conversational* ones (Grice 1989: 30): "A man who, by saying (or making as if to say) that p has implicated that q, may be said to have conversationally implicated that q, provided that (1) he is to be presumed to be observing the conversational maxims, or at least the Cooperative Principle; (2) the supposition that he is aware that, or thinks that, q is required in order to make his saying or making as if to say p consistent with this presumption; and (3) the speaker thinks (and would expect the hearer to think that the speaker thinks) that it is within the competence of the hearer to work out, or grasp intuitively, that the supposition mentioned in (2) is required". Sbisà (2006: 237) also observes: "It is harder to tell whether or to what extent Grice would also count conventional implicature as something rational".

https://doi.org/10.1515/9781501507731-006

> The presence of a conversational implicature must be capable of being worked out; for even if it can in fact be intuitively grasped, unless the intuition is replaceable by an argument, the implicature (if present at all) will not count as a conversational implicature; it will be a conventional implicature. (Grice 1989: 31)

In this quotation we can see all the complexity of Grice's inferential view of comprehension, specifically with regard to the tension between the normative and the cognitive levels of description. On the one hand, the essential defining feature of conversational implicatures appears to be the possibility to provide a rational argument that justifies the attribution of a certain communicative intention. On the other hand, Grice makes it explicit that in fact the addressee may not have actually had any (complete, explicit) argument in his mind. Conversational implicatures may be only "intuitively grasped", although "the intuition [must be] replaceable by an argument". This means that what is taken to be the defining feature of conversational implicatures does not prima facie concern the way in which these are actually obtained (i.e., cognitively processed). This is why Saul calls it the "Calcula*bility* Criterion": as Sbisà (2006: 239; her emphasis) noted, "calcula*bility* is not actual calculation".

There is here the potential for a great variety of different stances and for recurrent debates in the pragmatic tradition stemming from Grice. The general point is well summarized by Warner (2001: x; his emphasis) as follows:

> The problem, of course, is that people hardly ever reason this way when communicating. You did not reason in any such way when you read [a certain] sentence [S]. You read the sentence and understood – straightaway, without any intervening reasoning, without, indeed, thinking about it at all. So, what is the relation between the reasoning you *might* have engaged in and your understanding the sentence? How is there any explanatory power in the fact that, although you reached your understanding of the sentence *in some other way*, you *might* have reasoned your way to such an understanding? The question is critical for Grice's theory of meaning. [...] This facet of [Grice's] methodology was often noted and discussed at Berkeley during the 1970s. The worry was, of course, that people do not really reason explicitly in the way Grice would imagine. Once, when he was taken to task for this, he replied (with some exasperation), "But there must be a rational explanation!". He was committed to seeing persons as rational agents, and to seeing rational agency as, at least in part, revealed by explicit derivations of rational justifications for attitudes and actions.

Yes, this is, indeed, the point: "what is the relation between the reasoning you might have engaged in and your understanding of the sentence?". And, "how is there any explanatory power in the fact that although you reached your understanding of the sentence *in some other way*, you *might* have reasoned your way to such an understanding?".

Due to the tension that is inherent in the Calculability Criterion, the debate is bound to swing back and forth between two extremes. To be more precise, there are two ways in which the dichotomy can be formulated, and therefore two different theoretical issues at play.

First, there is the dichotomy between strict normativity and cognitive accounts. On the one hand, one may adopt the bare idea of post hoc "replaceability by an argument" (Sbisà 2006: 244) as sufficient in itself to characterize inferential comprehension, without any concern for the actual cognitive processes involved. In this perspective, rational reconstructions of conversational implicatures are presumed to have little to say about the online processing of implicatures. This is what I call the "divorce view" of (normative) pragmatics and cognition. On the other hand, one may assume that what Grice provides us with, when he formulates the calculability criterion, is (in one way or another) also a characterization of the actual cognitive processes. Let us call this the "isomorphism view".

Second, in the perspective of the isomorphism view, there is a further dichotomy to be considered. Since the ability to provide justifications for conversational implicatures lies at the conscious, personal level, it is possible to interpret the calculability criterion in the sense that consciousness and personal-level access are essential features of actual pragmatic processing (remember the notion of secondary pragmatic processes in Recanati). But it is also possible to keep apart, for this respect, actual processing and conscious rational reconstructions, even in case you adopt the isomorphism view. You may claim in fact that, although actual processing mirrors rational reconstructions for other respects (it is an inferential, rational affair), it is not conscious nevertheless (this it the position of RT).

In its general lines, my approach should already be clear. As to the first dichotomy, I adopt the isomorphism view. As to the second one, I claim that it is badly formulated: specifically, I reject the idea that, in order to account for pragmatic inferences, there is no third option between conscious reasoning and purely automatic processing. In what follows, I intend to address this set of issues, capitalizing on my previous proposals but also assessing them in the light of questions raised by the literature on rationality in pragmatic processing. In practice, I will first analyse the divorce view and provide arguments for the isomorphism view (§§ 5.2–5.3). Then I will consider the extent to which isomorphism holds (§§ 5.4 to 5.6).

More specifically, I will ask: which arguments have been provided for the divorce view, and against the thesis that the processes involved in comprehension mirror the structure of rational reconstructions? Do we have persuasive counter-arguments? And, in any case, do the arguments for the divorce view have something to teach us about the nature of actual pragmatic processing (as differing from rational reconstructions)? I will answer both the second and the third question in the affirmative. As I will try to show, there are good reasons to assume a structural isomorphism between conscious reasoning and actual pragmatic comprehension, and even reasons to think that this was Grice's own idea. On the other hand, I think it fair – and useful – to acknowledge that, in spite of that isomorphism, we may occasionally find actual processing wanting with respect to standards of rationality. And it is worthy of further investigation, also in a cognitive perspective, the suggestion that full standards of rationality require consciousness.

In general, the issue of automaticity and control in processing is key to the questions addressed in this chapter.

To start with, there is the fact that, compatibly with my view, conscious accessibility may serve as a criterion of demarcation in a sense that is not far from Grice's. He conceives conversational implicatures as genuine inferences insofar as they can be consciously recovered when needed. This intuition is straightforwardly translated by Recanati (2004) into the thesis that consciousness is a necessary feature of (pragmatic) inferences, even if only in a dispositional sense. I have argued that, under a certain interpretation, his thesis is inconsistent (a process is said to be conscious because of the fact that it might have been substituted for by a conscious one!), although it has the merit to suggest the need for an intermediate notion between entirely conscious and entirely unconscious processing. In fact, I have claimed that pragmatic inferences normally involve conscious attention – which is something less than conscious reasoning. But, interestingly, this is not incompatible with the claim that Recanati's view specifies a minimal condition for having inferences (be they pragmatic or not). This is because the dispositional property of being accessible to consciousness can be held to intrude into the very notion of inference. Conscious access*ibility* (but not necessarily actual conscious access, be it in the form of conscious attention or conscious reasoning) provides the minimum threshold, under which automatic associative activation does not support inferences at all (except in a loose, and probably metaphorical, sense). The basic idea is that there are conceptual (propositional) contents only to the extent that the representations at issue are consciously accessible. And conceptual contents can be taken to license inferences even by means of *automatic* associative activation – although they license inferences in a stronger sense when conscious attention is involved, and in an even stronger one when conscious reasoning is at play.

This is important for my view, in that I assume that associative activation of neural patterns is sufficient to produce inferences, due to the schematic structure of our representations. And this assumption potentially exposes me to a very undesirable consequence, which is that any transition between patterns of activation in the brain counts as an inference. As I hope to show, a quite natural way to avoid this consequence is to adopt conscious accessibility as a demarcation criterion between the transitions that are inferences in a reasonably strict sense and the ones that are not.

This hypothesis will be part of a more general picture, by which I sketch an answer to a problem which traces back to Hume and Kant: the problem of predication, that is, how associations might account for the propositional integration of our representations. There is an intrinsic relation between our faculties of being rational on the one hand, and being able of propositional integration of contents on the other. What I will provide is a sort of "ladder of (propositional) integration and inference": associative activation allows for different kinds of integration, and these in turn account for progressively more demanding notions of "inference" – ranging from transitions between mental contents that are conscious access*ible*, to transitions that are actually performed with the help of conscious attention, then to transitions that are performed in the form of fully conscious reasoning.

In the light of the above considerations, the fact that pragmatic processes allow for rational reconstructions is no coincidence. These processes involve schematic (i.e., inferential) representation structures, which are in principle consciously accessible, and that as a matter of fact are also, in normal cases, consciously attended – in the sense that some of their components are in the focus of consciousness. When needed, the key premises and conclusions of the involved inferential structures can be made entirely explicit by conscious reasoning. In this sense, I submit, there is substantial isomorphism between actual pragmatic processes and their rational reconstructions.

On the other hand, I will consider two aspects for which isomorphism fails.

In the first place, the notion of (conversational) implicature seems to be based on a sharp distinction between implicatures and lexical access. But this might be just a rough simplification of the actual cognitive processing. Let me explain.

I proposed (in chapter 3) that between automaticity and control there is not a simple opposition. On the contrary, there is a continuum,[52] where the two mix in different proportions – while entirely automatic and entirely conscious processes are little more than pure virtualities. But I intend to show that the idea of such a continuum is also implicitly present in Grice's model and in the tradition stemming from it. Conventional meanings, conventional implicatures, generalized and particularized conversational implicatures, may be thought, at a first approximation, as rungs of a ladder that extends from a maximum of automaticity to a maximum of control. Although the consensus is that even (spontaneous) particularized conversational implicatures

52 But see the qualification at fn. 34, § 3.6.

are definitely *not* cases of conscious reasoning, it is not entirely inaccurate to say that they are closer to personal-level, conscious reasoning than any of the previous rungs of the ladder: they seem to be manifestations of something very similar to a personal-level project or plan. At the other extreme, the recall of conventional meaning appears to be sub-personal and merely causal in a rather clear sense – it is something that (normally) occurs to speakers and hearers in an automatic fashion.

But, I will argue, the idea of a continuum is, in the end, a better guide than the metaphor of the ladder. The rungs of the ladder are not exactly rungs; rather, there is something like a continuous transition between certain reference points. This consideration affects the very notion of implicature. The point is that, since implicatures can be more or less conventionalised, the distinction between lexical meaning and implicature tends to become somewhat blurred. As I will argue, lexicalisation (or conventionalisation) comes in degrees, and it seems to depend on a complex interaction between a number of factors. I will consider two specific cases to this effect: the case of generalized conversational implicatures (with scalar implicatures as a special case), and that of implicated politeness. Especially in the first case, there is a lively debate also involving significant experimental effort. But the existence of a sharp and quite general distinction between lexical meaning and implicature is mainly assumed as obvious. The debate seems still swayed by Grice's assumption that linguistic forms must possibly have one single lexical meaning, with little consideration of how repeated use (and the consequent conventionalisation) of implicatures can be expected to affect meaning. Looking at these issues from the perspective of the implementation in associative networks may help us to shed a new light on the probabilistic and nuanced nature of both implicatures and lexical meanings.

Finally, there is a second aspect for which isomorphism fails, which is well described by Sperber and Wilson (2015) in terms of the notion of "impression" we presented above (§ 2.13; see also Sperber and Wilson 1995: 59). When we look at how inferences can be implemented by a concrete biological substrate – constituted by associative networks through which waves of activation travel – it becomes clear that they cannot *prima facie* be described in terms of standard logical derivations, constituted by successive steps in a linear sequence. They are better described in terms of competition between alternative conclusions, whose result is determined by a hardly determinable number of changes in the system's pattern of activation. This means that rational reconstructions can only be rough simplifications of what really happens in actual processing of conversational implicatures – although, as I will claim, this simplification has an important role to play in our mental life.

5.2 Divorce or isomorphism? The normativity issue

One way to interpret the calculability criterion is as follows: the spontaneous process of comprehension admits of a rational reconstruction (it "is replaceable by an argument") but this – both in Grice's mind and objectively – does not impose any specific constraint on its actual functioning. In Sbisà's (2006: 246) words:

> in cognitively oriented approaches to linguistic communication, it should no longer be taken for granted that the processes actually leading to comprehension mirror the rational justifications we may give for our understanding of an utterance or text.

In general terms, what is at stake is

> whether the Gricean inferential path for the calculation of a conversational implicature is meant to have the nature of an actual psychological process [...] or that of some kind of abstract, logical model giving the grounds for the recognition of the implicature as conversational. (Sbisà 2006: 238)

In sum, under a certain interpretation of the criterion, the inferential structure that is integral to rational reconstructions of conversational implicatures has not to be present (and presumably *is not present*) in spontaneous pragmatic processing. As a consequence, Grice cannot be blamed for the psychologically unrealistic aspects of its account of comprehension: this kind of criticisms arises from a fatal misconception of his actual purpose. Specifically, according to Saul (2002a: 347), "Relevance theorists [in their criticisms to Grice] systematically misunderstand Grice by taking him to be engaged in the same project that they are: making sense of the psychological processes by which we interpret utterances".

The argument provided by Saul (2002a, 2002b) to this effect is based on the consideration that "Grice's characterizations of speaker meaning and conversational implicatures are cast in very different terms–the former completely in terms of speaker intentions and the latter incorporating a good deal about the audience" (Saul 2002a: 229). As a consequence, the notion of conversational implicature would lend itself to a normative account where what does really matter is the fact that the speaker *makes available* a certain thought to the audience, independently of the actual speaker's intentions. This has not to be understood, however, as if the audience rather than the utterer were responsible for implicatures. In fact, Saul thinks that neither "utterer implicature" (what the speaker has tried to implicate) nor "audience implicature" (what the audience takes to be implicated) in themselves may determine conversational implicature, which is "a more normative notion than utterer&audience implicature" (idem: 244).

In sum, the content "made available" by an utterance in a context may diverge from both what the utterer actually had in mind to convey, and what the audience actually thinks that the utterer had in mind to convey. Seen from the perspective of the hearer, this amounts to saying that rational reconstructions put a normative constraint on comprehension that is not compatible with a scientific (psychological) description:

> Actual hearers make every kind of mistakes. But of course, it must be possible to determine what implicature a certain utterance (in a certain context) should be recognized to carry, independently of whether actual hearers manage to derive the implicature. Were it not so, it would be impossible to distinguish correct from incorrect implicature comprehension. If, instead, we take into consideration only those hearers who succeed in grasping the implicature, we implicitly introduce a normative criterion. Hearers who understand well approximate ideal, "rational" hearers. So claims about how conversational implicature is derived are in fact claims about how hearers approximating ideal rational hearers derive it, and *therefore, are deprived of any empirical character*. They are claims about how the implicature should be derived. (Sbisà 2006: 239; emphasis mine)

To this line of reasoning inspired by Saul (2002a, 2002b), Sbisà (2006) adds a further argument based on the distinction between two notions of rationality that would be of unequal importance in Grice's theory of implicature. One is what she calls "instrumental rationality", which is defined as follows:

> A course of behavior is rational if it is characterized by the agent's non-accidental use of effective means, or of means believed to be effective, for achieving his or her goals. (idem: 241)

The other notion, called "argumentative rationality", is extracted from Grice's posthumous writings on rationality and value, and its definition is the following:

> Rationality is a concern that one's moves are justified and a capacity (to some degree) to give effect to that concern. (idem: 242)

Now, the claim is that instrumental rationality does not require any involvement of our personal-level ability to provide reasons and arguments; it only requires an automatic ability to appropriately match means and ends. As such, this notion allows for accounts of comprehension that are both psychologically plausible and rational in that minimal sense: "Under the instrumental conception, sub-conscious mental processes can nevertheless count as rational, if they succeed in providing efficient and economic means to the given ends" (idem: 242).

However, according to Sbisà, this notion is not at the core of Grice's theory of conversational implicature. What Grice cherished was a quite different theoretical project, that is, the project to ground comprehension in a wider understanding of rationality as a personal-level value. This is why it is so important to draw a sharp distinction between mere instrumental and truly argumentative, personal-level, rationality:

> That such a distinction should be drawn [...] is strongly suggested by the comparative consideration of the two conceptions. Instrumental rationality [...] does not presuppose self-awareness, while concern for justification does. Instrumental rationality bears no relationship to values, or rather, has effectiveness as its only value, so that it is of value only derivatively, while argumentative rationality may be claimed to be itself a value. Finally, instrumental rationality cannot raise questions about goals, except insofar as they are the means for other goals. That is a main source of dissatisfaction with instrumental rationality, which argumentative rationality may prove able to cope with. So we can safely enough admit that, within Grice's thought but also beyond it, a distinction between argumentative and instrumental rationality is not otiose. (idem: 245)

Now, in my opinion the distinction is indeed interesting and important. And I am also convinced that Grice, especially in certain periods of his life, has been strongly engaged in the project of grounding communication in argumentative rationality and values. But none of this, I submit, speaks in favour of the divorce view. The crucial point is whether the differences invoked by Sbisà actually prevent isomorphism between spontaneous comprehension and rational reconstructions.

For one thing, of course "instrumental rationality [...] does not presuppose self-awareness, while concern for justification does". But why should this difference imply that rational reconstructions say nothing about the structure of spontaneous comprehension? On the isomorphism view, the reason why we can provide conscious inferential reconstructions of spontaneous comprehension is precisely that the latter *actually has* an inferential structure. This is, at the very least, a logical possibility. So, unless Sbisà can show that the above difference bars the way to isomorphism, she is simply begging the question.

What about the other differences, and specifically the fact that instrumental rationality is only interested in effectiveness of means-end relations, while argumentative rationality is interested in the intrinsic value of ends? We should not forget that what is at issue are conversational implicatures and their rational reconstructions, and these properly concern effective inferences from means (utterances) to ends (implicated communicative intentions), irrespective of considerations of value about the ends. Although one may concede that conscious reconstructions also allow for explicit considerations of value, this is a different issue (to which Grice turned his attention in later years).

In other words, the argument seems to be that rational reconstructions have little to say about spontaneous comprehension because, while the latter only concerns means-end structures, the former concern instead the intrinsic value of ends. But this is clearly not the case: I know of no rational reconstruction of conversational implicatures in which the intrinsic value of ends, not the means-end structure, is focussed.

On the other hand, even on general conceptual grounds, it is not clear why Grice's concern in intrinsic values should speak against his interest in means-end considerations – in other words, why these interests should be part of two different explanatory projects.[53] Assessing the intrinsic value of ends would be of no use for subjects who are not able to manage means-end chains. In this sense, instrumental rationality (of which conversational implicatures are just a special case) is integral to argumentative rationality, and everyone who cherishes the latter should, for exactly the same reasons, appreciate the importance of the former as well.

Finally, even on textual grounds there are reasons to think that Grice had a specific interest in instrumental rationality. This is made apparent by our previous quotations from Grice (see especially § 1.3 and 1.11), in which mention of the "purposes" of communication (and the surrounding actions) is incessant. Allott (2005: 235) observes that "for Grice, reasoning was essentially activity in pursuit of a goal", and in this vein he quotes Warner (2001: xxx): "Grice emphasizes that reasoning is a goal-directed activity: we engage in reasoning with (typically at least) the intention of producing reasons relevant to some end in view". In all these cases, no mention of the ends' value is made; only the effective pursuit of purposes is considered.

In sum, the distinction between instrumental and argumentative rationality, and the differences between the two, does not seem to justify the divorce view. Quite on the contrary, on both logical and textual grounds, Grice's calculability criterion is best interpreted as follows. In spontaneous comprehension, there are conversational implicatures only if the underlying structure is such that it can be replaced by an argument. This underlying structure is a means-end inference, and therefore a manifestation of instrumental rationality, which can be made explicit by conscious reasoning.

On the other hand, it is of no help for Sbisà to invoke the issue of normativity, by insisting that argumentative rationality lies at a normative (versus psychological) level of description. Argumentative rationality is implemented by a specific cognitive ability, that is, the ability that we called conscious reasoning.

---

53 I am not unaware that, when moral perspectives are at issue, the difference between being concerned in the effectiveness of means-end relations and being concerned in the intrinsic value of ends is paramount. Nevertheless, instrumental and argumentative rationality seems not to imply incompatible perspectives *in the explanation of communication*.

So when we replace spontaneous comprehension with an argument, what we have is in fact a different psychological process, not an abstract norm. That this is the case is shown by the fact that it is possible to be mistaken both in spontaneous comprehension and in rational reconstructions: we have two different processes, both subject to norms.

This said, the issue of normativity raised by Saul is still left open. We have only argued that one cannot contrast (the explanatory project based on) argumentative rationality and (the one based on) spontaneous comprehension with the argument that the former, but not the latter, has a normative dimension: actually, both are subject to norms. But then, we can nevertheless ask – as Saul invites us to do – whether being interested in conversational implicatures *as norms* (applying to both spontaneous comprehension and rational reconstructions) underlies a different theoretical project from being interested in their psychological processing.

I think that this claim does not hold either. The reason is that, contrary to what is suggested, the norms at issue are not of the kind that cannot be part of empirical descriptions or explanations. For one example, norms that allow for deviations are standard in biological descriptions. If one, for instance, has to describe the (normal) way of locomotion of a given species, she will not consider a variety of possible abnormal cases (e.g., wounded or genetically deviant individuals). One might object that, in contrast with locomotion, in the case of conversational implicatures the norms at stake have to do with arguments and reasons, not with mere causes. In this perspective, Saul's argument might be seen as a variant of a Frege-style anti-psychologist argument: being interested in the validity of reasons has little to do with being interested in how people actually reason.

But it is hard to believe that Grice's project is correctly characterized in those terms and, even if that were the case, it is far from evident that the divorce view would be vindicated anyway.

First of all, it is important to note that Saul has to tailor quite unusual examples in order to make her case. For instance, she modifies the well-known Grice's example of a reference-letter by which a professor, without saying it, wants the addressee to understand that a certain student should not be hired as a philosopher. In Saul's version, unbeknownst to the professor the student is applying instead for a job as a typist. So, when the professor writes that the student is talented as a typist, the actual conversational implicature is not the one he intends to communicate – that the student should not be hired as a philosopher – but instead the one that is made available in context – that the student should be hired as a typist.

Now the point is that, although (as Saul shows) many examples of this kind may be constructed, *these are not the sort of examples that Grice had in mind (and actually used)* – and for good reasons. Grice's aim was to analyse communication, not miscommunication. And he was deeply convinced that communication, in the normal case, is a manifestation of rationality. Let me repeat part of the previous quotation from Warner (2001: x):

> The problem [...] is that people hardly ever reason this way when communicating. [...] The worry was, of course, that people do not really reason explicitly in the way Grice would imagine. Once, when he was taken to task for this, he replied (with some exasperation), "But there must be a rational explanation!". He was committed to seeing persons as rational agents, and to seeing rational agency as, at least in part, revealed by explicit derivations of rational justifications for attitudes and actions.

It is thus wrong to suggest that Grice was interested in abstract norms of rationality, as in the Fregean project of addressing the pure laws of reasoning. Grice was interested, instead, in the fact that communication *actually is* a rational enterprise, and communicators *actually are* rational in the normal case. This claim has two components. First, as we already know, it has to do with the fact that the relation between what is said and what is meant (or between explicit and implicit meaning) has the structure of an inference. But, second, the specific inferences performed by speakers and hearers are, in normal cases, justified in (and by the) context. Not only is this clearly what Grice had in mind; but also, there are strong reasons to think that this is the case. Human inferential communication – with its coordination between speakers and hearers – could not even exist if most of the times speakers did not provide, and hearers did not recover, conversational implicatures that are *justified by the context.*[54] More analytically, a speaker would have no reason to convey a conversational implicature in a context unless that is the implicature the hearer can normally be expected to draw (otherwise, the speaker would not be understood); and the hearer would have no reason to draw a conversational implicature in a context unless that is the implicature the speaker can normally be expected to convey. But the reason why, in a given context, the speaker can normally expect the hearer to draw a certain implicature, and the hearer can normally expect the speaker to convey the very same implicature, is that *that is the implicature justified by the context*.

In sum, if we take conversational implicatures to be subject to norms in the sense that they are justified by contexts, then in normal cases communicators actually conform to such norms. It is, therefore, not right to suggest that Grice was interested

---

54 I am focussing here on context because this is the factor of interest in Saul's example. However, conversational implicatures are also justified or not with respect to linguistic and world knowledge. In general terms, the point is that the inferential structures constructed by communicators are most of the times consistent with the mutually available information.

in the normative dimension of rationality *instead of* the psychological dimension of actual comprehension. Grice thought – and he was presumably right to think – that actual comprehension normally conforms to standards of rationality. In slightly different terms, we should not contrast the normative domain of reasons with the psychological domain of causes.[55] As a matter of fact, Grice did not contrast the former with the latter: "in some sense of 'reason' the recognition of the intention behind [an utterance] x is for the audience a reason *and not merely a cause*" (Grice 1957: 385; my emphasis). In Allott's (2005: 221) words, for Grice "the utterance is both a reason for the hearer to think that the speaker believes some proposition p and a cause of the hearer's coming to think that".

To sum up, in this section I have considered the divorce view from the side of normativity and rationality. Grice has been accused of providing a psychologically unrealistic account of actual comprehension. According to Saul and Sbisà among others, however, the objection misses the target in that Grice did not even intend to provide such an account; he was concerned instead with a different, normative project. I have analysed the relevant notions of rationality and normativity and argued that they are entirely compatible with the project of accounting for actual comprehension. In Grice's opinion, the structure of rational reconstructions reveals the underlying, rational structure of spontaneous comprehension.

Though not purely exegetical, this conclusion was nevertheless based on arguments somehow internal to Grice's philosophical perspective. In the next section I will consider the opposition between divorce and isomorphism views from the perspective of cognitively oriented approaches. In other words, while up to now we have considered conceptual reasons for thinking that actual comprehension mirrors the structure of rational reconstructions (and specifically, that actual comprehension has a means-end structure that is normally justified with respect to contexts), in the next section we will consider more closely *how* this is to be accounted for in terms of cognitive processing. This will allow us to go deeper into the associative view of inferences that I have presented so far.

5.3 Divorce or isomorphism? The cognitive issue

The psychological reality of Grice's account of comprehension has been recently discussed in Geurts and Rubio-Fernández (2015) – which is mainly focussed on the role of mindreading in comprehension. Their line of reasoning formally

55 The alleged opposition between causes and reasons with regard to performing inferences is addressed in some more detail in Mazzone (submitted).

parallels the argumentative structure of normative approaches. In fact, the authors observe that "one of the standard objections against the Gricean approach is that it makes communication impossibly hard from a psychological point of view" (idem: 450). But, in their opinion, this objection is ill-directed since "Gricean pragmatics is not concerned with the psychological processes" involved in comprehension (idem: 449). In sum, as in normative approaches a sharp distinction is drawn between two domains, with the implication that the description of one of them is not expected to reveal anything decisive about the functioning of the other. But, differently from normative approaches, the distinction is here conceived as internal to the cognitive domain. In practice, Geurts and Rubio-Fernández appeal to the general framework provided by Marr for describing computational systems, and specifically to his distinction between computational and algorithmic levels of description – although they find those labels potentially confusing and prefer to speak of W- and H- levels, which respectively stand for *what/why* and *how*.

The aspect under which Grice's account appears "impossibly hard from a psychological point of view" is well summarized, according to the authors, by the following passage of Wilson (2000: 415–6; my emphases):

> Grice seems to have thought of the attribution of meaning as involving a form of *conscious, discursive reasoning* [...]. It is hard to imagine even adults going through such *lengthy chains of inference* in the attribution of speaker meanings.

Now, Geurts and Rubio-Fernández' claim is that such complex descriptions at the W-level must not imply a comparable complexity at the H-level. This does not mean, however, that the authors indiscriminately adopt the divorce view. On the contrary, in their opinion "it is not unreasonable to expect that, to some degree at least, a process model will mirror the corresponding W-level description" (idem: 458). Their overall view can thus be summarized as follows:

> We have seen that, in principle, a W-level theory and its H-level counterpart need not constrain each other very strongly, but we have also advocated the view that, in fact, pragmatics and processing are coupled relatively tightly. In particular, we have argued that propositional attitudes and their representations figure essentially on the W- and H-levels, respectively. (Geurts and Rubio-Fernández 2015: 467)

In the philosophical tradition, mental states are conceived in terms of propositional attitudes, that is, general attitudes (beliefs, desires, intentions and so on) which apply to specific contents expressed by propositions: for one example, a subject S may have the propositional attitude expressible as "S believes that p". Now, when the authors claim that, in comprehension, propositional attitudes figure at the W-level and their representations at the H-level, it is quite clear that they assume those levels to have a common structure. On the other hand, spontaneous comprehension as described at the H-level is (relatively) automatic and effortless; as such, it must not have the same complexity of conscious processing. Thus, their conclusion is that the kind of mindreading involved in comprehension does not require conscious effort, but it can nevertheless count as genuine mindreading to the extent that it involves representation of propositional attitudes: to this effect, it is *structure* what really matters.

In a similar vein, Allott (2005) argues that between the structure of rational reconstructions and that of spontaneous comprehension there is "more than a parallel: for Grice, arriving intuitively at a conversational implicature is an instance of reasoning" (Allott 2005: 228). Allott quotes a passage from Grice (2001) where a distinction is drawn between a hard and a quick way of reasoning, both of which allow for "inferential moves": "We have [...] a 'hard way' of making inferential moves: [a] laborious, step-by-step procedure [which] consumes time and energy [...]. A substitute for the hard way, the quick way, [...] made possible by habituation and intention, is [also] available to us" (Grice 2001: 17). What makes the quick way a case of reasoning, too, is precisely the fact that it involves inferential moves: that is, it shares the structure with hard reasoning, even if the former is automatic and the latter conscious. Thus, Allott draws the following conclusion, which he assumes to be "congruent with work in cognitive sciences": "what makes pragmatic interpretation count as reasoning is that it involves (perhaps tacit) mental representation *of steps that constitute an argument*" (idem: 230; my emphasis).

These views are substantially consistent with the approach I have proposed so far. In my approach, spontaneous comprehension and conscious reconstructions have the same structure in that both depend on the schematic organization of memory. In general, associative activation permits inferences to be drawn, either in the automatic or in the conscious way, thanks to the bottom-up/top-down dynamic described above. This approach also applies to mindreading, since, I submit, the attribution of mental states is dependent on mental concepts that can be identified with schemata.[56]

This said, Allott raises an issue that seriously calls into question my approach, and whose consideration permits to shed light on the notion of inference adopted.

56 An important difference with Allott (2005) is that his explanation for the rationality of spontaneous comprehension is (at least tentatively) embedded in a modular view: comprehension might be rational, he suggests, because it is a goal-directed activity and these goals "are built in to a pragmatics module by evolution, that is, they are tied up with the function of the pragmatics module" (Allott 2005: 235). I have argued instead that the modularity thesis is untenable unless in a trivial sense that is compatible with my proposal.

The general point is that one should distinguish between genuine inferences and pseudo-inferences, with the latter characterized by the fact that their inputs have "the wrong form to perform inferences on" (idem: 236). To be sure, as noted by Recanati (2004: 41) there exists "a liberal notion of inference in contemporary cognitive science", as in Marr's (1982: 68) claim that "the true heart of visual perception is the inference from the structure of an image about the structure of the real world outside". However, a more restrictive notion of inference is advisable, according to which in order to have a genuine inference there must be a truth-preserving transition from a conceptual representation to a conceptual representation. On the contrary, in Allott's (2005: 236) words,

> the input to the visual system is patches of light on the retina and corresponding activation of rods and cones in the eye, not propositions or proposition schemas. One cannot run *modus ponens* on an activation pattern.

Now, if – as I propose – schemata are identified with patterns in the brain, then any transition mediated by such neural patterns seems to count as an inference. And I agree that this notion of inference is too loose to support the claim that a process is inferential in any interesting sense.

But there is more. My claim that our representations are generally organized in a schematic way, and that this is sufficient to ensure inferences, makes it difficult to draw a boundary between conventional and conversational implicatures – and, more generally, between conventions and reasoning. According to Grice's calculability criterion, what distinguishes the latter is the fact that they can be inferentially reconstructed. But, as I will show, my account of inferences is such that even conventional implicatures can easily be reconstructed in inferential terms.

In sum, we have here two questions: how can we distinguish a) between genuine inferential transitions and mere conventions on the one hand, and b) between genuine inferential transitions and schematic transitions that are not conceptual on the other? I think, however, that the associative account I propose has the resources to answer both questions. Specifically, it allows us to describe different levels of accessibility and integration between representations, accounting for different notions of inference. The core of the proposal has already been explored in § 3.10. Let me repeat it and reframe the above problems in its terms.

When (first case) connections between representations are sufficiently strong and direct, associations alone can make the representations accessible to each other by means of simple spreading activation. For less direct or weaker associations (second case), representations are reciprocally accessible only if contexts contribute further activation: let us call this contextual spreading activation. On the other hand (third case), when associations are significantly indirect or weak, spreading activation (whether simple or contextual) may not be sufficient at all, and conscious attention (with the related sustained activation) is required in order to ensure reciprocal access and integration. Finally, when indirectness is such that not even conscious attention may suffice, conscious reasoning is needed (fourth case): that is, a condition in which each of the related representations and their connections are consciously attended.

Thus, as a first approximation, the four dynamics – simple spreading activation; contextual spreading activation; conscious attention; conscious reasoning – can be thought to form a one-directional scale with regard to their range of accessibility: any of them has a shorter range than the ones at its right, and a longer range than the ones at its left. I take this picture to be correct, except for the following qualification: as we already said, conscious attention is better described as *including* automatic components as well. In other words, it requires cooperation between automatic processing (both simple and contextual spreading activation) and consciousness in a low-effort mode.[57] Most cognitive processes of reasonable complexity can be described as cases of conscious attention thus conceived, while conscious reasoning is a rather costly and rare activity (see, for instance, Kahneman 2011).

Given this picture, there are inferences in the strictest, prototypical sense when all the inferential steps are in the focus of consciousness – which is the fourth case (conscious reasoning). When we provide rational reconstructions in Grice's style, the inferential steps that we make entirely conscious correspond to (at least part of) the inferential structure that was actually involved in spontaneous comprehension. Specifically, the inferential structure that in actual comprehension was under the partial focus of conscious attention must now be addressed by conscious reasoning. I have proposed that this inferential structure is ensured by schemata. The problem is that, under this hypothesis, even conventional implicatures can easily be accounted for in inferential terms. It is sufficient that there is a schema representing the relation between the implicit content and the words conveying it, and this in turn seems to be the case whenever subjects can provide a conscious reconstruction of the implicature. This means that at least students of pragmatics (or linguistics in general), who master that relation and are able to reconstruct it consciously, must have the appropriate schema. And therefore, at least for students of pragmatics, conventional implicatures are no more conventional, after all: since they can be reconstructed consciously,

57 This directional inclusion from left to right in the scale can presumably be generalized: contextual spreading activation includes simple spreading activation as its component, and conscious reasoning includes conscious attention as its component.

they are turned into conversational implicatures. Something seems to have gone wrong here.

In order to overcome this problem, I propose to consider more closely the distinction between the first and the other three cases analysed above – that is, between directly and less directly associated mental contents. One way to intend this distinction is in terms of contents that are, respectively, directly associated versus related through schemata. To be more precise, for the relevant distinction to hold it is not even required that in the former case there are no schemata at all. It is sufficient that, even when a schema is present, there is a direct association between contents that is strong enough to make the schema practically ineffective in normal processing: it is the direct association between content A and content B that accounts for the activation of the latter from the former, while the schema connecting them is actually not involved in the transition. With this qualification, the existence of a schema does not imply inferential processing (i.e., a schematic transition), and therefore the Gricean boundary between conventional and conversational implicatures is safe.[58]

There is, however, the other problem. How can I account for the fact that not every schematic transition between neural patterns should be taken to count as an inference? In my proposal, schemata are representation structures constituted by a certain number of components and their relations, where both the structures and their components are, in the end, nothing but neural patterns. For one example, under the hypothesis of a hierarchical and schematic organization of the entire cortex (see chapter 2, especially §§ 2.8 and 2.9), even vision can be conceived as schematic in this sense. To be sure, some local transitions might involve direct associations instead, in the sense we just specified above; but a major role, in vision as elsewhere, is likely to be played by higher-level patterns prescribing the organization of lower-level ones. To this extent, if any transition that is mediated by a schema counts as an inference, then we are using "inference" in the loose sense that Allott criticized.

However, nothing prevents me from limiting the use of "inference" to cases in which both the schema and its components are concepts, with concepts defined as schemata that are consciously accessible (as I actually suggested in footnote 22). This puts a second, quite natural constraint on what counts as an inference. First,

58 Of course, this argument does not commit me to adopt the highly debated notion of conventional implicature. It may be taken as a conditional argument: if there were conventional implicatures, my approach would allow one to draw the distinction. Since the argument applies to any distinction between conventional and inferential relations, it will be useful when we will turn to the issue of conventionalisation (see below § 5.4).

as I said above, there are no inferences in cases of simple spreading activation mediated by direct associations. Second, there are not even inferences in cases of automatic activation mediated by schemata, unless the transition involves concepts – specifically, the component *A* activates the schema, which in turn activates the component *B*, and all the three elements (the component *A*; the schema; the component *B*) can be accessed consciously. It is important to note that, based on the first constraint, the existence of a schematic and consciously accessible association between *A* and *B* does not imply that every actual transition between *A* and *B* is inferential: in addition, the actual transition must have been mediated by that indirect association, not by a direct one.

In practice, the above picture is compatible with Grice's proposal that "replaceability by an argument" is a *necessary* condition for conversational implicatures, but in my view more than this is required. In order for there to be a conversational implicature, and more generally an inference, it is not sufficient that the relevant transition can be accounted for by a schema which is consciously accessible in each of its steps; it is also required that the transition has actually been mediated by that schema. It is interesting to compare, once again, this proposal with RT and Recanati's view.

According to Recanati, genuine inferences require conscious accessibility, which is conceived as a weak mode of consciousness, intermediate between purely automatic processing and conscious reasoning. In my view, these two aspects must be kept apart. Conscious access*ibility* is a precondition of inferences, in that it is definitional of the kind of things on which inferences can be performed. But the existence of a consciously accessible schematic structure is not sufficient evidence that an inference has occurred, insofar as a direct association might account for the transition instead. In order for there to be an inference, it is required that the indirect, schematic association has actually played a role. Given the fact that schematic associations are indirect, this presumably implies that the process cannot be one of simple spreading activation: at least contextual spreading activation, and possibly conscious attention, must be involved. Thus, apart from conscious accessibility, there are reasons to believe that actual conscious processing is (mostly) involved; but this presupposes the notion of a low-effort mode of conscious processing, that is different from (even dispositional) conscious reasoning.

On the other hand, relevance theorists, in line with their underestimation of consciousness (see above, especially § 4.8), do not impose the condition that (pragmatic) inferences require either conscious accessibility or conscious attention. This is related to their view of concepts. Under the assumption that an inference is a truth-preserving transition from one *conceptual* representation to another, one needs to know what makes a representation conceptual, in the first place. RT's answer is based on the Fodorian view of concepts. Although it is a common assumption in cognitive science that concepts are consciously accessible, Fodor defines them instead as atomic and amodal labels (see § 4.5 above) acting as components of thoughts, with no definitional role assigned to consciousness (in line with what we said in § 4.8, fn. 43). In my view, however, concepts are (at least in part) sensorimotor schematic representations (see §§ 2.7 and, again, 4.5), so the question arises as to whether all sensorimotor schematic representations are concepts. My proposal is instead that they are concepts only insofar as they are accessible to consciousness.

Thus, in my view Grice was importantly right in considering rational reconstructions (and therefore, conscious reasoning) as a necessary condition for the attribution of pragmatic inferences. Not only are rational reconstructions the prototypical cases of inferential processing; but they also ensure that, even when the actual process is not one of conscious reasoning, there is nonetheless a relevant schematic structure that is entirely accessible to consciousness. I take this to be the minimum threshold for there to be inferences, even if the schematic structure is only involved in contextual spreading activation, or in conscious attention. Schematic transitions that are *not* consciously accessible cannot count as genuine cases of inferential processing – at least, not in a sense that is similar enough to conscious reasoning to enable robust generalizations. On the other hand, the calculability criterion leaves only implicit the requirement that the schematic structures appealed to in rational reconstructions have actually played a role in the transition. This qualification is nevertheless crucial, if we want to take the isomorphism view as a serious cognitive claim on actual comprehension. Thus, in my view, rational reconstructions are a test of the conscious accessibility of schemata, but they also convey an implicit assumption that those schemata play a causal role in the actual process. This causal role, I submit, can be described in terms of the bottom-up/top-down dynamic of activation described above, especially in the mode of activation that I called conscious attention.

The above account also allows us to address the issue of what distinguishes inferential from associative processing – in the behavioural sense – in much greater detail than we did before. This can be framed in terms of a traditional problem tracing back to Hume and Kant, known as the problem of predication. A recent formulation, inspired by Fodor (2003), is the following:

> For a pure associationist, association is "semantically transparent" (see Fodor 2003), in that it purports to add no additional structure to thoughts. When a simple concept, *X* and a simple concept *Y*, become associated one acquires the associative structure *X*/*Y*. But *X*/*Y* has no additional structure on top of their contents. Knowing that *X* and *Y* are associated amounts to knowing a causal fact: that activating *X*s will bring about the activation of *Y*s and *vice versa*. However, so the argument goes, some of our thoughts appear to have more

> structure than this: the thought BIRDS FLY predicates the property of flying onto birds. The task for the associationist is to explain how associative structures can distinguish a thinker who has a single (complex) thought BIRDS FLY from a thinker who conjoins two simple thoughts in an associative structure where one thought, BIRDS, is immediately followed by another, FLY. [...] In Fodor's terms the problem boils down to how association, a causal relation among mental representations, can affect predication, a relation among intentional contents (Fodor 2003). (Mandelbaum 2016)

My claim is that now we have all the main theoretical resources that are needed to address this problem. One way to understand the issue is in terms of our previous distinction between associative and inferential processes at the behavioural level (chapter 2): associationism is inadequate to account for predication *to the extent that* it is a thesis about associations in the behavioural sense. In other words, Fodor (as well as Kant before him) is definitely right about this: one cannot explain the construction of propositional structures in terms of local activation with rapid decay, which can only account for automatic recall of very simple co-occurrences (see § 2.12). Automatic processes of this kind include both simple and contextual spreading activation. In fact, there cannot be predication even in case schemata are involved in entirely automatic transitions between contents, as is presumably the case with contextual spreading activation: although such schemata provide structure "on top of" concepts, this does not yet allow a thinker to have a single complex thought. In order for this to happen, there must be controlled, conscious activation of schematic information.

Our previous considerations on conversational implicatures allow us to be more precise about what this appeal to "conscious activation" amounts to. First, for there to be a complex thought, there must be a consciously accessible schema relating the concepts at issue. Second, this consciously accessible schema must actually play a role in processing – otherwise, it is hard to see why we should speak of a complex thought at all. Third, consciousness must be actually involved, although it is at least conceivable that not every component of the schematic structure (component *A*-schema-component *B*) is consciously focussed. In practice, conscious attention, not conscious reasoning, is often involved. In sum, the general idea is that in predication the concept *X*, the concept *Y*, and the "additional structure on tops of their contents" are all accessible, and they actually play a role in the conscious attentional process involved. On occasion, the entire schematic structure can be consciously focussed.

As a final comment, let me note that this proposal involves uncertainty about which representation structures are properly inferential. This is especially due to the requirement that schematic structures play a role in actual processing: it seems far from easy, and perhaps impossible, to draw a sharp boundary between the structures that satisfy this requirement and the ones that do not, in an episode of conscious attention. However, as I will argue below, this is as it should be: a certain degree of vagueness is integral to inferential processes as performed by conscious attention (versus conscious reasoning).

This is certainly the case with conversational implicatures, especially because the conclusion of the inference is only implicit. Predication seems different for this respect, because both the components related by the schema are stated explicitly. For instance in the case of BIRDS FLY, the intuition is that the schematic transition at issue is quite evident: it is the one that has BIRDS and FLY as its components. Predication, however, raises other problems. For one thing, the utterance "birds fly" admits of at least two different interpretations, one of which involves universal quantification while the other has a local domain of reference. It is in fact reasonable to assume that two different schemata are needed. For another thing, it is not easy to provide a description of the additional structure on tops of the concepts BIRDS and FLY. Rather, the predication seems here to imply a modification of the concept BIRDS. These and similar problems are definitely outside the scope of the present enquiry. I just want to emphasize that my approach is flexible on a couple of relevant dimensions. As to the first aspect, the approach does not commit me to claim that every schema must have a sensorimotor representation. It is possible that schemata emerge on *linguistic* experience: for instance, universal quantification seems to be a consciously accessible schema only as a linguistic refinement of pre-linguistic expectations of regularity. As to the second aspect, the fact that in BIRDS FLY the concept FLY seems to act as a modification of BIRDS may be explained by the fact that the schema experientially precedes the formation of the concepts. We perceive birds while they fly, and while they do not, and we also perceive bees that fly. Then, we can abstract the concept BIRDS and the concept FLY in terms of what underlies some but not others of those experiences. Thus, it is no surprise that certain schemata are impossible to represent unless as modifications of concepts: they are in fact patterns of experience from which concepts are abstracted away. But let me leave all those complexities aside. My general point was simply that the general framework provided above makes the idea of an associative (at the implementation level, and therefore not *associationist* in the traditional sense) account of predication far less mysterious than it may seem at first sight. We have schemata "on top" of concepts, these schemata may play a role in the dynamic of associative activation, and the relative schematic structures (concept-schema-concept) are consciously accessible as a whole.

5.4 Schematic and direct associations: a continuum

In the previous section, I proposed that there are conversational implicatures on condition that i) there are schematic associations actually playing a role in the transitions at issue, and ii) the entire schematic structure can be reconstructed consciously. This twofold cognitive characterization (let me call it shortly CC) of conversational implicatures has consequences that deserve to be further analysed. I will especially address a limitation of what I called the isomorphism view. On the one hand, CC accounts for the structural similarity between spontaneous comprehension and rational reconstructions, by assuming that the latter make consciously explicit the schematic associations actually employed by the former. On the other hand, the condition i) poses a constraint on which rational reconstructions count as indicators of genuine implicatures: there are implicatures only when the schemata employed in rational reconstructions did actually play a role in spontaneous comprehension. In this sense, rational reconstructions are not entirely reliable as indicators of implicatures. Now, I want to emphasize that the constraint i) is vague, in two different senses. As a consequence, the notion of conversational implicature is itself vague: it is indeterminate which transitions, among the ones for which schemata are consciously accessible, deserve to be counted as implicatures.

The first kind of vagueness depends on the distinction between schematic and direct associations. I proposed that schematic associations play no role in spontaneous comprehension whenever there is a direct association that is strong enough to make the schema – even if present – practically ineffective in normal processing. However, the respective strengths of direct and schematic associations can be expected to vary in degrees, and therefore there will be cases in which it is indeterminate whether the transition counts as schematic or direct, which means in turn that it is indeterminate whether there is an implicature.

The second kind of vagueness depends on the fact that a great number of schemata might be involved in spontaneous comprehension, so that the implicature might result not from one single schema but from the combined effect of many of them. For this aspect, too, the assumption of a systematic correspondence between comprehension and conscious reconstruction might be faulty.

Let me start from the first kind of vagueness. The existence of a continuum between direct and schematic associations threatens the very idea of a sharp boundary between lexical access and rational inferences. More generally, the associative account I propose suggests a non-standard view of lexical meaning. In this section I am going to address the boundary issue, in the next I will focus on lexical meaning.

As we already saw, the distinction between schematic and direct associations can be used to tell apart conversational from conventional implicatures: an implicature is conventional when the transition depends on a direct, conventionalised association, instead of an indirect schematic one. To be sure, the notion of conventional implicature is nowadays far from uncontroversial (see especially Bach 1999; 2006). According to Grice, there is a conventional implicature when a word form regularly conveys a meaning independently from the context (which makes the implicature *conventional*), but that meaning does not affect the truth-conditional content of the utterance (and therefore it is thought to be *implicated* instead of literally said). For one example, "but" is supposed to differ from "and" because the former regularly conveys an idea of contrast between the conjoined phrases: compare "She was poor but honest" with "She was poor and honest". Nevertheless, the truth conditions of those sentences are not presumed to differ, that is, the sentences are thought to be true in exactly the same situations.

This point has been questioned by Bach (1999), who argues that conventional implicatures as described by Grice imply a change in truth-conditional meaning after all – for instance, "but" has different conditions of truth than "and". A distinct concern is that the notion of conventional implicature has little cognitive significance: even if "but" and "and" had the same conditions of truth, they may play different cognitive roles nevertheless, and in this respect the idea of contrast conventionally conveyed by "but" behaves as a normal component of its lexical meaning.

If this is correct, as I think it is, then the notion of conventional implicature should be dismissed: we do not need such an intermediate notion between lexical meaning and conversational implicatures. Nevertheless, the distinction I proposed between direct and schematic associations does not lose its grip as a demarcation criterion. In fact, it still accounts for the distinction between conventional transitions and implicatures, with the former conceived in terms of associative recall of lexical meaning. The issue I want to address is whether this distinction supports the standard view of implicatures. More precisely, the point is whether implicatures are sharply distinct from lexical recall, in that the former (but not the latter) allows for rational reconstructions, which in turn ensures that they are properly inferential. I maintain that, from a cognitive point of view, this picture is at the very least imprecise.

In the first place, what distinguishes implicatures from lexical access is not the fact that the former but not the latter allows for rational reconstructions. On the contrary, we can easily provide a rational reconstruction of lexical access in terms of an inference from the fact that people conventionally use the word "x" to mean X to the fact that, in the current situation, the speaker is probably using "x" to mean X. The point is rather that it is not this inference that is likely to account for lexical access, but a more direct association between "x" and X. In other words, it is the condition i) – not ii) – of CC which accounts for the distinction between lexical access and implicatures. The condition ii) is responsible instead for the distinction between inferences (which can be accessed consciously) and non-conceptual transitions (which cannot). But both lexical access and implicatures satisfy the condition ii): they involve consciously accessible contents that are components of consciously accessible schemata. They are rather distinguished by the fact that lexical access, although it allows for rational reconstructions, is presumably explained by direct associations, while implicatures are explained by schematic ones.

Now, if lexical access and implicatures are distinguished by the criterion i) of CC, then in principle there cannot be a sharp boundary between them, because, for any two contents that are related by both direct and schematic associations, the relative strength of the direct association compared to the schematic one can be increased gradually by conventionalisation. However, it is not entirely clear the extent to which Grice and the tradition stemming from him are aware of this issue.

On the one hand, implicatures may be (and are actually often) conceived as based on mechanisms which are quite different from lexical recall. For one example, one way to frame this intuition is in terms of the modular approach proposed by RT: implicatures require inferential mechanisms of a different nature than associative recall. But then, it is hard to think of intermediate cases between lexical recall and implicatures. This is indeed suggested by Grice himself, with his Modified Occam's Razor. As a way out of the debate between those who claimed that, even in ordinary language, the meanings of logical connectives are the ones described by logics and those who claimed instead that ordinary meanings are different, Grice proposed that we should not multiply meanings beyond necessity: in a strict sense, the meaning of connectives is the logic one, but their use in ordinary language is accounted for by the inferential procedures that he called implicatures. Now, implicatures are described as a form of practical reasoning, and this is suggested to be something essentially different from meaning conventions – at least, if one takes the functional distinction between reasoning and lexical recall at its face value.

On the other hand, although the distinction between practical reasoning and meaning conventions may intuitively seem sharp, this is not mandatory: we provided a cognitive account which allows for gradual transition between them. The idea is that there is a common associative mechanism (not two mechanisms, as in the modular view), while the distinction is made to depend on gradual differences in the dynamics of activation (direct versus schematic associations, automatic versus conscious processing). Interestingly, Grice has provided at least one suggestion in this direction: his thesis that semantics is reducible to psychology. The idea is that conventional meanings develop from communicative intentions, as a result of repeated use. But then, communicative intentions are subject to processes of conventionalisation, and conventionalisation comes in degrees: so we can expect a continuum of cases between purely conventional meanings and purely inferential recognition of communicative intentions.

As a matter of fact, the Gricean tradition has acknowledged the existence of intermediate cases between purely conventional and purely inferential (implicated) meaning in terms of some sort of conventionalisation. This is in fact suggested by Searle (1975), who speaks in this sense of "conventions of usage" that must be kept distinct from meaning conventions – and therefore from lexical meanings. In the same vein, Morgan (1978) has introduced the notion of short-circuited implicatures, that is, implicatures that are somewhat conventionalised as a result of past use (see also Horn and Bayer 1984). Bach (1995, 1998) has proposed that the term "conventionalisation" should be reserved for cases in which precedent serves to make a given use possible, while one should speak of "standardisation" – and "standardised implicatures" – with regard to cases in which precedent merely facilitates the inferential process licensing a certain use (Bach 1995: 677). As may be seen, in all these approaches the intuition of intermediate cases between (particularised) implicatures and conventional meaning is accounted for in terms that are very close (as is the case for Bach's "standardisation"), if not identical, to the notion of conventionalisation.

The notion of short-circuited inference has been introduced in order to account for a special kind of conversational implicatures, that is, the ones that Grice called generalized conversational implicatures (GCIs). These are described by Grice (1989: 37) as cases in which "the use of a certain form of words [...] would normally (in the absence of special circumstances) carry such-and-such an implicature or type of implicature". An example he made is the following utterance:

(9) A man came to my office yesterday afternoon.

The hearer of this utterance would be surprised to discover that the man was the speaker's husband, since by using the indefinite phrase "a man" an implication is conveyed that the speaker is not intimately related to the man (Bezuidenhout and Morris 2004). The assumption is that such an implication is normally conveyed by the use of the indefinite without being part of its lexical meaning, so that it may be cancelled when the implication is in contrast with co-textual or contextual information: this is why it is considered an implicature, in the first place. However, the fact that GCIs are normally conveyed in the absence of specific circumstances make them different from particularized conversational implicatures (PCIs), which are instead implications carried on particular occasions "in virtue of special features of the context" (Grice 1989: 37).

In sum, PCIs are the prototypical case of pragmatic reasoning, conceived as essentially dependent on context and not affected by the brute force of conventions. GCIs, on the other hand, may be seen as a step back towards conventional meaning: they are still a case of reasoning, but of the kind that is called *default* reasoning, that is, reasoning based on rules that are sensitive to what is likely to happen (i.e., to precedents), and therefore produce "default", defeasible outcomes. This default reasoning – or reasoning to defaults – is what Morgan (1978) accounts for in terms of short-circuited implicatures, and Bach (1995) in terms of standardised implicatures: a phenomenon that retains something of lexical recall, although it is closer to inferential reasoning.

The point is whether those notions are compatible with the existence of a continuum extending from lexical meaning to pragmatic inferences. And again, the verdict is mixed. On the one hand, there seems to be some recognition of the fact that conventions and inferences can both contribute to comprehension in certain cases, which leaves open the possibility that the weight of their relative contributions changes from case to case. For instance, Levinson (2000: 23) adheres to Searle's idea that some pragmatic phenomena are "both partially conventional and inferentially motivated". But on the other hand, there is a difficulty in conceiving these as genuinely intermediate cases, due to the underlying intuition that reasoning and lexical access are essentially different processes. As a consequence, short-circuited inferences tend to be conceived as a uniform category modelled on standard reasoning.

One very clear example of this attitude is Bontly (2005). He first voices the intuition that a default interpretation may seem indistinguishable from a new lexical meaning. In practice, he notes, there is

> an interesting difficulty that (to my knowledge) Griceans have never adequately addressed, for it is now quite unclear why this default interpretation should be considered an implicature rather than an additional sense of the expression. To say that it is a default interpretation is, after all, to say that speakers learn to associate that interpretation with the type of expression in question [...]. 'Short-circuited' implicature-calculation is thus hard to differentiate from disambiguation. (Bontly 2005: 308)

This said, Bontly attempts to get rid of the difficulty by observing that conventional meanings are inherently arbitrary while default implicatures are not: "Familiarity with [a given] use [...] can remove the need to go through the canonical inference, but it doesn't change the fact that the use has a 'natural' (i.e., nonconventional) explanation. It doesn't change the fact that it is calcul*able*" (Bontly 2005: 308, his emphasis).

I do not want to deny that Bontly is right on this point: there are intermediate cases which cannot be entirely assimilated to lexical recall. However, once this is acknowledged, one should resist the temptation to fall at the other extreme by concluding that, if those are not cases of lexical recall, then they must be clear-cut cases of reasoning – though possibly of a special kind. This conclusion is generally justified by an appeal to the Calculability Criterion, as in the previous quotation from Bontly and, for another example, as in Bach (1998: 713):

> The inference is compressed by precedent. But where there no such precedent, in which case a more elaborate inference would be required, there would still be enough contextual information available to the hearer for figuring out what is being conveyed. That is why special conventions are not needed for these special cases.

I think this view is problematic for at least two reasons.

One is a general, theoretical issue concerning the Calculability Criterion. My analysis in § 5.3 was meant to show that calculability – which is just a dispositional property – is not sufficient to characterize inferences. Even lexical recall can be replaced by an argument: as we saw, one can provide a rational reconstruction in terms of an inference from the fact that people conventionally use the word "x" to mean X to the fact that, in the current situation, the speaker is probably using "x" to mean X. But no one actually thinks that lexical recall is based on such an inference, and for good reasons. It is not enough that subjects are able to recall schemata which can be used to provide rational reconstructions; in addition, those schemata must be presumed to play a role in the actual process we want to account for. This is why I introduced condition i) in CC, that is, the condition that schematic (versus direct) associations must have played a role in processing.

If this is correct, the argument from calculability – that is, the main argument for the claim that short-circuited inferences are genuine inferences – falls short of its goal. We should be able to show not only that a consciously accessible, schematic association is available, but also that this association is stronger than the corresponding direct association. And this leads us to the second issue, which is, whether the notion of short-circuited inferences is clear-cut and whether it licences the sort of robust pragmatic generalizations it is used to make.

A case in point is that of scalar implicatures, which are considered a special case of GCIs, with the underlying assumption that there are both a conventional meaning and a short-circuited inference associated to the relevant form of words. However, I submit, it is hard to see by which general criterion one might prove that, in all cases of scalar implicatures, there is a short-circuited inference instead of a new conventional meaning. The only argument for this conclusion, as far as I can tell, is the intuition that the default meaning is calculable; but, in the light of our previous considerations, calculability is far from being a reliable indicator that an inference is in place. Let us analyse the issue in more detail.

Scalar implicatures are thought to be based on the existence of "implicational scales", that is, sets of lexical items that may be ordered in accordance with their informative value, so that the use of a less informative item (a weaker value) on the scale implies that stronger values on the scale do not apply (Horn 1972, 1984; Gazdar 1979). An example of implicational scale is "all, most, many, some, etc.". Given this scale, in the sentence

(10) John ate some of the cake

the presence of "some" suggests that John did not eat all of the cake, since otherwise the speaker should have chosen the more informative "all". Specifically, the assumption is that the conventional meaning of "some" is something like SOME AND POSSIBLY ALL, but that tacit comparison with the possible alternative "all" triggers an inference (based on Grice's Maxim of Quantity): if the speaker had had reason to presume that John ate all of the cake, she should have chosen the more informative "all" instead; if she did not, then she intends to claim that John ate some *but not all* of the cake.

Now, the question is, what happens when scalar implicatures are conventionalized, and therefore short-circuited?[59] As in the above quotation by Bach (1998), one might say that "the inference is compressed by precedent": in other words, a direct association is formed, so that a "more elaborate inference" is no more required. However, Bach insists that there is still an inference in place, to the extent that the "more elaborate inference" can always be recovered. But this is again the Calculability Criterion, and it carries with it the by now familiar problem: it is not a reliable indicator of inferences. We need in addition to ask which association, the direct or the schematic one, is stronger: if it is the latter, then there is reason to claim that an inference is in place; but if the former is stronger, then the process is actually based on the recall of a new conventional meaning. And my suggestion is that there is no general answer to this question. There are a variety of implicational scales, and it is hard to see how one might decide in principle, for any item in any scale, whether the direct or the schematic association is effective in actual spontaneous processing. With regard to our specific example, it should be considered an empirical question whether the conventional meaning associated to "some" is SOME AND POSSIBLY ALL, SOME BUT NOT ALL, or both.

Generally speaking, I propose that conventionalisation (lexicalisation) of meanings is a process depending on a variety of factors. Together with the frequency with which a word form conveys a meaning, other plausible factors are

59 Many pragmaticists think that this is the case: scalar implicatures are considered a typical instance of short-circuited, default inferences. But even for those, such as relevance theorists, that reject the notion of default inferences the issue remains: what happens when implicatures are used again and again?

the frequency of previously lexicalised meanings, the absence of synonyms, the independence of new uses from old meanings, the determinacy of word uses, the grammatical category – and possibly others. An interesting illustration is the case of lexicalisation of figurative expressions. Let us consider, for instance, the metaphorical sentence

(11) Juliet is the sun.

Could the phrase "the sun" come to be lexically associated to – let us say – the concept BEAUTIFUL, even in case it were frequently used in that sense? The answer must be mostly negative, for in this case almost all the factors cited above disfavour lexicalisation. The word form "sun" is basically used to express the concept SUN (as to the factor frequency of previously lexicalised meanings); the concept BEAUTIFUL is already lexicalised in English (presence of synonyms); the phrase "the sun" in contexts such as (11) has a much more indeterminate meaning than BEAUTIFUL (determinacy of word uses); the phrase "the sun" belongs to a different grammatical category than the meaning BEAUTIFUL would require.

For another example, let us consider the metonymic sentence (discussed in Nunberg, 1977):

(12) The ham-sandwich left without paying.

The phrase "the ham-sandwich" is intended as referring to the person who ordered the sandwich, thanks to a transfer from one component to another of a café/restaurant schema. Now, it is not only that the literal meaning is no less (and probably more) frequent than the figural one (frequency of previously lexicalised meanings); moreover, this case is so construed that the literal meaning is salient in the context and presumably has a role in retrieving the figural meaning (there is little independence of new uses from old meanings). Frequency of use presumably favours lexicalisation of secondary meanings in inverse proportion to how much the contexts of use evoke primary meanings as well.

In sum, in both the examples (11 and 12) above, one should not expect a significant amount of conventionalisation. Compare (11) with the expression "the legs of the table". Here the conveyed meaning is quite determinate, there are no synonyms available, and the grammatical category is the standard one for referring to concrete objects. As a consequence, the fact that this expression is lexicalised – while the metaphoric use of "the sun" is not – is no surprise.

The lesson to be drawn, in my opinion, is the following. There is no reason to presume that items in implicational scales behave any differently from figural expressions: the extent to which a certain scalar implicature is conventionalised – that is, short-circuited by a direct association – is likely to depend on a variety of factors as the ones described above, and therefore it should be determined empirically on a case-by-case basis. More generally, we should always consider that frequently performed implicatures are likely to be lexicalised to some extent – and also, that there are intermediate cases in which both the direct and the schematic association contribute to activate the meaning. As a matter of fact, I know of no empirical study showing that the (alleged) scalar implicatures which are most frequently tested are not lexical meanings instead. As far as I can tell, this is simply assumed, and the only reason I know for such an assumption is the Calculability Criterion and the principle based on it, the Modified Occam's Razor. But the latter is just a methodological principle of parsimony ("do not posit lexical meanings whenever you can calculate them by implicature"), which has little to say about what is the case for any specific word's meaning, while the former is, as we said, insufficient to ensure that implicatures (versus lexical recall) are actually involved.

Similar considerations apply to other pragmatic domains, as for instance politeness. In their seminal work, Brown and Levinson (1987) proposed that polite forms/strategies provoke a deviation from rational efficiency, as defined by Grice's norms (the Cooperative principle and maxims), and such deviation has the effect of producing an implicature which communicates politeness. Against this view, Jary (1998: 2) argues that "polite forms often go unnoticed by the participants". This suggests, in accordance with a distinction proposed by Kasper (1990), that what is at play is not "strategic politeness" but instead a process of "social indexing" – that is, the automatic selection of forms that are appropriate to social contexts. In other words, politeness mostly involves "unselfconscious adherence to sociocultural constraints" instead of self-conscious and "strategic manipulation of these towards egocentric ends" (Jary 1998: 18).

We can rephrase this in terms of our previous considerations. Since polite forms are highly standardized, their original implicatures are to some extent short-circuited: they are no more calculated starting from what used to be the literal meaning. Instead, polite forms acquire a new – social-indexed – literal meaning. For instance, "Can you pass me the salt?" acquire the new meaning of a request to pass the salt in relatively formal situations. This amounts to saying that the polite form and the implicated content become directly associated with each other. At the same time, polite forms are open to be used strategically thanks to the fact that, although the polite use of "can" seems to be highly lexicalized, the primary use is no less frequent. This implies that the primary meaning remains strongly associated to the word and competes for activation with the secondary one, thus making the former easily accessible and salient, and its relationship with the latter easy to be noticed. The general point is that, although short-circuiting of polite forms makes available a more direct route for the activation of the secondary meaning, the less direct route is also strong (though possibly to a lesser extent), and thus easily accessible in any circumstance.

5.5 Lexical meaning

Let us take stock. In this chapter, my line of reasoning has been the following. Implicatures allow going beyond lexical meanings in a way that not only can be reconstructed inferentially, but also is inferential in essence. This means that a cognitive explanation of implicatures has to account for the isomorphism between spontaneous implicatures and their rational reconstructions. I propose to explain this isomorphism in terms of the fact that, in genuine implicatures, the schemata employed in rational reconstructions have actually played a role in spontaneous comprehension, and specifically in the activation of the implicated meaning. However, this view implies that replaceability by an argument is not sufficient as a criterion for detecting implicatures. As a matter of fact, when scholars of pragmatics provide rational reconstructions they heavily rely on their intuitions about which cases are genuine implicatures and which are not; in particular, they do not provide rational reconstructions for lexical recall not because this cannot be done, but because of their intuition that in lexical recall there are no schematic transitions actually involved.

A further claim I have made is that, to the extent that repeated use causes progressive conventionalisation (short-circuiting) of implicatures, schematic associations tend to be substituted for by direct ones. As a consequence, even in cases in which a sound rational reconstruction is available, one should ask whether, due to the degree of conventionalisation, what actually accounts for the activated meaning is the direct, not the schematic, association: and this can only be decided case by case.

One may be convinced or not that this account of implicatures is correct and, in particular, that it may count as a proper interpretation of Grice's view. To be sure, it brings our understanding of implicatures closer to what is known about associative memory and the way in which repeated use modifies it. But these considerations can also be expected to affect our view of lexical meaning as well. This is not the place to discuss the issue in details, though, on the other hand, it can neither be escaped entirely: cognitive pragmatics is more and more involved in addressing the organization of lexicon, as is shown by the research on what is called "lexical pragmatics", due to the now prevalent view that explicit meaning requires pragmatic modulation of lexical meaning in context. My purpose here is only to sketch the general lines of a probabilistic, associative approach to lexicon.

In lexicon studies, it is rather standard to assume that lexically encoded meanings are concepts, that concepts are simple (or even atomic) entities, and that in the normal case there is just one encoded meaning or, at least, a limited and well-defined number of them. As to the assumption that concepts are simple entities, the most extreme version is the Fodorian view of concepts as atomic mental labels (Fodor 1975), a variant of which is the proposal that concepts are mental file names (Fodor 2008). In this variant, there is information associated to word forms, but only indirectly: this information is contained in the file, but it is the file name that is directly associated to the word form and constitutive of the concept.

A related issue is whether simple recall of concepts is sufficient to provide the explicit content of utterances (see § 1.7). According to contextualists, this is not the case. In their view, explicit content is strongly underdetermined by lexical meaning, and one main reason for this is that lexicalised concepts are often not the ones that are fed into this layer of meaning: what happens instead is that they are "modulated" in context, which means that some related concept is selected instead as more appropriate to the context. The relation with the previous issue is the following: if one thinks, as contextualists do, that in spontaneous comprehension we do not form a proposition containing lexicalised concepts, but instead the first proposition actually constructed already contains modulated concepts (i.e., concepts resulting from modulation), then the thesis that lexical concepts are names of mental files is of little help. Specifically, it is not clear that, in that case, lexicalised concepts can play a genuine explanatory role.

This is actually argued for by Carston (2012). She quotes Nunberg (1979: 154), according to which "there is a substantial class of cases where we have no principled grounds for deciding which of several uses is conventional, i.e., licensed entirely by linguistic rules, [and which are derived]". What Nunberg has in mind are not cases of ambiguity between clearly different senses, but instead cases of polysemy, that is, cases in which there is a family of strictly related senses but none of them appears to be the basic one from which the others are derived. For one example, the word "window" can be used to refer to the frame, the glass pane, the open space in the wall, something one can see through, and an indefinite number of other things. Since none of those senses appears more basic than the others, which of them should be considered the lexicalised concept for "window"? One might be tempted to argue that there is some more abstract sense than those, which is the genuine lexicalised concept and acts as a pointer to different concepts. The problem with this view, as Carston observes, is that there does not seem to exist any thought containing such an abstract lexicalised concept, instead of the more specific ones it points to. Consequently, it is not even clear that this alleged concept behaves as such, that is, as a potential component of thoughts. This has been pointed out by Sperber and Wilson (1998: 185): "quite commonly, all words behave as *if* they encoded pro-concepts: that is, whether or not a word encodes a full concept, the concept it is used to convey in a given utterance has to be contextually worked out". In sum, Carston (2012) calls our attention to the fact that lexical meanings are contextually fine-tuned "in the interpretation of *almost every word*" (Wilson and Carston 2007: 231), and therefore they do not behave as concepts (i.e., as components of the uttered proposition), but instead as pro-concepts (i.e., as pointers to concepts, or rules to determine concepts in context). But, as Carston observes, there is another related aspect for which lexical meanings do not behave as concepts. Concepts are in fact supposed to conform to the principle of compositionality, while lexical meanings clearly don't: combinations of words often require reciprocal modulation of meanings, not their simple composition in accordance with syntactic rules.

In brief, according to Carston (2012), in many cases it is hard to pick out *the* lexicalised concept among an indefinite number of uses and, however, lexical meanings do not seem to behave as concepts. Her conclusion is that we should consider seriously the possibility that word forms do not encode concepts, conceived as simple components of the thoughts conveyed by utterances. In other words, Carston proposes to take seriously one of the two views proposed by Recanati (2004) under the names of "wrong format view" and "meaning eliminativism". According to the former view, concepts have the "wrong format" to be lexical meanings; word meanings are, instead, abstract schemas or sets of constraints or rules for use, thanks to which speakers determine context-relevant concepts. According to the latter view, word forms (*qua* types) do not have meanings at all, only their specific utterings in context have meanings.

Carston also claims that the boundary between wrong format view and meaning eliminativism may not be easy to draw. An example of the first position is the idea that meanings are too rich to be concepts, in that they incorporate a host of (possibly incompatible) semantic features which can be cancelled by contextual and pragmatic considerations. However, a liberal interpretation of this view collapse into what Rayo (2013) called the "grab bag" view, which according to Carston is a clearly eliminativist position. In Rayo's (2013: 648) words:

> With each expression of the basic lexicon, the subject associates a "grab bag" of mental items: memories, mental images, pieces of encyclopaedic information, pieces of anecdotal information, mental maps, and so forth.

As Carston notes, this is very much like the information that is presumed to be contained in mental files, in accordance with the view of concepts as mental file names proposed by Fodor (2008) – except that, in the "grab bag" view, no file name is present: the appropriate information is directly associated to the word form.

My claim is that Carston's conclusions are largely coherent with the view I am advocating here, according to which the associative organization of memory is key to the explanation of cognitive processes. In particular, the assumption that there is one single and simple invariant meaning (i.e., the lexicalised concept) associated to the lexical form flies in the face of the fact that words are used in a variety of senses, some of which occur with significant regularity. As a consequence, there are reasons to expect that the most frequent uses become "extra lexical senses", as is acknowledged by Wilson and Carston (2007):

> lexical adjustment may be a one-off process, used once and then forgotten, creating an ad hoc concept tied to a particular context that may never occur again [...]. However, some of these pragmatically constructed senses may catch on in the communicative interactions of a few people or a group, and so become regularly and frequently used. In such cases, the pragmatic process of concept construction becomes progressively more routinised, and may ultimately spread through a speech community and stabilise as an extra lexical sense.

In the associative account I propose, this lexicalisation of a new sense amounts to the formation of a direct association with the word form, instead of an indirect association mediated by the primary sense. Assuming that "almost every word" needs to be contextually fine-tuned, and that there are regularities in the way this occurs, a single lexicalised concept is likely to be an exception. Instead, what we expect is that most lexical forms are directly associated with a number of different but related senses, due to the fact that meaning is frequently, and somewhat regularly, adjusted in contexts. To be sure, there can be cases in which a lexical form is used in a quite technical sense, and/or in which it has little frequency of use in a language, so that there is a basic meaning that stays rather invariant in use. But in most cases the word form is likely to be directly associated to a certain number of different and related senses, not to one lexicalised sense giving only indirect access to a variety of other senses.

A couple of qualifications are in order.

First of all, we have to consider whether the views of lexical meaning as a rich collection of semantic features, as a "grab bag" and the like are equivalent to Wilson and Carston's (2007) suggestion that more than one sense may be lexicalised. One problem is that the notion of "grab bag" – as well as that of mental file – is, in the end, a metaphor: associative memory is a network, with no boxes in it for isolating chunks of information. Thus, one should ask: what does it mean that there is a collection of mental items associated to a given lexical form? Does it mean that each of them (that is, in accordance with Rayo's description of a grab bag, the entire collection of memories, mental images, pieces of encyclopaedic information, pieces of anecdotal information, mental maps and so on) is *directly* associated to that lexical form? My guess is that this is very implausible, given what we know about associative memory. It is much more likely that there are a certain number of direct associations, due to regular uses of the word, and a host of other information that is accessible only indirectly, *via* the directly associated nodes. The "grab bag" of a given word form can therefore be conceived as the area of the semantic network (be it either directly or indirectly associated to that word form) that is easily accessible from it – which presumably includes what is accessible not only by simple spreading activation but also by contextual spreading activation, in the terms introduced in § 5.3.

In a sense, if compared to the notion of mental file name, the notion of "grab bag" is in danger of going too far in the opposite direction. While the former makes the implausible assumption that, in the normal case, only one node is directly associated to the lexical form, the latter might be taken to mean that any node which is easily accessible from the lexical form is also directly associated to it – which is equally implausible. It is reasonable to assume instead that there is a limited number of nodes that are directly associated, and a vast area of indirectly and yet easily accessible information. Also, an associative account suggests that even among directly accessible nodes there may be differential strength of association: as a consequence, whenever one of those nodes has a significantly stronger association than any other, it may act as the default meaning of the lexical form.[60]

Second, if the "grab bag" is an instance of the wrong format view in the sense of Recanati (2004), then what is associated to lexical forms is not concepts. As Carston (2012) notes, this raises a question: since concepts are the entities out of which thoughts are composed, how can a non-conceptual entity provide the concepts to be fed into the intended proposition? The question, however, seems especially hard to answer when the assumption is made that concepts and world knowledge are qualitatively different kinds of things, and that the entire content of the "grab bag" is thus constituted by non-conceptual world knowledge. But in the associative view I defend here, world knowledge is entirely constituted by associative schemata (higher-level mental entities prescribing the organization of lower-level ones) some of which count as concepts (the ones that are accessible by consciousness). Together with the assumption that word forms are directly associated not to "grab bags" as a whole, but to a relatively limited number of their components, this means that word forms may be thought to have direct associations with a certain number of *concepts*, and indirect (but easily accessible) associations with an even greater number of them.

This view, however, does not preclude the possibility that word forms are also associated to non-conceptual contents. Let us assume, for example, that there exist pro-concepts, that is, mental entities that are too abstract to be component of thoughts but serve as pointers to a variety of concepts. Such pro-concepts meet my definition of schema, and – if detection of regularities at growing levels of abstraction is indeed a general law of human cognition (see above, §§ 2.7–2.11) – there are reasons to think that they are actually formed. However, there is no reason

60 More on this in Mazzone (2013b).

to presume that those schemata are consciously accessible, and therefore they cannot be components of thoughts: thus, they are directly accessible but non-conceptual contents of lexical forms.

Based on the above considerations, it is not entirely true that concepts have the wrong format to be lexical meanings. What is true instead is that lexical forms do not have, as a rule, an exclusive relationship with a basic concept (although this may happen occasionally, and although in other cases a concept may provide the default meaning): rather, lexical forms can be associated with a variety of conceptual and non-conceptual entities. This conclusion is largely compatible with Wilson and Carston's (2007) suggestion that a lexical form may have more than one lexical sense, and with Carston's (2012) arguments to the effect that in most cases there is no single invariant concept providing *the* lexical meaning. On the other hand, this is a substantial departure from the view that is standard in RT – as Carston (2012) acknowledges. According to that view, the meaning of a lexical form is an encoded concept, that is, a node in memory that a) provides access to mentally represented information and b) is a constituent of thoughts about the individuals in the extension of the concept (see also Wilson and Carston 2006: 411). But, as we saw, in most cases there are too many things apt to satisfy those requirements, and word forms can also be directly associated to mental entities that do not satisfy them.

5.6 Inferences or impressions? How consciousness makes a difference

If what we have said so far is correct, rational reconstructions tell us something important about the structure of spontaneous comprehension – specifically, that it is inferential or schematic in essence – but, nevertheless, the calculability of the intended meaning is not a completely reliable indicator of its actual calculation. There are cases in which pragmatic implicatures are short-circuited, and in fact substituted for by direct associations between lexical forms and new senses; and presumably there are also cases that are intermediate between full-fledged implicatures and complete lexicalisations. As a consequence, the isomorphism between spontaneous comprehension and its rational reconstruction has some limitations: the latter is a faithful description of the former only in case the schemata it appeals to have actually played a role in the derivation of the intended thought.

Finally, I want to focus on another aspect for which isomorphism may be expected to fail, that is, the fact that most of the times the inferences involved in spontaneous comprehension are not standard logical derivations, but instead what Sperber and Wilson (2015) called "impressions" (see above, § 2.13): competitions between alternative conclusions, one of which is selected as a result of "activation or inhibition caused by brain states that represent information in all kind of ways (from consciously entertained propositions to unconscious weightings of features [...])" (Sperber and Wilson 2015: 137). In their view, such a mechanism accounts for "the vast majority of inferences made by humans and other animals" (ibidem), and it counts nonetheless as inferential to the extent that it tends to favour warranted conclusions.

As I noted earlier (§ 2.13), this amounts to explaining inferences in terms of activation of, and competition between, information in memory, which is entirely coherent with my general associative account. But I also noted (§§ 3.1, 5.5) that, in my account, it is possible to provide stricter criteria for inferential processing than the capacity to produce warranted conclusions (or, equivalently, than "replaceability by an argument"). Spontaneous processes not only produce the same results that could have been obtained through inferences, but they may *actually* perform inferences, in the sense of conceptual transitions based on the same schemata involved in their rational reconstructions. More precisely, I proposed that the minimum threshold for having genuine inferences is that schemata (not direct associations) are responsible for the transition, and that those schemata and their components are consciously accessible: while the latter condition equates to the possibility to provide an explicit argument, the former is no less required.

To repeat, inferences can be short-circuited to the point that they are no more inferences, which in turn implies a breakdown of the isomorphism between spontaneous comprehension and rational reconstruction. Now, the notion of "impression" raises a related but different issue. Even when a schema plays a role in spontaneous processing, and specifically in the activation of the relevant conceptual contents, if Sperber and Wilson (2015) are right it may be the case that this schematic activation is only part of a more complex pattern of activation, presumably involving a host of both schematic and direct associations. Thus, it is a reasonable assumption that any rational reconstruction requires the selection of schemata which did not play, in fact, an exclusive role: by selecting those schemata, the assumption is made that they have played a prominent role in processing, but other associations are likely to have contributed to the outcome as well.

This is consistent with the general view of automatic processing as a "spreading cascade of activity" (Kahneman 2011: 97) – due to associative activation in a network – that in dual model theory is referred to as "System 1". In this theory, mechanisms for controlled processing are called "System 2", and in normal circumstances they operate in a comfortable low-effort mode and are prone to adopt the suggestions of System 1 with no modification (idem: 24). This low-effort mode is very much like the condition I have called conscious attention (versus conscious reasoning): a condition in which there is a flow of automatic activations (presumably both simple and contextual spreading activations) that are only lazily monitored by consciousness. As a consequence of its way of working, System 1 is subject to what Kahneman calls the "mental shotgun":

> We often compute much more than we want or need [...]. It is impossible to aim at a single point with a shotgun because it shoots pellets that scatter, and it seems almost equally difficult for System 1 not to do more than System 2 charges it to do. (Kahneman 2011: 95)

The mental shotgun is responsible for the fact that our cognitive processes are often far from being examples of rigorous thinking. In particular, Kahneman (2011: 97) focuses on what he calls "substitution", that is "the operation of answering one question in place of another": "If a satisfactory answer to a hard question is not found quickly, System 1 will find a related question that is easier and will answer it". And the interesting point is that System 2 will not even notice the difference, unless a special effort is made to this end.

When applied to spontaneous speaking and understanding, these considerations suggest (in line with the notion of impression in Sperber and Wilson 2015) that pragmatic inferences may be much less determinate than rational reconstructions make them appear to be. At the very least, a number of convergent factors, only a few of which are captured by conscious reasoning, participate in producing explicatures and implicatures. And it is also possible that what is implicated is not entirely determinate even for the speaker, a fact that leaves room for negotiation of the intended meaning in the course of the interaction (see Mazzone 2010: § 7).

For all these reasons, rational reconstructions can only be rough simplifications of what really occurs in spontaneous comprehension. However, this simplification – that is integral to rational reconstructions and, more generally, to conscious reasoning – is in a sense an important virtue. In fact, not even conscious attention is sufficient to prevent major flaws in reasoning, as Kahneman (2011) makes apparent whit his notions of "mental shotgun" and "substitution". When we want to check for possible errors, proper conscious reasoning is required: for any specific task at hand, we need to maintain a somewhat complete representation of it so as to check whether the right components are in place. In other words, we need to keep active – so to speak – the question, in order to be able to assess whether what we are providing is indeed the answer to it.

So, beyond the kind of automatic and spontaneous inferencing that Sperber and Wilson call "impression", our associative networks should better be able, after all, of serial, standard inferencing, as in fact they seem to be on occasion. Consciousness is, for sure, the key to this unique capacity of our species for explicit reasoning. In the synthetic formulation of Dehaene (2014), although associative activation in its basic functioning is far from operating as a Turing machine capable of serial operations, consciousness is the brain's trick by which linear representations (schemata and chains of schemata) are isolated from the flow of automatic activity and specifically attended:

> The mighty unconscious generates sophisticated hunches, but only a conscious mind can follow a rational strategy, step after step. By acting as a router, feeding information through an arbitrary string of successive processes, consciousness seems to give us access to a whole new mode of operation – the brain's Turing machine. (Dehaene 2014: 109)

In the end the question as to whether spontaneous speaking and understanding are rational activities requires, after all, a mixed answer. On the one hand, they are rational insofar as they depend on the schematic structure of information in memory, which allows for *inferential* transitions, that is, transitions that are actually driven and logically motivated by the appropriate schematic associations. On the other hand, the extent to which spontaneous speaking and understanding are properly inferential should not be overestimated, for two reasons: first, they may depend on short-circuited, direct associations more than rational reconstructions suggest; and second, the schematic associations appealed to in rational reconstructions are likely to be just part of a "spreading cascade of activity" (Kahneman 2011: 97) or, equivalently, of what Sperber and Wilson (2015) call an "impression".

Conclusions

What I have presented in this book is a *general framework* for cognitive pragmatics, in the first place. As a matter of fact, my points of divergence with RT essentially depend on their commitment to a different theoretical framework, largely influenced by a quite traditional view in cognitive science, and especially by Fodor (1975) and (1983). If we move away from that theoretical background towards the core of RT, there is much that I have found worthy of being preserved.

In particular, the view I defended here is entirely compatible with the following of RT's claims: utterances raise expectations of relevance in their addressees; comprehension is an exercise in mindreading and requires the (largely) automatic construction of inferential structures; this construction involves competition between interpretive hypotheses and is performed by a two-way movement of forward and backward inferences; explicit content is largely underdetermined by linguistic information and, specifically, it needs modulation of concepts as part of the forward/backward construction of pragmatic inferences. These claims paint a robust theoretical landscape to which my work in pragmatics is deeply indebted.

However, at the point where this core meets Fodor's (1983) modularity thesis and Fodor's (1975; 2008) theory of concepts, I have argued, a number of problems arise.

First of all, the assumption that pragmatic processing is modular requires that the role played by associative activations is restricted to its periphery, in contrast with its genuinely inferential character. And this involves, I claim, a confusion between two different levels of explanation. In spite of the fact that associationism (as well as connectionism) has often been formulated (and criticised) as an alternative to rule-based computation, I have tried to show that two notions of associations must be distinguished, and that the alternative between rule-based and purely associative holds only with regard to the very restricted notion which applies at the behavioural level. In other words, "associative" is incompatible with "inferential" when understood in terms of the purely automatic activation of unsophisticated (i.e., non-schematic) associations, while it is entirely compatible with "inferential" when understood in terms of associative encoding and activation of schemata within memory networks.

A second problem concerns the possible role of consciousness in utterance understanding. In accordance with the traditional emphasis on unconscious processing in cognitive science, and especially in accordance with the modularity thesis, RT conceives pragmatic processing as essentially automatic and unconscious. However, I have provided reasons to think, both in general and with

https://doi.org/10.1515/9781501507731-007

specific regard to pragmatics, that a sharp distinction between conscious and unconscious processing is likely to be misleading: most of our cognitive life is characterized by conscious attention (weakly) monitoring and sustaining components of larger patterns of automatic activation.

Third, the modular approach invites RT to keep pragmatic comprehension separate from general mindreading (as well as from proper linguistic processing). This separation is intuitively based on the idea that different processes are involved: in other words, the distinction is taken to depend not on the organization of bodies of knowledge that provide the domain-specific rules operating on a common mechanism, but instead on genuinely different mechanisms. As a matter of fact, relevance theorists have always conceived of (communicative) relevance as ingrained in the internal functioning of a domain-specific pragmatic module, thus severing the intuitive link with the general purposes of the speakers. In the passage from Grice (1957: 387) I quoted in § 1.11, the speaker's communicative intention can be recognized on the basis of how much it "would fit in with some purpose [the speaker] obviously has" in that context. In other words, a communicative intention is (recognized as) relevant with respect *to goals*. It is this link with the recognition of non-communicative intentions that is severed when relevance is conceived as internal to the pragmatic module, and independent from general purposes or goals.

Finally, if concepts are conceived as mental labels that provide the lexical meanings of word forms, and that are fed into the thoughts expressed by utterances, one has to face the problem that most of the times there seem to be no such entities, as noted by Carston (2012). If, on the other hand, word forms are directly associated to non-conceptual world knowledge, the problem arises as to how this knowledge may provide the concepts to be fed into the intended proposition. These problems are not surprising. The very least we can say about the view of concepts as atomic mental labels is that it leaves seriously underspecified the relation with world knowledge. Even assuming that concepts are mental file names, and therefore that world knowledge is contained within such files, a number of key details are left unaddressed anyway. How is information conferred to the mental file in the first place? Is any bit of information within a mental file as accessible as any other? And most of all, when information within the mental file is accessed, how this guides the search for different contextually modulated concepts? To put it a bit differently, if we take seriously the idea that the organization of memory is key to how contextually relevant information is accessed (as proposed by Sperber and Wilson 1996; see above, § 1.9), then concepts and world knowledge had better be integrated within the same memory network, so that inputs to the network are able to activate the appropriate concepts to be fed into thoughts.

In my approach, this is easily obtained: information in memory is mainly organized in schemata, whose components can be schemata as well, and concepts are a subclass of such schemata, specifically the ones that are consciously accessible. Generally speaking, (long term) memory is thus conceived as a network containing both conceptual and non-conceptual information, while concepts are thought of as (consciously accessible) structures constituted by a node to which a certain number of other nodes is attached, in such a way that the former prescribes the organization of the latter.[61] In this view, the distinction between concepts and world knowledge is preserved anyway, in the following sense: nodes that are only indirectly related to a concept are part of our world knowledge about it, not part of the concept. This does not imply any absolute distinction between the two. What is world knowledge with respect to a concept can nevertheless be conceptual information in itself.

As it should be clear, the main points I have addressed in this book are strictly related to each other. First of all, the schematic organization of memory is what allows simple associative activation to ensure genuine inferential processing. Moreover, I have proposed that conscious accessibility is one essential feature of both concepts and inferences. Together with the consideration that conscious attention is key to active maintenance of information in most cognitive tasks (comprehension included), this implies that consciousness is crucial even in accounting for (partially) automatic processing, and suggests a significant continuity between automatic processing and conscious reasoning. Specifically, rational reconstructions in pragmatics are importantly different from spontaneous comprehension in more than one way (see §§ 5.4 and 5.6 above), but, on the other hand, the former may succeed on making explicit the core structure of the latter precisely because spontaneous comprehension recruits the same schemata that are available to conscious reasoning. And, finally, mindreading is based on mental concepts that are themselves associative schemata, so that a common bottom-up/top-down dynamic of activation may account for the construction of interpretive hypotheses that cross the boundaries between language and action, the self and others.

In fact, I submit, one major methodological fault of modularism is that it does not encourage efforts to make use, in accounting for our cognitive abilities, of all

61 In speaking here of "nodes" I do not intend necessarily a single neuron or something similarly simple. In the account I provided in this book, schemata can be patterns of various complexity, but they count nevertheless as schematic nodes to the extent that they act as unitary entities prescribing the organization of other patterns in the network.

we know about basic mechanisms such as the associative and schematic structure of memory, the mechanism of associative activation (in the implementation sense), and its two modes of operation, that is, rapidly decaying versus sustained activation (automatic versus controlled processing). In the end, what I have tried to do here is just to examine which parts of RT are compatible with a general framework based on that well-established knowledge. The result is a picture in which comprehension is understood as a special case of spontaneous practical reasoning, as distinct from explicit, conscious reasoning – but with important structural similarities between the two.

If coherence in science is a virtue, this attempt should have some interest of its own, and we should take seriously the possibility to revise the received wisdom about the importance of the modularity thesis, nativism, and the atomic theory of concepts for cognitive science.

References

Allott Nicholas. 2005. Paul Grice, reasoning and pragmatics. *UCL Working Papers in Linguistics* 17. 217–43.
Atmaca, Silke, Natalie Sebanz & Günther Knoblich. 2011. The joint flanker effect: sharing tasks with real and imagined co-actors. *Experimental Brain Research* 211. 371–385.
Atmaca, Silke, Natalie Sebanz, Wolfgang Prinz & Günther Knoblich, 2008. Action co-representation: The joint SNARC effect, *Social neuroscience* 3(3–4). 410–420.
Baars, J. Bernard & Nicole M. Gage, N. 2010. *Cognition, brain and consciousness*. Amsterdam: Academic Press.
Bach, Kent. 1995. Standardization vs. Conventionalization. *Linguistics and Philosophy* 18. 677–686.
Bach, Kent. 1998. Standardization revisited. In Asa Kasher (ed.), *Pragmatics: Critical concepts. Vol IV*, 712–22. London and New York: Routledge.
Bach, Kent. 1999. The myth of conventional implicature. *Linguistics and Philosophy* 22. 327–66.
Bach, Kent. 2006. The top 10 misconceptions about implicature. In Betty J. Birner & Gregory Ward (eds.), *Drawing the Boundaries of Meaning: Neo-Gricean Studies in Pragmatics and Semantics in Honor of Laurence R. Horn*, 21–30. Amsterdam: John Benjamins.
Badre, David. 2008. Cognitive control, hierarchy, and the rostro-caudal organization of the frontal lobes. *Trends in Cognitive Sciences* 12(5). 193–200.
Badre, David. 2013. Hierarchical Cognitive Control and the Functional Organization of the Frontal Cortex. In Kevin N. Ochsner & Stephen Kosslyn (eds.), *The Oxford Handbook of Cognitive Neuroscience: Volume 2. The Cutting Edges*, 300–317. Oxford: Oxford University Press.
Baillargeon, Renée, Scott, Rose M., & Zijing He. 2010. False-belief understanding in infants. *Trends in Cognitive Sciences* 14. 110–118.
Baldwin, Dare A., & Jodie A. Baird, J. 2001. Discerning intentions in dynamic human action. *Trends in Cognitive Sciences* 5. 171–178.
Bargh, John A. 1989. Conditional automaticity: Varieties of automatic influence on social perception and cognition. In James Uleman & John Bargh (eds.), *Unintended thought*, 3–51. New York: Guilford Press.
Bargh, John A. 1990. Auto-motives: Preconscious determinants of social interaction. In Edward T. Higgins & Richard M. Sorrentino (eds.), *Handbook of motivation and cognition (Vol. 2)*, 93–130. New York: Guilford Press.
Bargh, John. A. 1994. The four horsemen of automaticity: Awareness, efficiency, intention, and control in social cognition. In Robert S. Wyer Jr & Thomas K. Srull (eds.), *Handbook of social cognition (2nd ed.)*, 1–40. Hillsdale, NJ: Erlbaum.
Bargh, John A., Gollwitzer, Peter M., Lee-Chai, Annette, Barndollar, Kimberly, & Roman Troetschel. 2001. The automated will: Nonconscious activation and pursuit of behavioral goals. *Journal of Personality and Social Psychology* 81. 1014–1027.
Barsalou, Lawrence W. 1982. Context-independent and context-dependent information in concepts. *Memory & Cognition* 10(1). 82–93.
Barsalou, Lawrence W. 1983. Ad hoc categories. *Memory & Cognition* 11. 21–27.
Barsalou, Lawrence W. 2005. Situated conceptualization. In Henri Cohen, & Claire Lefebvre (eds.), *Handbook of categorization in cognitive science*, 619–650. St. Louis: Elsevier.
Barsalou, Lawrence W. 2010. Ad hoc categories. In Patrick C. Hogan (ed.), *The Cambridge Encyclopaedia of the Language Sciences*, 86–87. Cambridge: Cambridge University Press.

https://doi.org/10.1515/9781501507731-008

Bartlett, Frederic C. 1932. *Remembering: An experimental and social study*. Cambridge: Cambridge University Press.
Bezuidenhout, Anne L. & Robin K. Morris. 2004. Implicature, relevance and default pragmatic inferences. In Dan Sperber & Ira Noveck (eds.), *Experimental Pragmatics*, 257–282. Palgrave.
Bongers, Karin C. A., & Ap Dijksterhuis. 2009. Consciousness as a trouble shooting device? The role of consciousness in goal-pursuit. In Ezequiel Morsella, John A. Bargh & Peter M. Gollwitzer (eds.), *Oxford handbook of human action*, 589–604. New York: Oxford University Press.
Botvinick, Matthew M. 2008. Hierarchical models of behavior and prefrontal function. *Trends in Cognitive Sciences* 12(5). 201–208.
Botvinick, Matthew M., Niv, Yael, & Andrew Barto. 2009. Hierarchically organized behavior and its neural foundations. A reinforcement learning perspective. *Cognition* 113(3). 262–280.
Botvinick, Matthew M., & David C. Plaut. 2006. Such Stuff as Habits Are Made On: A Reply to Cooper and Shallice. *Psychological Review* 113(4). 917–928.
Bratman, Micahel E. 1987. *Intention, plans, and practical reason*. Cambridge, MA: Cambridge University Press.
Brennan, Susan E., Alexia Galati & Anna Kuhlen. 2010. Two Minds, One Dialog: Coordinating Speaking and Understanding. *Psychology of Learning and Motivation* 53. 302–344.
Brown, Penelope & Stephen C. Levinson. 1987. *Politeness: Some Universals in Language Usage*. Cambridge: Cambridge University Press.
Buckner, Cameron. 2011. Two approaches to the distinction between cognition and 'mere association'. *International Journal of Comparative Psychology* 24(4). 314–348.
Carston, Robyn. 1997, Relevance-theoretic pragmatics and modularity, *UCL Working Papers in Linguistics* 9, 1–27.
Carston, Robyn. 2002. *Thoughts and utterances. The pragmatics of explicit communication*. Oxford: Blackwell.
Carston, Robyn. 2007. How many pragmatic systems are there? In Maria Frapolli (ed.), *Saying, Meaning, Referring. Essays on the Philosophy of Fançois Recanati*, 1–17. New York: Palgrave.
Carston, Robyn. 2012. Word meaning and concept expressed. *The Linguistic Review* 29(4), 607–623.
Carver, Charles S., & Michael F. Scheier. 2009. Action, affect, and two-mode models of functioning. In Ezequiel Morsella, John A. Bargh & Peter M. Gollwitzer (eds.), *Oxford handbook of human action*, 298–327. New York: Oxford University Press.
Christensen, Wayne, & John Michael. 2016. From two systems to a multi-systems architecture for mindreading. *New Ideas in Psychology* 40. 48–64.
Choudhury, Suparna, & Sarah-Jayne Blakemore, S. 2006. Intentions, actions, and the self. In Susan Pockett, William P. Banks & Shaun Gallagher (eds.), *Does consciousness cause behavior?*, 39–51. Cambridge, MA: MIT Press.
Clark, Herbert H. 1996. *Using Language*. Cambridge: Cambridge University Press.
Cohen, Jonathan D., Dunbar, Kevin, & James L. McClelland. 1990. On the control of automatic processes: A parallel distributed processing account of the Stroop effect. *Psychological Review* 97. 332–361.
Cohen, Jonathan & Andrew Kehler. submitted. Conversational eliciture.
Coltheart, Max. 1999. Modularity and cognition. *Trends in Cognitive Sciences* 3. 115–120.

Cooper, Richard & Tim Shallice. 2006. Hierarchical schemas and goals in the control of sequential behavior. *Psychological Review* 113(4). 887–916.

Dehaene, Stanislas. 2014. *Consciousness and the Brain. Deciphering How the Brain Codes Our Thoughts*. New York: Viking Press.

Dehaene, Stanislas, Jean-Pierre Changeux, Lionel Naccache, Jérôme Sackur & Claire Sergent. 2006. Conscious, preconscious, and subliminal processing: a testable taxonomy. *Trends in Cognitive Sciences* 10(5). 204–11.

Dijksterhuis, Ap, Tanya L. Chartrand & Henk Aarts. 2007. Effects of priming and perception on social behavior and goal pursuit. In John A. Bargh (ed.), *Social psychology and the unconscious: The automaticity of higher mental processes*, 51–132. Philadelphia: Psychology Press.

Epstein, Seymour 1973. The self–concept revisited or a theory of a theory. *American Psychologist* 28. 404–416.

Ferguson, Melissa J., Ran R. Hassin & John A. Bargh. 2007. Implicit motivation. In James Shah & Wendy Wood (eds.), *Handbook of motivation*, 150–168. New York: Guilford Press.

Fodor, Jerry A. 1975. *The Language of Thought*. Cambridge, MA: Harvard University Press.

Fodor, Jerry A. 1983. *The Modularity of Mind: An Essay on Faculty Psychology*. Cambridge, MA: MIT Press.

Fodor, Jerry A. 1987. *Psychosemantics: The Problem of Meaning in the Philosophy of Mind*. Cambridge, MA: MIT Press.

Fodor, Jerry A. 2003. *Hume Variations*, Oxford: Clarendon Press.

Fodor, Jerry A. 2008. *LOT 2: The Language of Thought Revisited*. Oxford: Clarendon Press.

Frege, Gottlob. 1952a. Function and Concept. In Peter Geach Peter & Max Black (eds. and trans.), *Translations from the Philosophical Writings of Gottlob Frege*, 21–41. New York: Philosophical Library.

Frege, Gottlob. 1952b. On Concept and Object. In Peter Geach & Max Black (eds. and trans.), *Translations from the Philosophical Writings of Gottlob Frege*, 42–56. New York: Philosophical Library.

Fuster, Jaquin M. 2001. The Prefrontal Cortex – An Update: Time Is of the Essence. *Neuron* 30. 319–333.

Fuster, Jaquin M. 2003. *Cortex and Mind*. Oxford: Oxford University Press.

Fuster, Jaquin M. 2014. The Prefrontal Cortex Makes the Brain a Preadaptive System. *Proceedings of the IEEE*. 417–426.

Gallese, Vittorio. 2007. Before and below 'theory of mind': Embodied simulation and the neural correlates of social cognition. *Philosophical Transactions of the Royal Society B: Biological Sciences* 362. 659–669.

Garrod, Simon & Martin J. Pickering. 2004. Why is conversation so easy?. *Trends in Cognitive Sciences* 8. 8–11.

Garrod, Simon & Martin J. Pickering. 2007. Automaticity in language production in monologue and dialogue. In Antje S. Meyer, Linda R. Wheeldon & Andrea Krott (eds.), *Automaticity and control in language processing*, 1–21. Hove, UK: Psychology Press.

Gazdar, Gerald. 1979. *Pragmatics. Implicature, Presupposition, and Logical Form*. New York: Academic Press.

Geurts, Bart & Paula Rubio-Fernández. 2015. Pragmatics and processing. *Ratio* 28(4). 446–469.

Gigerenzer, Gerd, Todd, Peter M., & the ABC Research Group. 1999. *Simple Heuristics That Make Us Smart*. Oxford: Oxford University Press.

Glenberg, Art & Vittorio Gallese. 2012. Action-based language: A theory of language acquisition, comprehension and production. *Cortex* 48. 905–922.
Gollwitzer, Peter M., Parks-Stamm, Elizabeth J. & Gabriele Oettingen. 2009. Living on the edge: Shifting between nonconscious and conscious goal pursuit. In Ezequiel Morsella, John A. Bargh & Peter M. Gollwitzer (eds.), *Oxford handbook of human action*, 603–624. New York: Oxford University Press.
Grafman, Jordan & Frank Krueger. 2009. The prefrontal cortex stores structured event complexes that are the representational basis for cognitively derived actions. In Ezequiel Morsella, John A. Bargh & Peter M. Gollwitzer (eds.), *Oxford handbook of human action*, 197–213. New York: Oxford University Press.
Grafton, Scott & Antonia Hamilton. 2007. Evidence for a distributed hierarchy of action representation in the brain. *Human Movement Science* 26. 590–616.
Grice H. Paul. 1957. Meaning, *The Philosophical Review* 64. 377–88.
Grice H. Paul. 1975. Logic and conversation. In Peter Cole & Jerry Morgan (eds.), *Syntax & Semantics 3: Speech Acts*, 41–58. New York: Academic Press.
Grice H. Paul. 1989. *Studies in the way of words*. Cambridge: Harvard University Press.
Grice H. Paul. 2001. *Aspects of Reason*. Oxford: Clarendon Press.
Hamilton, Antonia & Scott Grafton. 2006. Goal representation in human anterior intraparietal sulcus. *Journal of Neuroscience* 26. 1133–1137.
Hampton, James A. 2006. Concepts as Prototypes, in Brian H. Ross (ed.), *The Psychology of Learning and Motivation: Advances in Research and Theory, Vol. 46*, 79–113. Amsterdam: Elsevier.
Hampton, James A. & Martin L. Jönsson. 2012. Typicality and compositionality: The logic of combining vague concepts. In Markus Werning, Wolfram Hintzen & Edouard Machery (eds.), *Oxford Handbook of Compositionality*, 385–402. Oxford: Oxford University Press.
Happé, Francisca & Eva Loth. 2002. 'Theory of mind' and tracking speakers' intentions. *Mind & Language* 17(1–2). 24–36.
Haruno, Masahiko, Wolpert, Daniel M. & Mitsuo Kawato. 2003. Hierarchical MOSAIC for movement generation. *International Congress Series* 1250. 575–590.
Hassin, Ran R., Aarts, Henk, Eitam, Baruch, Custers, Ruud & Tali Kleiman. 2009. Non-conscious goal pursuit and the effortful control of behavior. In Ezequiel Morsella, John A. Bargh & Peter M. Gollwitzer (eds.), *Oxford handbook of human action*, 549–566. New York: Oxford University Press.
He, Zijing, Bolz, Matthias & Renée Baillargeon. 2012. 2.5-year-olds succeed at a verbal anticipatory-looking false-belief task. *British Journal of Developmental Psychology* 30. 14–29.
Heyes, Cecilia. 2014. False belief in infancy: a fresh look. *Developmental Science* 17. 647–659.
Hommel, Bernhard. 2003. Planning and representing intentional action. *The scientific World* 3. 593–608.
Hommel, Bernhard, Jochen Müsseler, Gisa Aschersleben & Wolfgang Prinz. 2001. The Theory of Event Coding (TEC): A Framework for Perception and Action Planning. *Behavioral and Brain Sciences* 24. 849–937.
Horn, Laurence R. 1972. *On the Semantic Properties of Logical Operators in English*. Bloomington: IULC.
Horn, Laurence R. 1984. Toward a new taxonomy for pragmatic inference: Q-based and R-based implicature. In Deborah Schiffrin (ed.), *Meaning, Form, and Use in Context*, 11–42. Washington: Georgetown University Press.

Horn, Laurence R. & Samuel Bayer. 1984. Short-circuited implicature: A negative contribution. *Linguistics and Philosophy* 7. 397–414.

Huang, Julie Y. & John A. Bargh. 2014. The Selfish Goal: Autonomously Operating Motivational Structures as the Proximate Cause of Human Judgment and Behavior. *Behavioral and Brain Sciences* 37(2). 121–135.

Huey, Edward D., Krueger, Frank, & Jordan Grafman. 2006. Representations in the human prefrontal cortex. *Current Directions in Psychological Science* 15. 167–171.

Iacoboni, Marco, Istvan Molnar-Szakacs, Vittorio Gallese, Giovanni Buccino, John C. Mazziotta & Giacomo Rizzolatti. 2005. Grasping the Intentions of Others with One's Own Mirror Neuron System. *PLoS Biology* 3(3). 529–535.

Jackendoff, Ray. 2007a. A parallel architecture perspective on language processing. *Brain Research* 1146. 2–22.

Jackendoff, Ray. 2007b. *Language, Consciousness, Culture: Essays on Mental Structure.* Cambridge MA: MIT Press.

James, William. 1890. *The principles of psychology* (Vol. 1). New York: Holt.

Jary, Mark. 1998. Relevance theory and the communication of politeness. *Journal of Pragmatics* 30. 1–19.

Jeannerod, Marc. 2006. Consciousness of action as an embodied consciousness. In Susan Pockett, William P. Banks & Shaun Gallagher (eds.), *Does consciousness cause behavior?*, 25–38. Cambridge, MA: MIT Press.

Jordan, Scott. 2009. Forward-Looking Aspects of Perception–Action Coupling as a Basis for Embodied Communication. *Discourse Processes* 46. 127–144.

Kahneman, Daniel. 2011. *Thinking, Fast and Slow.* New York: Farrar, Straus and Giroux.

Kahneman, Daniel, Tversky, Amos & Paul Slovic. (eds.). 1982. *Judgment Under Uncertainty: Heuristics & Biases.* Cambridge: Cambridge University Press.

Kasper, Gabriele. 1990. Linguistic politeness: Current research issues. *Journal of Pragmatics* 14. 193–218.

Kecskes, Istvan. 2010. The paradox of communication. Socio-cognitive approach to pragmatics. *Pragmatics and Society* 1(1). 50–73.

Kehler, Andrew & Jonathan Cohen. 2016. On the presuppositional behavior of coherence-driven pragmatic enrichments. *Proceedings of SALT (Semantic and Linguistic Theory)* 26. 961–979.

Kiefer, Markus. 2007. Top-down modulation of unconscious 'automatic' processes: A gating framework. *Advances in Cognitive Psychology* 3(1–2). 289–306.

Kintsch, Walter. 2000. Metaphor comprehension: a computational theory. *Psychonomic Bulletin & Review* 7. 257–266.

Kintsch, Walter. 2001. Predication. *Cognitive Science* 25. 173–202.

Knudsen, Eric I. 2007. Fundamental components of attention. *Annual Review of Neuroscience* 30. 57–78.

Koechlin, Etienne & Thomas Jubault. 2006. Broca's area and the hierarchical organization of human behavior. *Neuron* 50(6). 963–974.

Koechlin, Etienne & Cristopher Summerfield. 2007. An information theoretical approach to prefrontal executive function. *Trends in Cognitive Sciences* 11(6). 229–235.

Levelt, Willem J. M. 1989. *Speaking: From intention to articulation.* Cambridge MA.: MIT Press.

Levinson, Sephen J. 1992. Activity types and language. In Paul Drew & John Heritage (eds.), *Talk at work: Interactions in osservational settings*, 66–100. Cambridge: Cambridge University Press.

Levinson, Stephen J. 2000. *Presumptive meanings: The theory of generalized conversational implicature*. Cambridge MA: MIT press.
Libet, Benjamin. 1992. The neural time–factor in perception, volition and free will. *Revue de métaphysique et de morale* 97(2). 255–271.
Lieberman, Matthew D., Ruth Gaunt, Daniel T. Gilbert & Yaacov Trope. 2002. Reflection and reflexion: A social cognitive neuroscience approach to attributional inference. *Advances in Experimental Social Psychology* 34. 199–249.
Mandelbaum, Eric. 2016, Associationist theories of thought. The Stanford Encyclopedia of Philosophy, Edward N. Zalta (ed.), URL = <https://plato.stanford.edu/archives/sum2016/entries/associationist-thought/>.
Mandler, George. 1979. Organization and repetition: Organization principles with special reference to rote learning. In Lars-Göran Nilsson (ed.), *Perspectives on memory research*, 293–327. Hillsdale, NJ: Erlbaum.
Marr, David. 1982. *Vision: A computational investigation into the human representation and processing of visual information*. New York: Freeman.
Mazzarella, Diana. 2011. Accessibility and relevance. A fork in the road. *UCL Working Papers in Linguistics* 1. 11–20.
Mazzarella, Diana. 2013a. Associative and inferential approaches to pragmatics: The state of the art of experimental investigation. *Methode. Analytic Perspectives* 2(2). 172–194.
Mazzarella, Diana. 2013b. 'Optimal relevance' as a pragmatic criterion: the role of epistemic vigilance. *UCL Working Paper in Linguistics* 25. 20–45.
Mazzarella, Diana. 2014. Is inference necessary to pragmatics? *Belgian Journal of Linguistics* 28. 71–95.
Mazzarella, Diana. 2016. Pragmatics, modularity and epistemic vigilance. *Argumenta* 1(2). 181–193.
Mazzone Marco. 2006. Linguistica cognitiva. In Antonino Pennisi & Pietro Perconti (eds.), *Le scienze cognitive del linguaggio*, 93–134. Bologna: il Mulino.
Mazzone, Marco. 2009. Pragmatics and Cognition: Intentions and Pattern Recognition in Context. *International Review of Pragmatics* 1. 321–347.
Mazzone Marco. 2010. Intentions in Spoken Communication. Strong and Weak Interactionist Perspectives. In Massimo Pettorino, Federico Albano Leoni, Isabella Chiari, Francesca M. Dovetto & Antonella Giannini (eds.), *Spoken Communication between Symbolics and Deixis*, 53–76. Cambridge: Cambridge Scholars Publishing.
Mazzone, Marco. 2011a. Intentions as Complex Entities. *Review of Philosophy and Psychology* 2(4). 767–783.
Mazzone, Marco. 2011b. Schemata and associative processes in pragmatics. *Journal of Pragmatics* 43. 2148–2159.
Mazzone, Marco. 2013a. Attention to the speaker. The conscious assessment of utterance interpretations in working memory. *Language & Communication* 33(2). 106–114.
Mazzone, Marco. 2013b. A pragmatic Pandora's box. Regularities and defaults in pragmatics. In Frank Liedtke & Cornelia Schulze (eds.), *Beyond Words. Content, context, and inference*, 307–329. Berlin/Boston: Mouton.
Mazzone, Marco. 2014a. Language and action: a common intentional, generative, and inferential process. *Reti, saperi, linguaggi: Italian Journal of Cognitive Sciences* 1. 165–178.
Mazzone, Marco. 2014b. Mental states as generalizations from experience. A neurocomputational hypothesis. *Philosophical explorations* 17(2). 223–240.
Mazzone, Marco. 2014c. Crossing the associative/inferential divide: ad hoc concepts and the inferential power of schemata. *Review of Philosophy and Psychology* 5. 583–599.

Mazzone, Marco. 2015a. Being nativist about mindreading: More demanding than you might think. In Gabriella Airenti, Bruno Bara & Giulio Sandini (eds.), *Proceedings of the EuroAsianPacific Joint Conference on Cognitive Science (EAPCogSci 2015)*, 288–293. CEUR Workshop Proceedings.

Mazzone, Marco. 2015b. Trivializing modularity. An associative-representational account of cognition. *Epistemologia* 38(2). 201–215.

Mazzone, Marco. 2015c. Constructing the context through goals and schemata: Topdown processes in comprehension and beyond. *Frontiers in Psychology* 6(651). 1–13.

Mazzone, Marco. 2016a. What kind of associative and inferential processes? A response to Rubio-Fernández (2013). *International Review of Pragmatics* 8. 143–161.

Mazzone, Marco. 2016b. Is novelty of thought a mistery? Old schemata for new problems. *Rivista italiana di filosofia del linguaggio, Special Issue*. 78–91.

Mazzone, Marco. 2017. Why don't you tell it explicitly. Personal/subpersonal account of implicitness. In Piotr Cap, Marta Dynel (eds.), *Implicitness: from lexis to discourse*, 259–179. Amsterdam: John Benjamins.

Mazzone, Marco. Submitted. Is "associative inference" an oxymoron? Explaining inferences in pragmatics and reasoning.

Mazzone, Marco & Emanuela Campisi. 2013. Distributed intentionality. A model of intentional behavior in humans, *Philosophical Psychology* 26. 267–290.

Miller, Earl K. & Jonathan D. Cohen. 2001. An integrative theory of prefrontal cortex function. *Annual Review of Neuroscience* 24. 67–202.

Miller, Earl K., Freedman, David J. & Jonathan D. Wallis. 2002. The prefrontal cortex: categories, concepts and cognition. *Philosophical Transactions: Biological Sciences* 357. 1123–1136.

Morgan, Jerry. 1978. Two types of convention in indirect speech acts. In Peter Cole (ed.), *Syntax and Semantics, vol. 9, Pragmatics*, 261–280. New York: Academic Press.

Morsella, Ezequiel. 2009. The mechanisms of human action: Introduction and background. In Ezequiel Morsella, John A. Bargh & Peter M. Gollwitzer (eds.), *Oxford handbook of human action*, 1–32. New York: Oxford University Press.

Nunberg, Geoffrey D. 1977. *The pragmatics of reference*. PhD dissertation, City University of New York.

Nunberg, Geoffrey D. 1979. The non-uniqueness of semantic solutions: polysemy. *Linguistics and Philosophy* 3. 143–184.

Neumann, Odmar. 1990. Direct parameter specification and the concept of perception. *Psychological Research* 52. 207–215.

Onishi, Kristine H. & Renée Baillargeon. 2005. Do 15-month-old infants understand false beliefs? *Science* 308. 255–258.

O'Reilly, Randall C. 2010. The what and how of prefrontal cortical organization. *Trends in Neuroscience* 33(8). 355–361.

Pacherie, Elisabeth. 2006. Towards a dynamic theory of intentions. In Susan Pockett, William P. Banks, & Shaun Gallagher (eds.), *Does consciousness cause behavior?*, 145–167. Cambridge, MA: MIT Press.

Pastra, Katerina & Yiannis Aloimonos. 2012. The minimalist grammar of action. *Philosophical Transactions of the Royal Society B* 367. 103–117.

Penn, Derek C. & Daniel J. Povinelli. 2007. On the lack of evidence that non-human animals possess anything remotely resembling a 'theory of mind'. *Philosophical Transactions of the Royal Society B – Biological Sciences* 362. 731–744.

Perner, Josef. 2010. Who took the cog out of cognitive science? Mentalism in an era of anticognitivism. In Peter A. Frensch & Ralph Schwarzer (eds.), *Cognition and neuropsychology: International perspectives on psychological science (Vol. 1)*, 241–261. London: Psychology Press.

Perner, Josef. 2014. Commentary on Ted Ruffman's "Belief or not belief:. . .". *Developmental Review* 34. 294–299.

Perner, Josef, Huemer, Michael & Brian Leahy. 2015. Mental files and belief: A cognitive theory of how children represent belief and its intensionality. *Cognition* 145. 77–88.

Pickering, Martin J. & Simon Garrod. 2013. An integrated theory of language production and comprehension. *Behavioral and Brain Sciences* 36(4). 329–347.

Plebe, Alessio & Marco Mazzone. 2016. Neural plasticity and concept ontogeny, *Synthese* 193(12). 3889–3929.

Pockett, Susan. 2006. The Neuroscience of movement. In Susan Pockett, William P. Banks, & Shaun Gallagher (eds.), *Does consciousness cause behavior?*, 9–24. Cambridge, MA: MIT Press.

Rayo, Augustin. 2013, A plea for semantic localism. *Nous* 47(4). 647–679.

Reboul, Anne. 2017. Is implicit communication a way to escape epistemic vigilance? In Stavros Assimakopoulos (ed.), *Pragmatics at its interfaces*, 91–112. Boston/Berlin, De Gruyter.

Recanati, François. 2004. *Literal Meaning*. Cambridge: Cambridge University Press.

Recanati, François. 2007. Reply to Carston. In Maria Frapolli (ed.), *Saying, Meaning, Referring. Essays on the Philosophy of François Recanati*, 49–54. New York: Palgrave.

Rubio-Fernández, Paula. 2013. Associative and inferential processes in pragmatic enrichment: The case of emergent properties. *Language and Cognitive Processes* 28(6). 723–745.

Ruffman, Ted. 2014. To belief or not belief: Children's theory of mind. *Developmental review* 34. 265–293.

Ruffman, Ted, Taumoepeau, Mele & Chris Perkins. 2012. Statistical learning as a basis for social understanding in children. *The British Psychological Society* 30. 87–104.

Rumelhart, David & Andrew Ortony. 1977. The Representation of Knowledge in Memory. In Richard C. Anderson, Rand J. Spiro & William E. Montague (eds.), *Schooling and the acquisition of knowledge*, 99–135. Hillsdale: Lawrence Erlbaum Associates.

Saul, Jennifer. 2002a. Speaker Meaning, What Is Said and What Is Implicated. *Nous* 36(2). 228–248.

Saul, Jennifer. 2002b. What is said and psychological reality: Grice's project and relevance theorists' criticisms. *Linguistics and Philosophy* 25(3). 347–372.

Saul, Jennifer. 2010. Speaker-meaning, conversational implicature and calculability. In Klaus Petrus (ed.), *Meaning and Analysis: New Essays on Grice*, 170–83. Houndmills: Palgrave Macmillan.

Satpute, Ajay B. & Matthew D. Lieberman. 2006. Integrating automatic and controlled processing into neurocognitive models of social cognition. *Brain Research* 1079. 86–97.

Sbisà, Marina. 2006. Two Conceptions of Rationality in Grice's Theory of Implicature. In Elvio Baccarini & Snježana Prijić-Samaržija (eds.), *Rationality of Belief and Action*, 233–247. Rijeka: University of Rijeka.

Schank, Roger C. & Robert P. Abelson. 1977. *Scripts, plans, goals and understanding*. Hillsdale, NJ: Lawrence Erlbaum Associates.

Schneider, Walter & Jason M. Chein. 2003. Controlled & automatic processing: behavior, theory and biological mechanism. *Cognitive Science* 27. 525–559.

Schneider, Walter & Richard M. Shiffrin. 1977. Controlled and automatic human information processing. I. Detection, search, and attention. *Psychological Review* 84(1). 1–66.

Searle, John. 1975. Indirect speech acts. In Peter Cole & Jerry Morgan (eds.), *Syntax & Semantics 3: Speech Acts*, 59–82. New York: Academic.

Sebanz, Natalie, Günther Knoblich & Wolfgang Prinz. 2003. Your task is my task. Shared task representations in dyadic interactions. In Richard Alterman & David Kirsh (eds.), *Proceedings of the 25th Annual Meeting of the Cognitive Science Society*, 1070–1075. Mahwah, NJ: Erlbaum.

Sergent, Claire & Stanislas Dehaene. 2004. Is consciousness a gradual phenomenon? Evidence for an all-or-none bifurcation during the attentional blink. *Psychological Science* 15(11). 720–728.

Shanks, David R. 2010. Learning: From association to cognition. *Annual Review of Psychology* 61. 273–301.

Shastri, Lokendra & Venkat Ajjanagadde. 1993. From Simple Associations to Systematic Reasoning: A Connectionist Representation of Rules, Variables, and Dynamic Binding Using Temporal Synchrony. *Behavioral and Brain Sciences* 16. 417–51.

Shiffrin, Richard M. & Walter Schneider. 1977. Controlled and automatic human information processing. II. Perceptual learning, automatic attending and a general theory. *Psychological Review* 84(2). 127–190.

Shintel, Hadas & Boas Keysar. 2009. Less is more: A minimalist account of joint action in communication. *Topics in Cognitive Science* 1. 260–273.

Sloman, Steven A. 1996. The empirical case for two systems of reasoning. *Psychological Bulletin* 119. 3–22.

Smith, Edward E. 1989. Concepts and induction. In Micahel I. Posner (ed.), *Foundations of cognitive science*, 501–526. Cambridge, MA: The MIT Press.

Smith, Linda B. 2000. Avoiding associations when its behaviorism you really hate. In Roberta M. Golinkoff & Kathy Hirsh-Pasek (eds.), *Becoming a word learner, A debate on lexical acquisition*, 169–174. Oxford: Oxford University Press.

Smolensky, Paul. 1988. On the proper treatment of connectionism. *The Behavioral and Brain Sciences* 11. 1–23.

Song, Hyun-joo & Renée Baillargeon. 2008. Infants' reasoning about others' false perceptions. *Developmental Psychology* 44. 1789–1795.

Sperber, Dan. 2005. Modularity and relevance: How can a massively modular mind be flexible and context-sensitive? In Peter Carruthers, Stephen Laurence & Stephen Stich (eds.), *The Innate Mind: Strucuture and Content*, 53–68. Oxford: Oxford University Press.

Sperber Dan & Deidre Wilson. 1986/1995. *Relevance. Communication and cognition*. Blackwell: Oxford.

Sperber Dan & Deidre Wilson. 1987. Precis of Relevance: Communication and Cognition. *Behavioral and Brain Sciences* 10. 697–754.

Sperber Dan & Deidre Wilson. 1996. Fodor's frame problem and relevance theory: A reply to Chiappe & Kukla. *Behavioral and Brain Sciences* 19. 530–532.

Sperber Dan & Deidre Wilson. 1998. The mapping between the mental and the public lexicon. In Peter Carruthers & Jill Boucher (eds.), *Language and Thought*, 184–200. Cambridge: Cambridge University Press.

Sperber Dan & Deidre Wilson. 2002. Pragmatics, Modularity and Mindreading. *Mind & Language* 17(1–2). 3–23.

Sperber Dan & Deidre Wilson. 2008. A deflationary account of metaphors. In Raymond W. Gibbs (ed.), *The Cambridge handbook of metaphor and thought*, 84–105. Cambridge: Cambridge University Press.

Sperber Dan & Deidre Wilson. 2015. Beyond speaker's meaning. *Croatian Journal of Philosophy* XV(44). 117–149.

Strack, Fritz & Roland Deutsch. 2004. Reflective and impulsive determinants of social behavior. *Personality and Social Psychology Review* 8. 220–247.

Strack, Fritz, Roland Deutsch & Regina Krieglmeyer. 2009. The two horses of behavior: Reflection and impulse. In Ezequiel Morsella, John A. Bargh & Peter M. Gollwitzer (eds.), *Oxford handbook of human action*, 104–117. New York: Oxford University Press.
Surian, Luca, Caldi, Stefania & Sperber, Dan. 2007. Attribution of beliefs by 13-month-olds infants. *Psychological Science* 18. 580–586.
Tomasello, Michael. 1999. *The Cultural Origins of Human Cognition*. Cambridge: Harvard University Press.
Tomasello, Michael. 2008. *Origins of human communication*. Cambridge, MA: The MIT Press.
Tomasello, Michael, Carpenter, Malinda, Call, Josep, Behne, Tanya & Henrike Moll. 2005. Understanding and sharing intentions: The origins of cultural cognition. *Behavioral and Brain Sciences* 28. 675–691.
Warner, Richard. 2001. Introduction: Grice on Reasons and Rationality. In Richard Warner (ed.), *Aspects of Reason*, vii–xxxviii. Oxford: Clarendon Press.
Wenke, Dorit, Silke Atmaca, Antje Holländer, Roman Liepelt, Pamela Baess & Wolfgang Prinz. 2011. What is Shared in Joint Action? Issues of Co-representation, Response Conflict, and Agent Identification. *Review of Philosophy and Psychology* 2(2). 147–172.
Whiten, Andrew. 1996. When does smart behavior-reading become mind-reading? In Peter Carruthers & Peter Smith (eds.), *Theories of theories of mind*, 277–292. Cambridge: Cambridge University Press.
Wilson, Deirdre. 2000. Metarepresentation in linguistic communication. In D. Sperber (Ed.), *Metarepresentations: a multidisciplinary perspective*, 411–448. Oxford: Oxford University Press.
Wilson, Deirdre. 2003. New directions for research on pragmatics and modularity. *UCL Working Papers in Linguistics* 15. 105–127.
Wilson, Deirdre. 2004. Relevance and Lexical Pragmatics. *UCL Working Paper in Linguistics* 16. 343–360.
Wilson, Deirdre & Robyn Carston. 2006. Metaphor, relevance and the emergent property issue. *Mind and Language* 21(3). 404–433.
Wilson, Deirdre & Robyn Carston. 2007. A unitary approach to lexical pragmatics. In Noel Burton-Roberts (ed.), *Pragmatics*, 230–260. New York: Palgrave.
Wilson, Deirdre & Tomoko Matsui. 1998. Recent approaches to bridging: Truth, coherence, relevance. *UCL Working Paper in Linguistics* 10. 1–28.
Wilson, Deirdre & Dan Sperber. 2002. Relevance Theory. *UCL Working Paper in Linguistics* 14. 249–287.
Wilson, Deirdre & Dan Sperber. 2004. Relevance theory. In Laurence Horn & Gregory Ward (eds.), *Handbook of Pragmatics*, 607–632. Oxford: Blackwell.
Wimmer, Heinz & Josef Perner. 1983, Beliefs about beliefs: Representation and constraining function of wrong beliefs in young children's understanding of deception. *Cognition* 13. 103–128.
Wolpert, Daniel M., Doya, Kenji & Mitsuo Kawato. 2003. A unifying computational framework for motor control and social interaction. *Philosophical Transactions of the Royal Society B* 358 (1413). 593–602.
Wood, Justin N., Glynn, David D., Phillips, Brenda C. & Marc D. Hauser. 2007. The Perception of Rational, Goal-Directed Action in Nonhuman Primates. *Science* 317. 1402–5.
Wood Jacqueline N. & Jordan Grafman. 2003. Human prefrontal cortex: processing and representational perspectives. *Nature Reviews Neuroscience* 4. 139–147.
Zufferey, Sandrine. 2010. *Lexical Pragmatics and Theory of Mind: The Acquisition of Connectives*. Amsterdam: John Benjamins.

Name index

https://doi.org/10.1515/9781501507731-009

Subject index

https://doi.org/10.1515/9781501507731-010